Industrial Relations
in Education

Routledge Studies in Employment and Work Relations in Context

EDITED BY TONY ELGER AND PETER FAIRBROTHER

The aim of the *Employment and Work Relations in Context Series* is to address questions relating to the evolving patterns and politics of work, employment, management and industrial relations. There is a concern to trace out the ways in which wider policy-making, especially by national governments and transnational corporations, impinges upon specific workplaces, occupations, labour markets, localities and regions. This invites attention to developments at an international level, marking out patterns of globalization, state policy and practices in the context of globalization and the impact of these processes on labour. A particular feature of the series is the consideration of forms of worker and citizen organization and mobilization. The studies address major analytical and policy issues through case study and comparative research.

1. Employment Relations in the Health Service
The Management of Reforms
Stephen Bach

2. Globalisation, State and Labour
Edited by Peter Fairbrother
and Al Rainnie

3. Sexualities, Work and Organizations
Stories by Gay Men and Women in the Workplace at the Beginning of the 21st Century
James Ward

4. Vocational Training
International Perspectives
Edited by Gerhard Bosch
and Jean Charest

5. Industrial Relations in Education
Transforming the School Workforce
Bob Carter, Howard Stevenson and Rowena Passy

Previous titles to appear in Routledge Studies in Employment and Work Relations in Context include:

Work, Locality and the Rhythms of Capital
The Labour Process Reconsidered
Jamie Gough

Trade Unions in Renewal
A Comparative Study
Edited by Peter Fairbrother and Charlotte Yates

Reshaping the North American Automobile Industry
Restructuring, Corporatism and Union Democracy in Mexico
John P. Tuman

Work and Employment in the High Performance Workplace
Edited by Gregor Murray, Jacques Belanger, Anthony Giles and Paul-Andre Lapointe

Trade Unions and Global Governance
The Debate on a Social Clause
Gerda van Roozendaal

Changing Prospects for Trade Unionism
Edited by Peter Fairbrother
and Gerard Griffin

Union Leadership and Unionization
Paul Smith

Restructuring the Service Industries
Management Reform and Workplace
Relations in the UK Service Sector
Gavin Poynter

Trade Unions at the Crossroads
Peter Fairbrother

Between Market, State and Kibbutz
The Management and Transformation
of Socialist Industry
Christopher Warhurst

**Globalization and Patterns of
Labour Resistance**
Edited by Jeremy Waddington

The State and "Globalization"
Comparative Studies of Labour and
Capital in National Economies
Edited by Martin Upchurch

**State Regulation and the Politics of
Public Service**
The Case of the Water Industry
Graham Taylor

Global Humanization
Studies in the Manufacture of Labour
Edited by Michael Neary

Women, Work and Trade Unions
Anne Munro

**The Global Economy, National
States and the Regulation of
Labour**
Edited by Paul Edwards and Tony
Elgar

**History of Work and labour
Relations in the Royal Dockyards**
Edited by Ann Day and Kenneth Lunn

**Japanese Management Techniques
and British Workers**
Andy Danford

Young People in the Workplace
Job, Union and Mobility Patterns
Christina Cregan

**Globalization, Social Movements
and the New Internationalisms**
Peter Waterman

Young Adult Women, Work and Family
Living a Contradiction
Ian Procter and Maureen Padfield

The Sociology of Industrial Injury
Theo Nichols

**Global Tourism and Informal Labour
Relations**
The Small Scale Syndrome at work
Godfrey Baldacchino

Industrial Relations in Education

Transforming the School Workforce

Bob Carter, Howard Stevenson and Rowena Passy

Routledge
Taylor & Francis Group
New York   London

First published 2010
by Routledge
270 Madison Avenue, New York, NY 10016

Simultaneously published in the UK
by Routledge
2 Park Square, Milton Park, Abingdon, Oxon OX14 4RN

Routledge is an imprint of the Taylor & Francis Group, an informa business

© 2010 Bob Carter, Howard Stevenson and Rowena Passy

Typeset in Sabon by IBT Global.
Printed and bound in the United States of America on acid-free paper by IBT Global.

Library of Congress Cataloging in Publication Data
A catalog record has been requested for this book.

ISBN10: 0-415-41454-7 (hbk)
ISBN10: 0-203-86164-7 (ebk)

ISBN13: 978-0-415-41454-8 (hbk)
ISBN13: 978-0-203-86164-6 (ebk)

Howard:
to Sue and Kate

Bob:
to Mary

Rowena:
to my daughter Rosanne, for her sense of humour,
and to David and Barbara who helped to make
life in Leicester so enjoyable

Contents

Acknowledgements xi

1 Teachers' Work and Teacher Unions: The Global Context 1

2 Transforming the School Workforce in England:
The Road to Remodelling 19

3 Research Methods: Processes, Issues and Implications 37

4 Setting the Agenda: The Emergence and Significance
of 'Social Partnership' at the National Level 45

5 Industrial Relations in Transition: The Changing Role
of Local Authorities 65

6 Transforming the Primary School Workforce 85

7 Workforce Remodelling in Secondary Schools:
Towards Extended, Accountable Management 103

8 Workforce Remodelling: Transforming Teaching? 126

9 Industrial Relations and Trade Union Renewal,
Rapprochement or Resistance 142

Appendix 159
References 163
Index 173

Acknowledgements

This book reports the results of an ESRC-funded research project—Workforce Remodelling, Teacher Trade Unionism and School-Based Industrial Relations (RES–062–23–0034-A). The project lasted two years, commencing in September 2006 and completing in Autumn 2008. As in all intellectual work, the debts we have incurred are widespread. Thanks are due to a number of people who commented on the proposal before it was submitted and particularly to Theo Nichols who, over a long period, has had a habit of making more pertinent points, in fewer words, than anyone else.

Data collection involved interviewing over 100 participants at national level, local authority level and in case study schools. Throughout the project we enjoyed enormous support and co-operation from all those who agreed to participate in the research, and we are extremely grateful that people were willing to give their time so freely. The irony of researching workload problems in schools, and in so doing, compounding those problems, was not lost on us and we are very appreciative that so many people found time to talk to us when their professional lives are so busy.

As well as the support of individuals, we received considerable support and assistance from a number of organisations involved in the workforce remodelling process. The Training and Development Agency for Schools, the Local Government Employers, the Association of School and College Leaders, the Association of Teachers and Lecturers, the National Association of Headteachers, the National Association of Schoolmasters Union of Women Teachers, the National Union of Teachers, Unison and Voice all provided considerable support, as did each of the three case study local authorities (identified in the project as London Borough, City and Shire).

We are particularly indebted to the project Reference Group that provided invaluable advice and comments at several stages of the project.

At various points in the project we had the opportunity to share our emerging and developing ideas with colleagues and we value in particular the support and advice we received from colleagues at the University of Leicester, and later at De Montfort University, Leicester and University of Lincoln. We are particularly grateful to members of the Teachers' Work and Teacher Unions Special Interest Group of the American Educational

Research Association (AERA) who have provided a welcome home for ideas we presented at AERA meetings in 2006, 2007 and 2008. We would also like to thank all those who contributed to the Remodelling Teaching: Rethinking Education Conference at the University of Lincoln in June 2008. This conference (financially supported by the British Educational Leadership Management and Administration Society) provided an opportunity to share our findings and to locate these in a wider context of education restructuring. We are particularly grateful to the keynote speakers on that day—Professor Mike Bottery, Professor Michael Apple, Dr Mary Bousted and Sarah Stephens.

Finally, we would like to thank our families. Writing makes the greatest demands on those closest to us and we would like to take this opportunity to record our gratitude.

1 Teachers' Work and Teacher Unions

The Global Context

INTRODUCTION

In recent years the work of schoolteachers in English and Welsh State schools has been subject to considerable restructuring, often presented in the name of workforce reform or 'workforce remodelling' (Ball 2008, Butt and Gunter, 2007). Significantly, the focus of the debates about remodelling has not been restricted to teachers, but has extended to the whole of the school workforce, and there has been suggestion of nothing less than the 'transformation' of the traditional roles undertaken by both teachers and support staff in schools (DfES 2002). Workforce remodelling has been seen as a key initiative in the continued drive to raise school standards through the more effective and efficient deployment of labour in schools, whilst simultaneously addressing problems of teacher recruitment arising from excessive teacher workload. School workforce remodelling, and the 'new professionalism' agenda for teachers that emerged from it (Rewards and Incentive Group 2005), have had a substantial and significant impact on the subsequent development of schools, and the work of teachers. This volume provides an exploration of the policies associated with workforce remodelling, and wider issues of workforce reform in schools, and locates these in the broader context of neo-liberal State restructuring and New Labour's commitment to 'modernise' public services. Specifically the work has two broad aims: first, it provides an assessment and analysis of recent development in teacher trades unionism and school sector industrial relations in England. It does so by exploring teacher union engagement with the policy of workforce remodelling and offering an analysis of how teacher unions both shape policy and are shaped by policy. Second, the work seeks to make explicit connections between the way teachers experience work (the labour process of teaching) and developments in the strategy and form of teacher trade unions. This volume thereby avoids a narrow focus on teacher unionism as an activity disconnected from the realities of teachers' work, linking developments in teacher unionism with school teaching as a very specific form of work.

Too often teacher unions are omitted from studies of education policy, and their influence on the processes of change are underestimated or ignored, even by authors with little sympathy for the managerial orientation of the Government (see, for instance, Ball 2008). A particular feature of workforce remodelling in England and Wales has been the central role that teachers' unions have played in its development. Emphasising the need to focus on policy as both process and product (Taylor *et al.* 1997), workforce remodelling has not only sought to effect substantial change in schools, but has also brought forth a new model of industrial relations in the school sector. Teacher unions, and unions representing support staff in schools, have joined forces with a range of employer representatives to form a 'Social Partnership' in which all parties seek to work together to explore agreed solutions to what are presented as common problems.

Neither the reforms that workforce remodelling has generated, nor the industrial relations model it has spawned, however, have proven straightforward. Key elements of the substantive content of workforce reform, and the model of social partnership itself, have provoked deep division within the teaching profession and these divisions have been played out in the policies and the actions of different teacher unions (Stevenson 2007b). This book explores these developments in school sector industrial relations in England and begins to evaluate the wider significance of the partnership model of industrial relations for teacher trade unionism. It does so by examining the link between workforce reforms and changing forms of industrial relations at three distinct 'levels' of the policy environment—at national, local and institutional levels—and seeks to locate these developments in a wider global context. The research material presented is based on an Economic and Social Research Council-funded project conducted between 2006 and 2008 (*Workforce remodelling, teacher trade unionism and school-based industrial relations*, RES-062–23–0034A). In this study data was collected at each of the three levels of analysis—central government, local authority and at individual institution level—by looking at case study schools in both the primary and secondary sectors. Within the book there are discrete chapters that explore each of these levels in detail. Although the reform agenda has been implemented across England and Wales there are differences between the two national contexts and, as our data were collected solely in England, comments and analysis are restricted to the development of workforce reform in England.

However, before presenting this data some of the key theoretical frameworks that inform our analysis are outlined. In particular, this case study from England is located in a wider, global context. The remainder of this chapter highlights and develops three central themes that underpin the analysis of the research, before locating these themes within an English context in the following chapter. The three themes are:

- The insistence that developments described in this study, located in England, take place in a global environment and in particular within a specific form of globalisation which is dominated by neo-liberal ideology. Workforce remodelling in England is a national policy shaped by a specific international environment, but also one capable of exerting in turn significant influence in other national contexts (Fitzgerald 2007).

- The recognition that teaching is work, and that those who undertake teaching are workers involved in a labour process. This utilisation of labour process analysis acknowledges that teaching takes place within a very specific set of social relations and that it is important not only to understand what teachers do and how teachers' work is regulated, but to understand how teachers' work is changing and how these changes are linked to wider policy contexts.
- The conviction that the neo-liberal restructuring of State education, and its concomitant impact on teachers' labour process, will not go unchallenged. A central thesis of this volume is that educational reform is political and contested. Reaction to reform may take many forms, but, in a context where very large numbers of teachers are unionised, then it is not only likely, but also inevitable, that teachers will engage with educational reform, directly or indirectly, through their unions. This is not to assert that teacher unions are uniform, nor that turning to them is the only, or even the default, response of teachers as they engage with the issues that face them in their working lives. However, it is to argue that understanding teacher union engagement with education reform is central to understanding how globally driven education reforms are played out in different countries (Stevenson 2007a).

In the following sections each of these three themes, and the links between them, are elaborated as the basis of subsequent chapters.

GLOBALISATION, NEO-LIBERALISM AND THE RESTRUCTURING OF SCHOOLS

There is nothing intrinsically new about the movement of people, materials, goods and services around the world and across borders. However, such movements now take place on a scale, and with such rapidity, that the claim is frequently made that qualitative changes have occurred—we now live in an age of 'globalisation'. Globalisation can take many forms (Bottery 2006) but a core belief is that developments in transport and technological communications in particular allow for the rapid global movement of everything from people to information. Whilst it is true to assert that many of these developments are facilitated by advances in technology, it is important to recognise that 'globalisation' is not simply about the movement of goods, services, capital and labour across national borders, but is also about the location of power, and in particular the transfer of power from some nation-states to supra-national institutions (Green 1997).

Although these institutions operate internationally, the dominance of individual nations, most notably the US (Ryner 2007), highlights the complex relationship between existing forms of geopolitics and new forms of globalisation. Contemporary globalisation is therefore not the product of a set of value-neutral technological breakthroughs, but is a political phenomenon driven by a specific set of social relations. In its current form, globalisation reflects the dominance of capital and the ascendancy of a range of ideas associated with neo-liberalism. Although the dominance of neo-liberalism has been challenged by the recent global economic crisis, there is little evidence that the forward march of neo-liberalism has been fundamentally halted. Whilst some on the left have argued that the problems of the world economy caused by the implosion of the banking system herald the prospect of neo-liberalism's demise (Milne 2008), our belief is that a more sober assessment is required. Whilst economic crisis clearly opens up opportunities to challenge the logic of contemporary capitalism, the inability to articulate and mobilise around a coherent political alternative leaves the neo-liberal orthodoxy largely intact. In the meantime the imperative of what has become known as the Global North (Fletcher and Gapasin 2008) to cross borders, to remove barriers to trade, to weaken the power of the nation-states of the Global South and to undermine the power of organised labour, continues to be driven by capital's need to secure resources and to develop low cost sources of production combined with the pursuit of new and expanded markets for the sale of goods and services.

Globalisation in its current form is itself an outcome of earlier economic and political crises of the advanced capitalist economies that occurred unevenly between the late 1960s and mid-1970s. Symptoms included a fiscal crisis of the State (O'Connor 1973) and a decline in profitability caused by increased international competition, particularly from Japan (Brenner 1998). Keynesianism, as an essentially national form of regulation, seemed incapable of resolving the combination of stagnation and rising inflation (Holland 2008), making it vulnerable to attacks from neo-liberal demands to reduce State activity, taxation and regulation, thus releasing the increasingly international aspirations of capital. What developed during this period was a much more fundamental political or 'organic' crisis (Gramsci 1971) in which the very values of post-war social democracy and welfarism were challenged. In Gramscian terms an organic crisis represents a particular historical juncture in which the balance of class forces is fundamentally realigned. Existing alliances fracture and collapse, whilst new alliances develop and form to assert leadership and direction (Hall 1987). In the 1970s this can be identified as the period in which post-war social democracy, and the settlement between capital and labour that underpinned it, came under significant and sustained challenge. At this point the 'New Right', spearheaded by Reagan in the US and Thatcher in the UK, emerged to impose its hegemonic leadership on a new world order. This new settlement was not restricted to the advanced capitalist economies, but through the increasing authority of supra-national institutions, such as the International Monetary Fund and the World Trade Organisation, impacted in different ways on all economies, at whatever stage of development. Only by recognising the trajectory of globalisation through this period is it possible to understand the specific ways that economic and political crises impacted on national contexts to influence the shaping and re-shaping of welfare states.

These crises challenged the principles that had informed post-war social policy across the advanced capitalist economies (including the US), reversing working-class welfare gains that had been achieved at both company and State level. The triumph of the New Right at this time depended to a substantial degree on the ability of those involved to knit together a diverse but formidable alliance in support of State restructuring and most specifically its welfare function. Apple (2006a) has characterized this alliance in the US as one of 'conservative modernization', bringing together neo-liberals, neo-conservatives, the 'religious right' and 'new managerialists' in a 'tense coalition' (2006a: 49) that has significant, and sometimes contradictory differences, but which is united by a commitment to challenge the principles of welfarism, defined broadly as a commitment to redistributive fiscal policies, public provision of welfare services and access to services based on principles of universalism. Conservative modernizers have sought to restructure the State so that it reinforces, rather than mitigates, the impact of the market on the lives of citizens. The dominance of neo-liberal ideas in the conservative modernizers' alliance has placed considerable emphasis on 'rolling back the frontiers of the State', and attacking so-called 'big government'—a process Jessop (2002) has referred to as 'destatization'. The consequent organisational changes in the form of the State have led to the State being variously described as the Enabling State (Gilbert and Gilbert 1989), the Contractual State (Harden 1992), and the Neo-Schumpterian Workfare State (Jessop 1994), all of which, with varying degrees of transparency, acknowledge neo-liberalism's core commitment to consummate free market solutions—opposition to progressive taxation, reduced public spending, de-regulation and privatization. Within the conservative modernizers' alliance presented by Apple, the group labelled 'new managerialists' stand apart. This is a group that Apple implies may not be ideologically committed to the goals of conservative modernization, but, at a pragmatic and opportunistic level, they have aligned themselves with the agenda. As a new order has emerged in State and public services, the alignment provides those who have embraced it with a means of furthering careers and personal aspirations. In so doing, this group plays a key role in the consolidation of the conservative modernisation agenda by making the reforms 'work'.

Within education the global consequences of neo-liberal domination have resulted in national policy agendas that reflect national differences, but which feature many striking similarities. A key feature of the neo-liberal restructuring of national education systems has been an emphasis on 'efficiency', 'value for money', 'competition' and 'choice'. Outputs, often measured by student test scores in standardised tests, not only need to be maximised, but brought into alignment with the requirements of capital. The consequence has been a shift towards much more utilitarian and functional curricula, combined with an increasing emphasis on the measurement and 'benchmarking' of performance—without which educational 'output' cannot be quantified. At the same time market forces are increasingly introduced as a disciplinary mechanism, either directly through privatization or indirectly through the use of quasi-markets. The intention is not only to curb costs but also to limit teachers' professional autonomy and the capacity of teachers to exert significant influence on the content and shape of the curriculum. Where free markets are unable to secure the desired outcomes, increasingly powerful inspectorates, reinforced by a phalanx of sanctions to penalise 'poor performers', provide regulation. This is illustrated by the identification of so-called 'National Challenge' schools in England (DCSF 2008a), or in the US, the designation of failure to make 'adequate yearly progress' under the No Child Left Behind legislation (US Department of Education 2008). (For a powerful critique of NCLB see Meier and Wood, 2004.)

All of these factors taken together highlight the need to develop a much more critical analysis of the drive to improve 'standards'. The focus on improving standards (and the associated denigration of past achievements) is often at the centre of education policy discourse. However, the apparently uncritical focus on 'effectiveness' masks much more profound political issues. The emphasis on 'standards' de-politicises a discourse which is about what is taught, what counts as 'real knowledge' and who decides. These are not neutral issues (Apple 2003), but raise fundamental questions about the nature and purposes of education. In this context, the focus on standards is not a debate about the effectiveness of education, but shorthand for a particular type of education. In this sense the conservative modernisers' emphasis on quantifying educational output ('standards') cannot be disentangled from the conservative modernisers' aspirations for education to be more functional for capital—they are one and the same.

The chapter thus far provides only a broad-brush sketch of the educational landscapes in a global context. There are inevitably appreciable differences according to national circumstances and it is vital that educational research recognises and reflects these. Nevertheless, the drive for 'standards' as reflected in the use of standardized tests, increasing centralized control of curricula, the use of (quasi) market mechanisms and privatisation and the increased emphasis on 'accountability' reinforced by inspectorates and associated sanctions are increasingly the dominant features of educational reform in many countries. Across the world, in a very diverse range of national and regional contexts, the broad features of education policy described earlier are widespread (Robertson 2008).

Whilst caution is necessary when treating broad trends as universal experiences, it is also important to recognise that the alliances that promote the 'conservative modernisation' of education are not static, but rather like tectonic plates, they move and shift. Sometimes they appear settled, but at others times they are uneven and disturbed. We would not want to suggest, for example, that the transition from a Conservative to a Labour Government in the UK in 1997 did not represent a significant and meaningful shift in important areas of policy. Rather New Labour represented a re-orientation of the conservative modernizers' alliance in which concerns about equity issues and the need for State intervention to develop human capital were acknowledged. However, addressing these issues within a fundamentally neo-liberal framework begins to generate new tensions and contradictions. For example, the inability of the relatively high cost economies of the advanced capitalist nations to compete with much lower cost economies elsewhere has resulted in increasing emphasis on the development of human capital as a means of competitive advantage. Within human capital theory (Becker 1964, Denison 1967, Schultz 1981) education policy is elevated to economic policy, as investment in skills through education is seen as the key to competitiveness in a globalised market. This investment in skills may suggest an expansion of public education, but at the same time the neo-liberal State points to the control of public expenditure and a commitment to the small State.

Trying to reconcile this apparent contradiction disturbs the alliances that previously underpinned policy and opens up the possibilities for new directions in education reform. Moreover, such a contradiction impacts directly on teachers and their experience of work. Teachers are caught in a vice between the need to increase output in the form of more credentialed labour (human capital), whilst simultaneously ensuring that public expenditure is contained and labour controlled (neo-liberalism). They are similarly pressured by the need to ensure that outputs are functional to the needs of the economy, a pressure that raises key questions about the curriculum and assessment. What is taught and who decides are not technical questions requiring technical solutions: they are profoundly political issues and they begin to raise important questions about the labour process of teaching—what do teachers do, and how is teachers' work controlled? (Ingersoll 2003).

SCHOOL RESTRUCTURING, TEACHER PROFESSIONALISM AND THE LABOUR PROCESS OF TEACHING

A common feature of the neo-liberal restructuring of schools in many global contexts has been a claim to increase 'accountability', either through the use of market mechanisms or formal evaluation systems supported by sanctions. A consequence of this development in policy has often been increased control over many aspects of teachers' work, as the drive for comparison has required standardisation. The need to compare 'like with like' drives the need for standardised testing, which in turn drives standardised curriculum content, and which in its turn is likely to lead to increasing uniformity in approaches to teaching. These developments may differ in form in different countries, but they provide the framework that underpins teachers' experience of work in many different contexts (Smyth *et al.* 2000, Tatto 2007). The drive for increased accountability, and the linked tendency for central authorities to specify more closely what teachers teach, how they teach it and how teaching outcomes are measured (and compared), has generated considerable focus on the changing nature of 'teacher professionalism' (Barber 2005, Bottery 2006).

Discourses relating to teacher professionalism are significant as they reveal much about contemporaneous constructions of what it means to be the 'good teacher'. However, it is equally important to recognise that notions of teacher professionalism not only change over time, but that at any one time they are contested and challenged (Ozga and Lawn 1981). Classical approaches to professionalism have emphasised traits such as professional autonomy, self-regulation and public service as the key determinants of a claim to professional status, but starting with Johnson (1972) there is equally a long tradition of criticism of the adequacy of this approach. In the neo-liberal State trust in 'the professions' reaches its nadir, trust being 'a concept largely lacking from the vocabulary of the market advocate' (Bottery 2000: 72). The classic liberal view is that professions will act in their own self-interest as producers, unless compelled to do otherwise. There is therefore a tendency towards re-casting professionalism in terms of 'professional standards' and increased accountability in relation to these standards (Rewards and Incentives Group 2005). However, in these circumstances, a move towards the increased specification of learning outcomes, for example, might be simultaneously presented as a promotion of professionalism (through increased accountability), or an attack on it (through the diminution of professional judgement), highlighting the potential for concepts of professionalism to be used in different ways in support of different ends. Our view is that discourses relating to 'professionalism', and the professional status of teachers, are important as they reveal much about how teaching is perceived and how it is struggled over. However, debates as to whether teacher professionalism is enhanced or diminished by particular developments in teaching are at best seen as a 'distraction' (Gunter 2008), and the contested nature of professionalism makes it a poor vehicle for analysing the changing nature of teachers' work. Rather than focus on what can be a frustrating debate about the nature of the teacher as a professional, it can be more productive to conceptualise teacher within an employment relationship and therefore as workers.

The approach adopted in this volume is to utilise labour process analysis to examine the changing nature of teachers' work and the workforce remodelling reforms that in England are integral to this change. Labour process analysis can be traced back to Marx's analysis of work in early capitalist society as set out particularly in the first volume of *Capital* (Marx 1990). However, labour process analysis emerged more prominently in contemporary analyses of work following publication of Harry Braverman's *Labor and Monopoly Capital* in 1974. Braverman's work provided a critique of Taylorist management methods (Taylor 1911) and offered a comprehensive analysis of how technological developments, shaped by the dynamics of the capitalist economy at the time, were re-shaping work, and, in turn, the composition of the working class. Central to Braverman's thesis was that the drive for capital accumulation was generating an increased division of labour: the labour process was being fractured and work was increasingly organised in ways that stripped out 'low skill' elements of the role and allocated these to less skilled, and cheaper, labour. What Braverman identified was a separation of 'conception from execution' (1974: 114), in which a restricted number of staff took responsibility for designing and organising work, whilst the task of 'doing' was distributed across the bulk of the labour force. Braverman concluded that the majority of workers, often despite increased education, were increasingly experiencing work as a process stripped of skill and the potential for fulfilment. Therefore, despite employees having many of the features of middle-class status, in particular among the growing white-collar sector, workers were likely to be 'proletarianised' by their experience of work, and would increasingly identify with working-class demands and forms of organisation.

In the years following publication of *Labor and Monopoly Capital* there was a substantial and lively interest in developing Braverman's work (Crompton and Jones 1984, Thompson 1983, Wood 1982), one feature of which were several efforts to apply labour process theory to teaching (Connell 1985, Carlson 1987, 1992, Ozga and Lawn 1981, Ozga 1988, Smyth 2001). Many of these contributions helped to develop a more sophisticated analysis of changes that were emerging in teachers' work, and provided a basis for better understanding an apparent growth in teacher's collective action and militancy. They were also better able to reflect the significance of factors such as gender and race when analysing teachers' work (Apple, 1983). However, increasing tensions within post-Braverman analysis generally, particularly that associated with post-structuralist analyses (Knights and Willmott 1989, O'Doherty and Willmott 2001), and, prompted by declining working-class militancy, the shift to a greater concentration on management, and the tendency to apply the concepts derived from other contexts in a way that did violence to the complexity of teachers' experiences, all contributed to the virtual abandonment of labour process analysis in education (Reid 2003). Recent studies of teaching and changes in teachers' work illustrate this shift in tending to eschew labour process analysis in favour of a series of well-informed and interesting analyses that ultimately fail to adequately explain the trajectory of change (see Tatto 2007). Such studies are often strong on the 'what' of change, but they are much weaker on the 'why'. Moreover, they are weaker still on what might be described as the 'so what?', with little attempt to assess the political significance of the reforms being described. These deficiencies highlight the need for research that can not only better explain the links between neo-liberal restructuring and teachers' work, but can identify the future consequences both for school reform and teachers as an occupational group.

This volume revisits labour process analysis, sharing Ingersoll's interest in 'teaching as a job, teachers as workers, and schools as workplaces' (2003: 1). This is not to fall into the trap identified by Reid (2003) of equating the labour process as no more than 'teachers' work', but rather it recognises that teachers' work takes place within a specific macro context (the key features of which have been outlined earlier), that it is underpinned by a specific set of social relations and that it is performed in very distinctive organisational contexts. At the core of our commitment to labour process analysis is a conviction that this is a study not only about control—that is, the control of individual teachers as workers—but also about the collective control of teachers as an occupational group.

This focus on occupational and workplace control connects teachers' experience with that of other workers elsewhere in the economy. The nature of the employment relationship is increasingly conditioned by the imperative to contain costs and maximise productivity in educational institutions as elsewhere. Indeed, in an increasingly marketised public sector some forms of pressure on teachers, such as the setting of crude targets, increasingly converge with the experiences of those working in the commercial sector. This observation has two provisos: (1) increased pressures bearing down on teachers does not justify the collapse of teachers into the category of 'productive labour' (Harvie 2006), certainly if the integrity of Marx's analysis is to be maintained; (2) stressing teachers' common experience with workers elsewhere in the economy must not prevent us recognising where there are differences. Central to the arguments presented in this volume is the belief that understanding the labour process of teaching, and the considerable changes that have taken place within it, must be based on recognising what is distinctive about teachers' work. In our view what separates teachers' work not just from workers in the private sector but often from fellow workers in the state sector, is the extent to which teachers' work is explicitly ideological work. Educational institutions are nothing if they are not about ideas. Workers in education have a central role to play in the production, transmission and the exchange of knowledge—and in a 'knowledge economy' these are not processes that can be left to chance, and this reinforces the need to assert control over teachers' labour.

The pressures to control teachers may be powerful and pervasive in their lives, but they are not always coherent, and at any one time they reflect both the complexities and the contradictions of the conservative modernizers' alliance. In much the same way, teachers' responses are similarly complex. We have presented a narrative of neo-liberal restructuring that not only intensifies teachers' work, but which asserts ever-greater control over the content and form of teaching itself. There is considerable and powerful evidence that teachers have reacted negatively to these developments—this can be found in the persistent existence of high levels of teacher stress and burnout (Kyriacou 2001, Woods and Troman 2001), the evidence of recurring recruitment crises (Barmby 2006) or the incidences of industrial action as teachers articulate their resistance through collective action (see, for example, Kerr 2006, Compton and Weiner 2008). Clearly, the evidence of high levels of stress would make it a simplification to suggest that teachers always openly resist these developments, or that if they do, opposition generates some visible, collective response. For many different reasons some teachers may be positively supportive of the neo-liberal agenda, whilst in other instances teachers may find themselves subtly drawn into supporting the restructuring. Even where teachers are more oppositional, their responses may still be apparently passive and even acquiescent (Yarker 2005). However, teachers do often engage with the restructuring of their work in collective ways, and in particular through their unions. Across the world teachers are very often highly unionised and integrally involved in responding to, and engaging with, educational reform. A central focus of this book is the link between the labour process of teaching and forms of union organisation and the exploration how teacher unions and teacher unionists engage in the process of policy development. How do teacher unions seek to shape education policy, and how are teacher unions themselves shaped by policy?

THE LABOUR PROCESS OF TEACHING, TEACHING AS WORK AND TEACHER UNIONS

Teacher unions are important to teaching and any attempt to analyse teachers' work, and teachers' responses to changes in their work, requires an understanding of teacher unions. Nearly 30 million teachers are indirectly members of Education International, the international federation of teachers' unions that has 394 affiliates in 171 countries (www.ei-ie.org), indicating the continued significance of teacher unions. Across the world teachers are frequently highly unionised, with density levels often being amongst the highest across all economic sectors. Moreover, despite a trend towards falling union membership generally, especially in the private and manufacturing sectors, teacher union membership has proved stable and resilient. In the US, for instance, Kasten and Fossedal's (1996) study indicated that union density rates for teachers were nearly seven times higher than the private sector average, and there is little evidence to suggest that there has been any appreciable change in these figures. This is not to be complacent about teacher union influence and the challenges facing teacher unions—there are still parts of the world, such as Columbia, where membership and activism within a teachers' union is an act of courage and defiance that risks harassment, intimidation and even assassination (Public Services International 2008). Even in contexts that are less obviously threatening, there are powerful and systematic efforts to weaken and marginalize teacher unions, often supported by considerable resources (see, for example, Center for Union Facts 2008 in the US). Such efforts to undermine teacher unions are not separate from, but inextricably linked to, the neo-liberal restructuring of education described in the opening of this chapter. However, despite this 'global assault' (Compton and Weiner 2008) teacher unions remain an enduring feature of the educational landscape, often wrestling with how to defend and extend their influence in difficult circumstances. Indeed a principal concern of this volume is exploring *how* teacher unions in England are responding to precisely this cold climate.

Teacher unions around the world face similar issues and there is much that is common in their response. However there are also important differences in the way different teacher unions are organised, both internationally and within particular countries and the issues around which they campaign. This observation is highlighted by a specific feature that is important in developing an understanding of individual teacher unions and the factors that shape what they do and why. The previous section drew attention to a distinction between the teacher as 'professional' and teacher as 'worker' and this distinction is mirrored in an historic tension in teacher unionism between the teachers' union as a professional association and as a labour union. As with many dichotomies, the distinction can be over-simplistic and unhelpful. Nevertheless identifying these opposing orientations as a tension within teacher unionism does have some merit for understanding the histories and development of teacher unions in different contexts. Almost everywhere it is possible to see a struggle as teacher unions have sought to reconcile a commitment to 'professional' concerns with a similar commitment to so-called 'bread and butter' concerns of pay and conditions. The history of teacher unionism in many different contexts can often be presented as a struggle between these agendas—frequently manifested as inseparable and complementary, but in reality often in conflict and difficult to reconcile (see Barber 1992 for England and Wales, Murphy 1990 for the US and Lawton *et al.* 1999 for Canada as examples of how these tensions have influenced teacher union development in three different contexts).

Acknowledging the tension between professional and industrial issues within teacher unionism not only offers an heuristic device that can help us understand how teacher unions engage with, and position themselves in relation to, education reform, but it can also draw attention to an important feature of teacher unionism in many countries, which is the co-existence of several unions representing teachers—multi-unionism. This phenomenon can look very different in different contexts. For example, in some cases separate unions exist to represent teachers in different sectors of the system. New Zealand provides just one example from many where separate teacher unions represent primary and post-primary teachers. These unions do not compete against each other directly for members, although the bargaining strategies of one clearly impact on the other (Jesson and Simkin 2007). In other cases different unions may represent different types of worker in the same sector. A common distinction, as in many Canadian provinces, for example, is that separate unions exist for principals/headteachers (Lawton *et al.* 1999). In yet other instances more than one union may exist, but in any one bargaining unit only one union is allowed representational rights. This is the case in many US states where the National Education Association (NEA) and the American Federation of Teachers (AFT) have to secure the right to be sole representatives by winning a ballot (see Cameron 2005 for accounts of how this has shaped teacher union strategy and action in the US). Understanding multi-unionism in its different forms is essential to understanding teacher unionism generally, and its specific development in different localities. This book is primarily concerned with developments in school sector industrial relations in England, a location in which several unions competing for the same membership co-exist in the same sector. Recognising and reflecting the specific significance of multi-unionism in England is crucial to understanding developments in school sector industrial relations. This involves acknowledging the deep ideological differences within teaching and teacher unionism that account for the enduring existence of several competing unions. Furthermore, comprehending these ideological tensions is essential to understanding capacities and potentialities as teacher unions frame their responses to neo-liberal restructuring. In the following section, three possible union approaches—*rapprochement*, resistance and renewal—are outlined as a basis for exploring data presented and analysed in subsequent chapters.

TEACHER UNION RESPONSES TO NEO-LIBERAL RESTRUCTURING: *RAPPROCHEMENT*, RESISTANCE OR RENEWAL?

Teacher unions cannot avoid responding to the attempts to restructure school sector education along neo-liberal lines. Classifying responses as *rapprochement*, resistance or renewal inevitably involves simplifications, but at this stage these three approaches provide a framework against which to assess the data presented in subsequent chapters. Moreover, an assessment of the literature relating to teacher unionism specifically, and public sector unionism more generally, justifies the presentation of these three broad approaches to neo-liberal restructuring. It is not claimed that these approaches are neat and tidy—on the contrary, our data will emphasise their complexity and sometimes the contradictions within them. But at this stage they provide a framework as the starting point of our analysis.

Rapprochement refers to those teacher union strategies that go with the grain of the new educational agenda and seek to maximise gains for their members within that. There is no attempt to fundamentally challenge the neo-liberal basis of reform policies—rather there is either an ideological or pragmatic acceptance of it. Recent examples of this approach to teacher unionism have their intellectual roots in the work of American scholars Kerchner and Mitchell (see Kerchner and Mitchell 1988, Kerchner and Koppich 2003). Within the *rapprochement* approach there is a strong emphasis on 'interest-based bargaining' (NEA 2003) whereby unions and employers seek ways to identify common solutions to what are seen as agreed problems. The outcomes where possible are so-called 'win-win' solutions (Keane 1996) in which both unions and employers can claim gains. Within this approach it is also possible to discern an emphasis on including professional issues in the bargaining agenda—what Kerchner *et al.* refer to as 'the other half of teaching' (1998: 11). Where this takes place however there is no fundamental attempt to challenge the direction of policy in professional areas such as the curriculum, testing or teacher evaluation, but rather a preparedness to discuss the details and form of their application.

The second approach may be best described as 'resistance'. Resistance is a rather over-worked, and often over-romanticized, word in the lexicon of labour unionism. Resistance can take many forms and be in response to many things. As Michael Apple (2006a) reminds us, there is nothing automatically 'progressive' about teacher union resistance and there are many examples of teacher unions mobilising powerful forces in support of sometimes reactionary causes (Seifert 1987). In this context the term 'resistance' is used to describe teacher union strategies that actively seek to challenge the trajectory of neo-liberal restructuring in education—to 'interrupt' the policy agenda of the conservative modernizers (Apple 2006b). These are teacher union strategies and actions that seek to oppose the implementation of neo-liberal reforms in terms of their impact on teachers' pay and conditions, but also often in 'professional' areas too. 'Resistance' therefore is wide-ranging and may extend to pedagogic reforms such as the use of standardized testing, or the break-up and privatization of school systems (Compton and Weiner 2008). The term resistance is chosen deliberately for the sense of conflict it conveys. If the *rapprochement* model goes with the grain of educational reform, then resistance goes against the grain. The latter approach to teacher unionism is predicated on a more conflictual concept of bargaining than that assumed in the *rapprochement* model and tends to reject forms of interest-based bargaining for more traditional forms of collective bargaining. Collective bargaining itself has often been a victim of the neo-liberal attack on trade unionism and notable examples of the resistance approach often involve a militant defence of traditional negotiating rights (see Poole's 2007 analysis of the struggles of teachers in British Columbia). What distinguishes resistance from renewal below is the conduct of unions is here characterised as largely traditional in form. Unions are opposed to many of the reforms, but in this instance resist in ways that mirror the organisational forms that were historically predicated on different relations with the State.

Resistance therefore contrasts with the third approach presented here— that of union renewal. The union renewal thesis was not developed with specific regard to union activism within education, but in response to neo-liberal restructuring across the wider State sector. Critics of government-inspired restructuring recognised that many features of the neo-liberal agenda (privatisation, quasi-markets, managerialism) were deliberately intended to weaken and undermine union organisation (Foster and Scott 1998). However Fairbrother (1996) suggested that these reforms, and in particular the tendency towards system fragmentation in which operational management decisions were decentralised to workplace level (manifest in schools as site-based management), could actually lead to union renewal or revitalization. At the heart of Fairbrother's argument was the belief that many public sector unions were centralised, bureaucratic and remote from their members. Their structures reflected their historical role in the centralised collective bargaining apparatus. In an environment where strategic control was held centrally, but where operational control was devolved to workplace level, Fairbrother argued that centralised union structures were no longer 'fit for purpose'. He further argued that decentralisation would bring many of the conflicts inherent in the employment relationship directly into the workplace. These would no longer be massaged away by bureaucratic and centralised procedures, to be dealt with by faceless managers and union officials. Rather these issues would become live in the workplace, and require workplace resolution. Fairbrother's argument was that under such conditions unions might break free of their bureaucratic structures and adopt more flexible, participatory and rank and file driven forms of organisation. Although the focus of this activity is rarely illustrated, the underlying assumption is that such activism would emerge from the contradictions and conflicts that workers experience in their working lives. In an age of site-based school management, attempts to increase control over the labour process of teaching, to restrict the scope for professional discretion or to worsen conditions of service (perhaps through privatization) are all potential sources of conflict, local involvement and hence union renewal. Given the centrality of the union renewal thesis to the concerns of this research, a more detailed analysis and critique of the union renewal thesis are provided in Chapter 2.

CONCLUSION

This chapter has attempted to sketch out with a broad brush the global picture that is the background to the empirical data presented in this volume. The arguments are based on a belief that school sector reform across the world is being driven by powerful neo-liberal imperatives. The emerging orthodoxy—that the development of human capital provides the key to competitive success in a global market—places education at the heart of the struggle over neo-liberal reforms. This reform agenda has profound implications for teachers as an occupational group and for teaching as work. That teachers represent such a large call on public spending makes them an obvious target for any attempt to make the State sector 'leaner and meaner'. But teaching is more than just a cost. Teaching is ideological work, and it is for this reason there have been such ambitious efforts by governments to assert ever-greater control of what is taught, who decides and how performance is evaluated.

All of these pressures bring the State into potential conflict with teachers. Such conflict may manifest itself in a myriad of ways, but in an environment where the workforce is highly unionised some form of collective response articulated by unions is not only likely, but also inevitable. It is precisely because of teacher unions' ability to interrupt the trajectory of neo-liberal reform that they have become the focus of such attention from those who seek to break-up the public sector for the purposes of opening it up to private enterprise. However, these are hard times for all unions and teacher unions face difficult decisions as to how they seek to defend and extend their influence in an environment where powerful forces continue to marginalise, undermine or incorporate them.

In setting out a framework for analysing teacher union responses to neo-liberal reform, it is not intended to posit a comprehensive model. Rather it offers a set of parameters against which to present our data. The aim is provide the detail and the nuance that this framework requires by drawing on the empirical data in our study of the Government's school reform agenda in England and the way in which teacher unions engaged with that reform. The reform, 'workforce remodelling', was not only significant because of its scale and its impact on teachers' labour process, but also for the way in which teacher unions were integrally involved in the formulation and implementation of policy. Indeed, as if to underline the argument about the significance of teacher unions and the labour process of teaching, remodelling emerged as an issue in direct response to industrial action by teacher unions in relation to excessive teacher workload.

However, the remodelling reforms proved highly contentious and they have divided the teacher union movement. In many ways they have exposed the tensions highlighted in this opening chapter, for example between *rapprochement*, resistance or renewal. This volume deepens the analysis of the role of teacher unions in education policy development by explaining how these tensions play out in the policies and practices of teacher unions and the lived experiences of teachers as both teachers and members of teacher unions. The context is distinctly national—remodelling is a policy largely 'Made in England'—and many of the contextual specificities, such as the peculiarly English experience of multi-unionism, are highly significant. However, the consequences and conclusions are definitely international. The focus of this volume is a policy case study in England. However, this cannot be cropped from the larger picture of which it is a part—and that picture is global. Chapter 2 sets out in more detail the specific context of workforce remodelling as a policy within England, providing details of the industrial relations context and the industrial relations structures that prevail in England.

Chapter 3 presents a summary of the research methodology undertaken when conducting this study. The research was undertaken between 2006 and 2008 when workforce reforms were becoming firmly established in schools. At the same time the Social Partnership between unions and employers (at central and local government level) was consolidating its position in the education policy process. The timing of the research, and the divisions between the teacher unions on core aspects of the remodelling process, made this sensitive research to undertake. Chapter 3 outlines the rationale for the research design and discusses some of the issues arising from undertaking politically sensitive research of this nature.

Chapters 4, 5, 6 and 7 focus on data from the research project, analysing the development of workforce remodelling as a policy at three different levels—national, local and workplace. Policy implementation is not a rational and linear process, but rather it is messy and complicated with policy being formed and re-formed by all those involved in the process of its development. In this volume, the data analysis attempts to capture the essence of policy as a refracted process (Taylor *et al.* 1997) and to do this in a context where unions are acknowledged as significant players in the policy development process. Chapters 6 and 7 present data at an institutional level and disaggregate these between the primary and secondary sectors. This focus is to reflect on the significant differences that emerged from the two sectors, in terms of how workforce remodelling policy impacted on both schools and the union infrastructure that existed within them.

In the final two chapters the empirical data presented previously are drawn together and an over-arching analysis of the broader issues is advanced, relating these to teachers' work and the labour process of teaching (Chapter 8) and to teacher union policy and organisation (Chapter 9). These chapters seek to present the broad trajectory of change that continues to impact on teachers and their work, and to connect this to wider questions of union strategy. In particular there is an assessment of the significance of the social partnership model in school sector industrial relations, and the possibilities that might exist for wider union responses of resistance and renewal.

A NOTE ON DATA PRESENTATION

When presenting data throughout the volume we have made substantial use of direct quotation. In order for readers to be able to identify different sources of data we have adopted the convention of labelling any quotes used with an appropriate anonymised identifier. Although individuals have been anonymised we do identify the organisational affiliation where appropriate. This format was discussed with all interviewees and recognises that this information is essential to be able to provide the level of analysis we require relative to our research aims. Within the text we adopt the following means of identifying interviewees:

National level—identified as 'National Official' followed by organisational affiliation, and where multiples interviewees participated from within a single organisation we differentiate further with a number. For example '*National Official 1, NASUWT*'.

Local authority level—we identify our three case study local authorities (LAs) throughout as City, Shire and London Borough. Quotations from LA interviewees are identified by the interviewee's role, followed by their LA. Unions have different terms for the official who represents the union at LA-level meetings and negotiations, and we refer to these throughout as *Branch Secretary*. It is also worth noting that several teacher unions refer to their local branches as local associations, and these terms can be considered interchangeable throughout. Where there are multiple interviewees with the same role in the same LA, we adopt the same convention as per national level interviews and include a number as a differentiator. Examples might include '*ATL Branch Secretary, Shire*' or '*LA Officer 2, London Borough*'.

School level—we identify interviewees by their role, followed by their LA, and the type of school (primary and secondary). To make it easier to differentiate data from primary and secondary schools, each primary school is numbered 1 or 2, and each secondary school is numbered 3 or 4. A typical example might be '*Headteacher, City Primary 1*'.

Note—whilst data analysis involved reviewing transcripts from all interviewees in the study, not all interviewees have been quoted directly in this volume.

Full details of all interviews undertaken are included as an appendix.

2 Transforming the School Workforce in England
The Road to Remodelling

NEO-LIBERALISM AND THE RESTRUCTURING OF SCHOOL SECTOR EDUCATION

In Chapter 1 it was argued that the economic crisis beginning in the late 1960s underpinned a much broader political and social crisis that developed in the 1970s. The significance of this 'organic crisis' (Gramsci 1971) was that it represented a rupture from the Keynesian and welfarist policies that had dominated the agendas of governments in the advanced capitalist economies in the post-war years. This period witnessed class and social forces re-alignment and the ideas associated with neo-liberalism assumed hegemonic significance. Rather than seek an accommodation with labour, in the way that capital had attempted since 1945, there was a more concerted attempt to directly challenge labour, and particularly in its organised form, trades unionism (Devine *et al.* n.d). As part of this strategy, there was also an attempt to roll back the frontiers of the State, and to weaken and undermine many of the public institutions that labour had campaigned for, both to enhance the social wage and to create institutions that might challenge social inequality. Whilst some countries, particularly those on mainland Europe, appeared more insulated from these developments, other countries such as the UK and New Zealand developed these ideas with particular enthusiasm, and education reform quickly emerged as a key battle ground in the struggle between the old and the new (Tomlinson 2001).

This chapter provides an analysis of how the global influence of neo-liberalism has shaped school sector education policy in England in the period since the mid-1970s, and in particular since the passing of the 1988 Education Reform Act (ERA)—a decisive and defining moment in the history of English education policy. The analysis recognises that education policy is developed in an environment in which teacher unions play a significant role and are capable of asserting substantial influence. A description of the unionised context in which policy is formed in England is therefore needed, and in particular some examination of the complex multi-unionism that is its defining feature. Neo-liberal restructuring has an explicit objective of weakening teachers' collective organisations, but the results of neo-liberal reforms are not predetermined or guaranteed, and in addition to threats there are opportunities. It is opportunity that is stressed by Fairbrother's (1996) union renewal thesis with the argument that increased managerialism and a de-centralised management framework might bring forth a more grassroots and participative form of unionism at the workplace. Similar arguments are presented by Ironside and Seifert (1995), specifically in a schools context, and the issues raised are explored in some detail. The chapter concludes by introducing the concept of workforce remodelling and the social partnership arrangement in industrial relations that has developed alongside it. These are major developments in the labour process of teaching and in school sector industrial relations, and their significance is explored in detail through the research presented and discussed in subsequent chapters in this book.

Early evidence of the shifting terrain of debate and the battles to come in education were Prime Minister Callaghan's launching of the Great Debate (Callaghan 1976) and disputes, such as those at William Tyndale School, which fuelled a moral panic about a crisis in public sector education (Ellis *et al.* 1976). Increasingly in debates, teachers were presented as the source of problems in public education, with their apparent autonomy over the curriculum, coupled with a willingness to resist wage restraint, placing them firmly in the sights of State restructuring (London Edinburgh Weekend Return Group 1979). These conflicts between teachers and the State were not purely economic (wages and jobs protection at a time of inflation and economic crisis), but were ideological, posing fundamental questions about the nature, purpose and future trajectory of schooling. They illustrate the extent to which education reform was central to the neo-liberal restructuring of the State during this period.

The momentum of restructuring increased significantly following the 1979 election of a Conservative Government, and the more explicit emergence of an English form of Apple's (2006a) conservative modernizers' alliance. Skirmishes over curriculum reform, teacher appraisal and budget cuts culminated in a protracted industrial dispute over pay between 1984 and 1986 (Lawn 1996), although at the time *The Times* newspaper correctly identified the dispute as 'not about money but management' (quoted in Ball 1988: 296). Industrial defeat, in part due to divisions between competing teacher unions, paved the way for significant reforms of both the school system and the teaching profession itself. The 1988 ERA represented the most significant reform of the English State school system since the 1944 Education Act and marked the beginning of a decisive phase in neo-liberal restructuring of education. This legislation indicated the direction of subsequent reform, and almost all the key features of education restructuring since that time can be said to have their origins in the 1988 Act. From that point governments began to radically reconfigure the whole of the school system, presaging what has become an almost permanent revolution in the organisation of schools and the labour process of teaching. At the time educational historian Brian Simon suggested the long-term aim was the dismantling of the system in preparation for privatisation, a suggestion that has grown more credible as time passes:

> Considered separately, there may be something to be said for some of these measures (for instance financial delegation to headteachers and governors). But considered as a set of interrelated measures, as they must be, each can be seen to provide it specific thrust towards the desired objectives—those of destabilising locally controlled 'systems' and, concomitantly pushing the whole structure of schooling towards a degree, at least, of privatization, so establishing a base which can be exploited later. There is no doubt that the combined effect of these measures would then mean the break up of the public system of education as we have known it since 1944.
>
> (Simon 1988: 48)

The reform of education was linked to the wider objectives of State restructuring. The ERA had the characteristics of what is commonly called new public management (NPM) (Cutler and Waine 1997, Ferlie *et al.*1996, Pollitt 1990). In broad terms NPM is characterized by centralisation through increased government control of finance and policy-making together with de-centralisation of implementation and accountability through the discipline of government targets. In the education sector, these broad features were manifest through both a weakening of the role of local authorities (LAs) and a sustained attack on the limited autonomy and professionalism of teachers as instanced by a series of measures, including the imposition of the National Curriculum, Standardised Assessment Tests and utilisation of examination results that simultaneously purport to judge teachers' performances, reinforced by a much more interventionist and punitive inspection regime. The publication of league tables of achievement was used to encourage parental choice and the development of a quasi-market in State education. Parental choice was introduced to stimulate competition between schools, while de-centralising responsibilities through local management of schools (LMS) has increased the powers of school governors and head-teachers, at the expense of LAs, and pressurised them to make school-based innovations. Notions of competition and hierarchy between schools were further encouraged, by allowing some schools to opt out of local education authority control and to establish themselves as semi-independent schools in the State sector. Amongst the changes that were encouraged were more school-based monitoring of teacher performance and increased use of capability procedures to remove weak teachers (Maclure 1992).

The election of the New Labour Government in 1997, with a clear commitment to increase investment in education, to an extent eased funding pressures on schools. Education policy, however, was linked ever more clearly to economic policy, with the strategic development of human capital seen as central to ensuring competitiveness in a global economy (Bell and Stevenson 2006). Moreover, although funding increased it did little to diminish the pressure on teachers, with New Labour not only remaining wedded to Conservative policies of choice and the market, but also layering over that a punitive system of national targets and benchmarks. Its claimed 'zero tolerance' of underachievement (DfEE 1997) elevated the policy of naming and shaming 'failing' schools to new heights, placing additional pressure on those schools which were often facing the most challenging circumstances. These pressures were compounded by national targets being cascaded down the system through LAs, individual schools and ulti-mately to individual teachers, a policy continued more recently through the National Challenge targets (Lipsett 2008). An early focus of New Labour attention was reform of the teachers' pay structure and the introduction of a more formalised process of performance management (PM), explicitly link-ing pay and performance. Alongside PM a national capability procedure, providing for the fast-track dismissal of incompetent teachers, was also introduced. Finally, weakened local education authorities (LEAs), which looked destined during the Conservative period to be abolished, instead have become transformed into transmission belts of central policies and initiatives, including ironically the expansion of academies largely indepen-dent of their control (Chitty 2008).

Many of the reforms were introduced within a rhetoric emphasising greater equality (Whitty 2008), especially in regard to student underperformance in urban areas, and New Labour's social democratic infused commitment to a measure of social justice did mark it apart from the previous Conservative administration. However, there is little evidence that gaps in performance have narrowed significantly. What is more apparent is that in choosing to reject Bernstein's (1971) contention that 'education cannot compensate for society' New Labour has added to the pressure on teachers by increasing the emphasis on performativity (Ball 2003), often placing the most pressure on teachers in those schools in the most difficult circumstances.

SCHOOL SECTOR RESTRUCTURING AND
THE CRISIS IN INDUSTRIAL RELATIONS

A feature of much of the reform agenda outlined here is that it has taken place in an environment in which schoolteachers are organized collectively in teacher unions, with relatively high density levels. At very least, and in contrast to the vast majority of books on education management (for example, Blandford 1997, Brighouse and Woods 1999), it is important to acknowledge the extent to which teacher unions engage with, are involved in, and are able to shape the processes of policy development. However policies in education are not politically neutral but rather the neo-liberal trajectory of policy reflects a political paradigm that promotes a particular set of class interests. Conversely, teacher unions are organizations that represent the collective interests of teachers as workers, and therefore, also possess a class dimension. Teacher unions therefore are not just 'players' in a policy process in which neo-liberal ideas drive policy: teacher unions do not just 'engage' with policy, but also become the focus of policy itself insofar as some policies have the express aim of weakening their influence. In this dynamic, it then becomes important not only to understand details of both the nature of individual unions and their histories, but also the ways in which they have responded to current policy approaches that have sought to weaken and undermine teacher unionism either through opposition or incorporation.

Teacher Unionism

Schoolteacher unionism in England exhibits a complex multi-unionism that has been characterised by fragmentation and division. One source of this division is that between employees in different grades. For example, two teacher unions draw their membership from the 'Leadership Group' in schools (primarily headteachers and principals and their deputies and assistants, but increasingly senior support staff such as school business managers). The Association of School and College Leaders (ASCL) (formerly the Secondary Heads Association) is one of the two headteacher unions, having 12,000 members (Certification Officer Report 2006) restricted to those working in the State sector. Local representation is provided by local lay officers, or, often, retired members who are paid on a retainer basis for carrying out casework. As its origins indicate, union membership is concentrated in the secondary sector, with primary sector headteachers largely members in the National Association of Head Teachers (NAHT), which has nearly 40,000 members. It faces similar problems of securing local representatives and again sometimes has to rely on retired members. Neither union is affiliated to the Trades Union Congress (TUC). In some cases members hold a dual membership, being members of ASCL or NAHT as well as one of the main classroom teacher unions.

Classroom teachers are primarily in one of three unions, all of which are TUC affiliated. Moreover, each of these unions has headteacher/principal members. According to Certification Officer Reports the National Union of Teachers (NUT) is the largest organisation with nearly 362,000 members in 2006. It has its origins in the elementary schools school sector and has continued to be stronger in the primary sector. The union's early campaigns were for national pay scales and opposition to payment by results (Tropp 1957), aims that still inform its policies today. The union has often adopted progressive policies on broader educational issues and was a leading contributor to the campaign for comprehensive education. Formed from local associations of teachers the union has a strong branch structure, although in many respects the union's organisation is highly centralised, reflecting the historic importance of full-time officials in national pay bargaining. Despite the centralised structure, policies and positions tend to be contested. A strong feature of the union has been the presence and influence of radical political organisation for much of its history. In the early part of the twentieth century there was significant radical socialist and feminist activity around the union (Kean 1990, Seifert 1984) and this has continued as a feature of NUT organisation. The union is therefore characterised by substantial factional activity with senior positions always being strongly contested by well-organised caucuses in the union.

The main competitor to the NUT has consistently been the National Association of Schoolmasters Union of Women Teachers (NASUWT), a union formed as its name implies, by the merger of the National Association of Schoolmasters and the Union of Women Teachers in 1976 (both organisations were originally splinters from the NUT, although each had broken away for very different reasons). The union has grown steadily since 1976, reaching almost 290,000 in 2006, with membership reflecting its historical strength in secondary schools where males predominate. Like the NUT it has a strong network of branches supported by regional offices. Unlike the NUT, the union has had less concern with educational issues as such, preferring to concentrate on terms and conditions of employment and being willing to take industrial action in their pursuit.

The third major teacher union is the Association of Teachers and Lecturers (ATL) (originally the Assistant Masters and Mistresses Association, AMMA), and formed in 1978 out of unions representing teachers in grammar schools. However, it also has a significant membership in the private and independent sector and also a small membership in further education. More recently it has expanded its membership in the primary sector and by 2006 had over 200,000 members in total. The union has made limited efforts to recruit support staff in schools, although maintaining good relations with fellow-TUC union Unison prevents this being an aggressive recruitment campaign. The union has a reputation for being moderate and concentrating on education policy rather than industrial relations and this latter absence is reflected in its relative lack of workplace representation and organisation.

The fourth union, Voice, representing largely classroom teachers, was until 2008 the Professional Association of Teachers (PAT). Established only in 1970, it emerged as a counter to the growing militancy of teachers and was overtly opposed to teachers taking strike action. A continuing feature of the union is its 'cardinal rule' that precludes its members taking industrial action. It is not affiliated to the TUC and its numbers are small, 33,500 in 2006, and consequently it has little representation at school level.

The NUT was the dominant union throughout the twentieth century and this was reflected in teacher representation in the national Burnham negotiating structure until its abolition in 1987. The union had 13 seats compared to the 7 of NASUWT and 4 of AMMA (ATL) (Seifert 1987:50),

Table 2.1   Teacher Union Membership 1985–2007/8

	1985	2001/2	2002/3	2003/4	2004/5	2005/6	2006/7	2007/8
NUT	235,000	314,174	331,910	324,284	330,709	361,987	368,006	374,170
NASUWT	127,000	253,584	265,219	304,762	327,953	289,930	298,884	313,350
ATL (AMMA)	95,000	186,774	202,585	201,845	195,511	203,241	207,075	208,568
NAHT				40,233	40,524	39,521	39,292	39,093
ASCL				11,084	11,557	12,341	12,760	13,217
Voice								37,689

(All figures from Annual Returns to the Certification Officer)

although in its latter years this balance of representation probably did not reflect relative membership strengths and partly accounts for the failure of other unions, such as NASUWT, to campaign for the restoration of Burnham-style negotiating rights. Moreover, with the abolition of the Burnham Committee the NUT's relative predominance has continued to weaken and there has followed a growth of other teacher organisations (Table 2.1). Acquiring accurate comparative figures for teacher unions is difficult due to the varied conditions of membership and geographical reach of the organisations. Most unions recruit in the schools sector only, but ATL and Voice also recruit in the further education sector and both unions are now taking into membership teaching assistants. The NUT recruits only in England and Wales, whereas the NASUWT recruits across the UK, including Northern Ireland.

The competition between unions, different emphases within their policies, in part reflecting their different constituencies, all provide predispositions that colour their responses to Government reforms. This becomes particularly apparent with regard to the workforce remodelling reforms discussed in this volume.

Teacher Unions and the State

Teachers' high levels of union organisation have traditionally been recognised by a central role in policy development. For example, the Burnham Committee that provided teachers with national collective bargaining rights was established in 1919. From about this time teachers, often through their unions, enjoyed significant influence in many areas of education policy. Pay and conditions of service were largely handled through national collective bargaining machinery (although pay and conditions of service were traditionally dealt with separately) whilst professional issues were in many ways left to individual teachers' professional judgement (Grace 1978, Lawton 1992). The post-war period is often presented as a form of tri-partism (Coates 1972) in which education policy was determined by LAs, teachers (through their unions) and central government, with the latter being very often a junior partner. Lawn (1996) describes this as a period of 'indirect rule' for teachers, in which responsible attitudes to pay and professional issues were rewarded with a relative absence of direct State intervention. Indeed the striking feature of this period was the lack of direct intervention by the central State, with LAs and the teaching profession appearing as the custodians of the system.

The equilibrium of this model came under increasing pressure as the early signs of capitalist crisis began to emerge. One of the first manifestations of this can be seen in 1965 when the Department of Education and Science (DES) significantly increased its voting power on the Burnham Committee, frustrated by what McCarthy described as a system with 'employers who do not pay and paymasters who do not employ' (quoted in Leopold and Beaumont 1986: 32). This development provided an early indication of the central State's desire to assert greater control over the level of public spending, and to wrest some of that control from LAs. Pressures on these arrangements grew as teachers became increasingly drawn into industrial action over issues of pay, pensions and redundancies (Seifert 1987). However, what in the 1970s were tensions between the unions and a Labour Government committed to social democracy, but increasingly buffeted by economic circumstances and dictated to by the International Monetary Fund, became very different when in 1979 the Thatcher Government was elected on a much more openly anti–organised labour agenda. One of the defining features of Thatcherism was its sharp political break with post-war welfarism and its developing, ideological critique of the institutions of social democracy (Gamble 1988). Within the new framework, organised labour was not something to be accommodated, but to be confronted and challenged. In the industrial sectors of the economy this challenge was to be driven by anti-union legislation and the use of a contrived recession to weaken union strength. In the services, and in public sector services in particular, the approach was different. Anti-union legislation clearly applied across the economy, but the public services were also presented as being the victims of 'producer capture', a conviction that professionals 'take over' public services and run them for their own benefit, rather than that of users (now reconstituted as 'consumers'). Here additional approaches were required (Demaine 1993).

The most obvious manifestation of the more overt conflict between teachers and the State was the 1984–1986 pay dispute, the significance of which was overshadowed by the higher profile miners' strike. The teachers' defeat in this dispute then made their unions vulnerable to further attacks. This became most obvious when the Government suspended the Burnham Committee and replaced it in 1987 with a temporary 'advisory committee' charged with investigating issues relating to teachers' pay and making recommendations to the Secretary of State. The establishment of the Interim Advisory Committee (IAC) effectively represented a statutory abolition of teachers' negotiating rights. This was the end of national collective bargaining for one of the most highly unionised groups of workers any-where in the workforce (Busher and Saran 1992). The temporary suspension subsequently became permanent when the IAC was replaced by the School Teachers' Review Body (STRB) advising on teachers' pay.

The 1987 abolition of negotiating rights was, however, not the only means by which the central State sought to curb the power of teacher unions. In 1988, the ERA introduced a raft of measures which created a much more hostile environment within which unions functioned. Perhaps the most significant element of this was the new relationship between schools and LAs as a result of the introduction of LMS, and grant-maintained status. LMS was a form of site-based management ostensibly intended to de-centralise decision-making to the point of delivery, thereby increasing efficiency and responsiveness. For teacher unions it not only represented a key element in the move towards establishing a quasi-market system (by linking school funding directly to student numbers), but it also weakened many formal links between schools and LAs. For example, LAs were no longer able to insist that local collective agreements between the LA and teacher unions were binding on local schools, but rather it was for school governing bodies to determine their own policies on issues such as redundancy, discipline and grievance. Grant-maintained schools pushed this a stage further by removing these schools from any form of local authority control. This school autonomy posed deliberate problems for teacher unions: their power base in the LAs (where local union officers were significant figures, supported by facilities agreements) was substantially undermined and teacher unions faced the prospect of dealing with thousands of individual schools.

Examining these developments, it is possible to construct a scenario in which the restructuring of public services, and the enforced marginalisation of teacher unions, point to a potential crisis in industrial relations from which teacher unions emerge stronger. The combination of membership retention, the loss of national bargaining, and concomitant changes to public sector labour processes, provided the bases for Fairbrother's (1994, 1996, 2000a, 2000b) contention that policies designed to weaken public sector unions could turn into their opposite through a process of union renewal. By encouraging de-centralised, workplace decision-making, the changes would effectively call forth local workplace-based trade union organisation to counter the development of local managers' power. By renewal Fairbrother envisaged 'forms of unionism where the emphasis is on decentralization rather than on centralization, egalitarian forms of organization and operation rather than hierarchy, and involvement and participation rather than passivity and remoteness' (1996: 112). While not an inevitable process, where union members do exploit the new circumstances in which they find themselves, 'there is the prospect that a process of union renewal will occur' (Fairbrother, 1996: 111). Despite qualifications, the suggestion was that unions in the State sector were 'in the process of reconstitution and reorganization' (Fairbrother, 2000a: 48).

As has been argued elsewhere (Carter 2004), Fairbrother's perspective is informed by both a description of claimed developments and a normative position that supports workplace democracy and workers' self-activity: both elements have been contested by those who, in different ways, perceive the future of effective trade unionism in continued or increased centralisation (Heery 1998, McIlroy 1997). The almost seamless movement within his works, from the possibility of renewal to the accomplished fact without much substantive evidence, has guaranteed that Fairbrother's claims have also faced more detailed challenges from those who, while not opposed to the idea of the need for renewal, have difficulty being convinced of the detail and extent of the process (see Carter and Poynter 1999, Gall 1998). In response to the contention that public sector unions would in effect become the crucible of union renewal, Colling (1995), for instance, countered that as far as Unison in local government was concerned, evidence was that 'rigor mortis' rather than renewal was a more accurate description.

Despite the lack of evidence to support the theory, it found some support within research on industrial relations within education. Ironside and Seifert (1995), in their study of school-based industrial relations in the period immediately after the ERA, document a series of changes that produce the kind of conditions outlined as precursors for the development of workplace-level industrial relations. Among these changes were the introduction of private sector management techniques; increased use of unqualified staff and the dilution of the workforce; the downgrading of teacher skills and a reduction in teachers' autonomy. As a consequence, they claimed that traditional industrial relations institutions 'are in disarray and have not been replaced by acceptable alternatives. This is to suggest that there is a deep crisis at the heart of the school system' (Ironside and Seifert 1995: 18). Elsewhere, they talk of the 'crisis facing school managers and employers' (Ironside and Seifert 1995: 120) because the reforms have pushed targets and accountability down to school level, forcing headteachers and governors to make difficult decisions, at the very point when the there was a 'breakdown of LEA-level personnel and industrial relations functions' (Ironside and Seifert 1995: 120). A second element accentuating the crisis was the pressure on schools to address the substantive problem of the cost of labour in schools. According to Ironside and Seifert this element could only be resolved through 'work intensification, de-skilling and selective reward management' (Ironside and Seifert 1995: 121). They note, for instance, that the loss of some peripheral roles leads to an intensification of teachers' work because 'they spend more time performing the demanding work in the classroom' (Ironside and Seifert 1995: 179). In short, reforms were required that would go to the very heart of later debates about workforce remodelling.

Ironside and Seifert maintain that the consequence of the reforms and the pressures on schools would be that 'schools will become the centre for conflict-laden issues' (Ironside and Seifert 1995: 213). Teacher unions therefore face practices that have major implications for pay and conditions and 'effective union organisation around school-based issues involves a new role for branches . . . the development of new networks and structures with a focus on workplace activity' (Ironside and Seifert 1995: 240). Despite claims of crisis and conflict, however, Ironside and Seifert were unable to show widespread discontent with, or abandonment of, traditional forms, and industrial relations still centred on the LA and union lay officials. There was little formal trade union activity in schools, with union representatives having neither the skills, nor the inclination, to become negotiators. Similarly, headteachers remained first and foremost professionals rather than managers.

Later research on the extent of changes in workplace practice and trade union organisation brought on by LMS by Carter (2004) and Stevenson (2003) could find neither evidence that industrial relations at LA level had changed appreciably, nor any growth in workplace-based organisation. One of the factors that framed this current research was the observation that workforce remodelling would add impetus to all the pressures identified by Fairbrother at a general public sector level and more specifically by Ironside and Seifert at school level. Thus, although no evidence could initially be found for an industrial relations crisis within education or a strategic union renewal response, the reforms might at last breach the dam of redundant tradition. It was also necessary for our research to take account of developments in school sector industrial relations that were very different to those anticipated by either Fairbrother, or Ironside and Seifert—principally the emergence of a national social partnership to fill the vacuum created by Burnham's abolition.

EDUCATION RESTRUCTURING, WORKFORCE REFORM AND THE 'NEW INDUSTRIAL RELATIONS'

New Labour's focus on education policy, famously articulated by Tony Blair describing his three highest priorities in government as 'Education, education, education', quickly generated significant, and potentially unsustainable, pressures. First, pressure emerged from heightened expectations, and in particular the Government's emphasis on achieving improved results against national targets in standardized tests. Second, the welter of new initiatives designed to drive forward the improvement in 'standards' produced an overload of demands. This latter pressure manifested itself not only in terms of major initiatives to influence teachers' pedagogy and practice (such as the national strategies for literacy and numeracy), but also in terms of a burgeoning bureaucracy associated with the growing pressures of accountability and the drive to raise standards. By early 2000 it was clear that the twin pressures to raise standards, and the associated increase in teachers' workload, were raising serious questions about the school sector's stability and sustainability (Barker 2008). These twin pressures in turn presaged the focus on workforce reform.

The Government's problems became clearer when it appeared that for all the proliferation of initiatives and strategies to drive forward improvements in target-driven standards, progress appeared to have stalled and results had plateaued. The very pressures to drive up performance, and the related accountability apparatus, were, however, a significant factor in creating a growing crisis in teacher supply (Morris 2001) with problems in a number of subjects (mathematics, science, modern languages), particular regions (London and the South East), and for specific posts (primary headships). The general factor of workload related to greater Government expectations of teacher performance was therefore central to the problem of recruitment and retention (Barmby 2006, Smithers and Robinson 2001).

The background and long-term pressure to address workload issues were transformed into an urgent political necessity by the threat of teacher industrial action in early 2001. When the General Secretary of the NUT was asked to comment on independent figures for student teacher recruit- ment (Cassidy and Hodges 2001) during the North of England Education Conference, he responded by saying that the union would take industrial action (interview, National Official 1, NUT). As a result the claim appeared as the front-page lead of the *Evening Standard* newspaper. The pressure on the Government mounted with a concerted move by all major classroom unions towards industrial action over workload. In a rare show of unity members of the NUT, the NASUWT and the ATL all voted for an identi- cal resolution demanding a 35-hour week at their 2001 conferences. The industrial action was scheduled to take effect in the autumn school term if the Government refused to meet the unions' demands. As a result of the growing pressure in March 2001 the Department for Education and Skills (DfES) commissioned PricewaterhouseCoopers (PwC) to undertake a review to:

> identify the main factors that determine teachers' and head teachers' workload, and to develop a programme of practical action to eliminate excessive workload and promote the most effective use of all resources in schools in order to raise standards of pupil achievement.
>
> (PwC 2001: 1)

The subsequent PwC report claimed that during term time teachers aver- aged a 52-hour working week, of which teaching time occupied only 35%. The report's findings both substantiated teachers' complaints about heavy workload and long hours, and strengthened the official view that teachers' jobs needed restructuring to increase the amount of teaching time. The report proposed a programme of reforms to address both constituencies, including the transfer of routine administrative work and some pasto- ral duties to support staff, and guaranteed time for teachers to plan and prepare. Amongst other recommendations were that 'the government and the main relevant bodies should seek to reach a common understanding over the main objectives' and that together they should:

> monitor the programme, ensure its effectiveness and ensure sufficient early momentum, as part of the overall drive to transform schools. The programme provides a basis for workload reduction through reforms at national level, and through work at the school level based on discussion between staff and managers, and in discussion where relevant with LEAs.

(PwC 2001: 2)

As such, it was not only the details of reforms that were to prove influential: the architecture for the processes of change broadly mirrored the Social Partnership arrangements subsequently adopted.

The same year, the Secretary of State for Education, Estelle Morris stated that it was time to 'remodel' the school workforce to take advantage of wider, adult skills. Classroom assistants, who would need neither a degree, nor to have undergone postgraduate teacher training, should be allowed to take classes under the supervision of qualified teachers (Morris 2001). In 2002, these ideas were developed through the DfES tendering a pathfinder project, *Transforming the School Workforce* (TSW), designed to explore new modes of delivery, so that teachers could spend more time teaching and thus raising standards. Reflecting the increasing penetration of private sector interests into the process of education (Ball 2007), the tender was won by a public-private partnership headed by the then Director of the London Borough Leadership Centre within the Institute of Education, Pat Collarbone. The private element was represented by *Consulting Strategies Ltd*, a company of change management consultants.

In contrast to the more national focus of the PwC report, the TSW project aimed to examine the potential of school-based innovation. The leaders of the project had a particular model of change management, focused on shifting organisational cultures, that involved five steps to successful change: Mobilization, Discovery, Deepening, Developing, and Delivery (Spooner 2006: 15), known as the M4Ds. The underlying premise of the model was that, once adopted, it could effectively be used to achieve any number of changes, not just ones directly related to workforce remodelling. It was essentially therefore about breaking down demarcations in order to increase flexibility and capacity: remodelling 'is a way of breaking down the cultural and organizational barriers to change' (Collarbone 2005c). As such, she contended that 'remodelling is different from other school initiatives. In fact rather than being just one initiative, it's the glue that binds the others together' (Collarbone 2005b: 5).

Collarbone's analysis of workforce remodelling places the objective of tackling teacher workload as a subsidiary goal to that of securing wider cultural change in schools. Such cultural change can be identified at several different levels, and includes the shift from a conception of the school workforce as one separated into teachers and 'non-teachers' to one that focuses on the whole school team. Linked to this wider conception of the school workforce was a conviction that workforce remodelling would help build capacity in schools by distributing leadership, and that these new and more inclusive ways of working would in turn generate a more flexible labour force. Such an analysis immediately generated tensions as some of these objectives had the support of teacher unions (a focus on the whole school workforce), whilst others (increased labour flexibility) did not. These points of agreement and disagreement subsequently played out in the ways that workforce remodelling was experienced in individual schools. These issues are explored in later chapters.

TSW selected 32 pathfinder schools with a view to identifying strategies to reduce teacher workload while raising standards. The standards agenda, therefore, was not the immediate concern, with teacher workload being the priority from which improved standards would follow. One remodelling consultant, who was also a primary headteacher, interviewed for the project had also previously been involved in a Pathfinder school:

> no-one mentioned standards particularly in that process. This was to do with workload . . . you could see that down the road a side-effect may well be to do with standards, but that was a later effect rather than a focus.
>
> (Remodelling Consultant, Shire)

Initially, the emphasis was very much on demonstrating the changes that could be wrought in schools and there were clearly defined ideas in advance:

> the DfES set up all these little stalls to direct us and these are the developments we want you to do. So there was a big thing on bursar training . . . this is what you're going to do. There . . . was a big thing on IT: this is what you're going to do . . . there was none of that real 'this interesting change process' . . . the action plan was almost written before the project (laughs).
>
> (Remodelling Consultant, Shire)

Amongst the innovations central to the pathfinder project were: the use of additional administrative and clerical staff to take on tasks that need not be carried out by teachers; the use of teaching assistants to provide non-contact time for teachers; and the holding of 'Blue Sky' staff events to devise radical remodelling solutions to alleviate excessive workload. As the project developed, there was more emphasis on cultural change. Importance was given to the formation of school-level change teams comprising representatives from all levels and functions in the school (Thomas *et al.* 2004: xxxiv), a feature that was to be prominent in later nationwide training. The emphasis on change teams, apparently unencumbered by notions of negotiations with unions, would be able 'to take ideas further than had previously been possible' (Thomas *et al.* 2004: li). The perspectives of the TSW project became more focussed on cultural change and capacity building. According to Gunter and Butt's evaluation (2007: 9), 'Reform is more than the employment and deployment . . . It involves dispositional change'. Tellingly there was no mention of unions in the evaluation of the project.

Whether the DfES lost some interest in the project is not clear. What is apparent is that events overtook the evaluation of TSW, which, according to Gunter and Butt (2007: 12), was marginalized 'with remodelling rolled out in advance of the evidence on which it was meant to be based'. The explanation of why the TSW project appeared to be left on the sidelines has probably more to do with political expediency than a wilful desire on the part of Government to ignore the evaluations of academic researchers. Industrial action by the teacher unions, and in particular cross-union united action, in which union members refused to undertake a range of administrative tasks or to attend more than one meeting or parents' evening per week, were causing some management problems in schools. More significantly, the industrial action created a political imperative on the part of Government to act, and resulted in the Government holding formal, national talks with the teacher unions. They were the first such talks in the 15 years since the abolition of teachers' negotiating rights in 1987 and marked a turnaround of New Labour's initial stance: 'David Blunkett's instructions in the DfES as far as we can ascertain were "Don't let the unions through the door!". Which I always thought was very interesting for a Labour Minister but there we are' (Senior National Official 1, NASUWT).

Despite an initially frosty relationship between Government and unions, therefore, discussions began to develop when Government recognized the need to work with, rather than against, the teacher unions. What followed were protracted discussions, involving the DfES, teacher unions, local government employers and support staff unions: 'It didn't start off as a negotiation. It actually started off as a set of discussions and scoping about what you could do in relation to Estelle Morris' [Secretary of State] very gloomy prognosis' [about teacher shortages] (National Official 1, NUT).

However, as these discussions developed, they increasingly incorporated issues around teachers' contracts of employment, ensuring a move towards more formal negotiations. The key to addressing the problem of teacher workload quickly became an enhanced role of support staff. This theme had been developing for some time, with the 1998 Green Paper *Teachers: Meeting the Challenge of Change* (DfEE 1998), for example, committed to increasing the numbers of support staff in schools. The PwC Report had also focused on this issue, but the details of this enhanced role now became formalized and consolidated in the discussions between Government, employers and unions and resulted in the first collective agreement between employers and unions since the abolition of negotiating rights. *Raising Standards and Tackling Workload* (DfES 2003), sometimes referred to as the National Workload Agreement, aimed to securing 'progressive reductions in teachers' overall hours over the next four years' (DfES 2003: 2) and introduced a number of contractual changes to teachers' duties in order to secure this. Principally these were:

- A requirement that a range of administrative tasks (the so-called '25 tasks') were to be performed by support staff and were not to be carried out by teachers. These included, amongst other things, bulk photocopying, data entry, collecting money from students and mounting displays.
- The provision of a guaranteed 10% of a teacher's normal timetabled teaching time for planning, preparation and assessment (PPA).
- A ceiling of 38 hours per year that a teacher could be required to cover for absent colleagues, with an expectation that over time there would be 'a downward pressure on the burden of cover' (DfES 2003: 7)

As has been indicated, the enhanced use of support staff was central to achieving these changes, and as a consequence changes were made to statutory orders governing teaching that allowed for staff without qualified teacher status (QTS) to assume responsibility for whole classes, under the supervision of a teacher. This provision allowed, for instance, cover supervisors to be established in schools to cover the classes of absent teachers. The extension of support staff roles to include the responsibility for taking whole classes proved to be particularly contentious, and the NUT, reflecting its historical commitment to an all-graduate profession, took the decision not to sign the agreement. Whilst this headline issue was the ostensible reason underlying the NUT's refusal to sign the agreement (NUT 2003), it is also the case that the NUT's broader opposition to the general direction of New Labour policy, as well as particular issues, made the union's support less likely. A senior official of the NUT indicated in interview that although the union appeared to reject the agreement on the basis of a single issue (the use of staff without QTS to have whole class teaching responsibilities), the reality was that the NUT's opposition was more complex.

> I think the real reason actually underlying it was that Doug McAvoy, the General Secretary at the time, but also the Executive, there was a feeling that there had been a number of initiatives which were contrary to NUT policy in general, particularly the 'naming and shaming' thing that Byers introduced in '98, but the obsession with structure rather than standards, the whole railroading through of what it believed to be a performance-related pay system without evidence that actually made Doug and the Executive disinclined to sign up to a blank cheque. And

that was the reason why we didn't sign actually, I think that was the basic reason why we didn't sign up. I think we could have signed on the agreement if the political environment in general had been different.

(National Official 1, NUT)

The NUT's refusal to sign the agreement assumed a double significance. Not only did the union set itself in opposition to key elements of the agreement, such as the use of cover supervisors, with potential implications for school level implementation, but the union also found itself outside of the body that had formally emerged from the Workload Agreement negotiations and had become known as the Social Partnership. The agreement itself refers to 'Government, in partnership with other Signatories to this Agreement' (DfES 2003: 11) and it this language that informed the metamorphosis of the group from signatories to an agreement to a more long-lasting and formalised body. This transformation was facilitated in the first instance by a body established to oversee implementation of the National Agreement—the Workload Agreement Monitoring Group (WAMG), which meets on a regular basis and is made up of signatories to the National Agreement. The WAMG has subsequently been supplemented by the formation of the Rewards and Incentive Group focused on aspects of teachers' pay (although pay itself remains the responsibility of the School Teachers' Review Body) and the Support Staff Review. The expanded role of the Social Partnership resulted in the development of the 'remodelling agenda' to embrace a major restructuring of teachers' pay in 2006 whereby generic Management Allowances (MA)s to reward teachers with additional responsibilities were replaced by new teaching and learning responsibility points, and later, in 2007, by the introduction of new PM regulations which strengthened the link between appraisal and pay.

The 'remodelling agenda' outlined here is both substantial and significant. In many ways it marks a decisive phase in New Labour's programme of education reform. However, many of its key elements had been a feature of education reform in the period since 1988. The increased use of non-QTS personnel, an enhanced role for 'middle leaders' and the increased use of appraisal and performance pay to evaluate and reward teachers had all been the subjects of significant policy developments prior to workforce remodelling. Whilst it is important therefore to analyse what is distinctive about workforce remodelling, workforce reform must be analysed as part of a much longer term trajectory that has shaped teachers' experiences of changes in their labour process. Workforce reform in the period following the signing of the National Workload Agreement is significant, but it is no 'watershed moment'—rather workforce remodelling is better viewed as a phase in a period of on-going restructuring in which State education and teachers' work are re-shaped by the exigencies of neo-liberal reform and its interface with wider social forces as it seeks to both accommodate and confront the forces that resist it.

CONCLUSION

Education reform in England has been radical and substantial in the years since 1988. In many ways England can be said to have acted as a laboratory for the neo-liberal experiment in restructuring the public services in general and schools in particular. Successive UK governments have demonstrated a particular willingness to introduce market features into school systems, to seek to enhance the role of the private sector, and to use the disciplinary mechanisms of powerful inspectorates and enhanced managerial controls to assert greater control over the system. A key feature of these reforms has been to secure greater control over teachers and their work, to reduce the scope for professional autonomy and to restrict teachers' ability to make decisive judgements about professional and pedagogical issues. However, the target of reforms has extended beyond teachers as individuals, and the reforms have also sought to weaken and undermine teachers' ability to organise collectively through their unions.

The undermining of teacher unions has been both direct and indirect. The former approach is exemplified by the removal of teachers' collective bargaining rights in 1987, something rarely seen elsewhere, even in countries adopting equally vigorous neo-liberal agendas. More indirect attempts to weaken union organisation lie in the restructuring of schools along autonomous and marketised lines—beginning in 1988 with LMS and the advent of grant-maintained schools, and developing more recently with the growth of academy and trust schools. Although the reforms have been designed to weaken trade union organisation, there have been several analyses suggesting that such reforms might actually prove a source of union renewal for public sector unions in general (Fairbrother 1996) and teacher unions in particular (Ironside and Seifert 1995). Whilst these perspectives have found both supporters and critics there is a need to subject these claims to a robust empirical study. This need has become even greater in an environment in which school sector industrial relations have developed in very different ways to those envisaged by Ironside and Seifert. In particular the emergence of a specific form of social partnership model has profound implications for school sector industrial relations at national, local and workplace levels. In the chapter that follows, research is described that provides the basis for these developments to be analysed.

3   Research Methods
Processes, Issues and Implications

INTRODUCTION

The two opening chapters set out the theoretical and conceptual contexts that underpin our research and presented a discussion of these general conceptual issues as they relate and apply to the workforce remodelling agenda in England. This chapter provides an account of the research process and some of the issues that arose from it. Given the issues being researched, and the time at which the fieldwork was conducted, the investigation was clearly politically sensitive. This chapter reflects on how this context impacted on the ways in which the project changed and developed over its two-year lifetime. In doing so the rationale for the research and the difficulties encountered during the fieldwork are discussed, and an account of the theoretical framework for the data analysis is developed.

RESEARCH DESIGN

As outlined in Chapter 1, the principal aim of the research was to explore how teacher trade unions have engaged with workforce reform and within this to investigate, on the one hand, the ways in which teacher trade unions have been involved with the process of workforce remodelling and on the other, the ways in which trade unions themselves have been shaped by the remodelling policy agenda. The second, related, aim was to explore the relationship between this agenda and teachers' work and thereby to establish the link between teacher trade unions and the nature of teachers' work as implementation of remodelling was passed from national to local level. Whitty and Edwards (1994) argue that the sometimes conflicting aims of policy, the interaction of interest groups and individuals, and the relative influence that each might bring to bear at particular times, mean that policy implementation is a complex process with no guaranteed outcomes (see also Scott 2000), and this observation is particularly relevant to workforce reform: there are relatively high numbers of stakeholders at the different levels of policy generation and implementation, potentially offering considerable scope for differing interpretations and outcomes. Thus, rather than attempting a broad overview of developments through surveys, we wanted to be able to capture the nuances and details of workforce remodelling as the agenda was shaped by different actors in different political and educational arenas. Our fieldwork therefore consisted of interviews in which participants could take time to explore relevant issues and to reflect on the implications of workforce reform for the education system in general and their own organisation in particular.

The aims of the project were to be achieved through interviews with:

- national-level teacher trade unionists, both inside and outside the Social Partnership, to gain their views on recent developments in teacher industrial relations, on the formation of the workforce remodelling agenda and the impact this agenda might be having on their own union;
- other non-union members of the national Workload Agreement Monitoring Group (WAMG) to gain a broader view of its remit and modus operandi;
- Local authority (LA) level teacher trade unionists in three case study authorities to discover how local industrial relations were conducted and the impact that remodelling was having on those structures and relationships;
- other members of the local WAMG—now known as Local Social Partnerships (LSPs)—to gain a broader view of developments in local industrial relations;
- staff and union representatives in two primary and two secondary schools in each of the three case study authorities to discover how schools engaged with the reforms together with the effects they were having on the school workforce.

Data collection at these three levels was supplemented by scrutiny of available documentation to provide a more rounded view of the processes under investigation.

The value of qualitative research is often considered to be controversial, partly because—in contrast to the quantitative approach—there are no explicit criteria on which it can be judged (Hammersley 2007) and partly because it does not well serve what has been called the 'science of school management' (Pring 2000a: 247). Consequently, results are not easily translated into an applied model for best practice. In addition, as Pring (2000a, 2000b) has argued, there is a dichotomy between quantitative and qualitative methods, with the former regarded as objective, rooted in the scientific method and somehow more rigorous, while the latter are seen to be based on a kind of social constructionism that sees all social life is negotiated, which has the effect of negating concepts such as truth and reality.

These charges against qualitative research can be addressed in two ways. The first is to draw on Pring's argument that our understanding and explanations of the social world are more complex and subtle than either of the previously mentioned approaches. He suggests that the type of constructionism in which all social life is negotiated fails to take account of differing power relations within any social grouping, of inherited conceptualisations and categorisations, or of an understanding of what it means to be a person—which he defines as 'a centre of consciousness capable of intentional action, rational behaviour, emotional response and potential for assuming some level of responsibility' (Pring 2000b: 53). Arguing that conceptualisations and categorisations provide a framework for meaning and, subsequently, for negotiation of meaning (Pring 2000b: 52), he is suggesting that, rather than being trapped in the hermeneutic circle where there is no 'bedrock 'fact of the matter'' (Scott and Usher 1999: 26), people interpret and construct their world within certain features of reality; there are not multiple realities but different ways in which reality is conceived. He uses the example of family, but the example of schools or industrial relations could be used equally well as they are a feature of social life, they change over time, but they are indisputably there and open to differing interpretations of the functions and processes within. Our approach follows Pring's lead and, while recognising that there are different forms of both constructivism and realism (see, for example, Scott 2000), is realist and interpretivist in Pring's sense; one in which we are seeking to understand changes and developments that arise from the policy of workforce remodelling from the perspectives of the research participants. Thus, while we cannot offer one definitive truth on the matter, we can analyse our different participants' stories to interpret developments and, in the spirit of Somekh's (2007) exhortation, engage in 'speculative knowledge' to assess the future position of teacher trade unions within the education system.

The second response is to be transparent over the research process itself. Thomas and Gorard argue that there are measures that researchers can take to ensure that their work is 'done properly' (Thomas and Gorard 2007: 240) in the sense that the research is conducted in good faith, with integrity (see, for example, British Educational Research Association [BERA] 2004) and employs a process of reflection on, defence of, and responsibility for, decisions and judgements made during the course of the project (Gewirtz and Cribb 2007). One part of this involves including consideration of the values of the research team. Research is political (Scott and Usher 1999: 1) and openness over such matters allows the reader to see how the researchers' backgrounds have framed the questions, methods and decisions taken during the course of the project and how they may impact upon the analysis. As the opening chapter suggests, the research is underpinned by a critique of neo-liberal reforms within the school sector that link into, and are part of, the process of globalisation. However while all three researchers accept that globalisation is in process and that it takes a neo-liberal form, there is no unanimity between us on interpretation of these developments, and we each found our views interrogated as our assumptions were challenged during the course of the project. We believe these thought-provoking discussions, in which we have each had to explain and justify particular points or approaches, have made a positive contribution to the conduct and the integrity of the research.

Another element of conducting the research 'properly' involves careful consideration of the methods of data collection. The first step in this case was to create a set of ethical guidelines that concerned issues of confidentiality and anonymity together with arrangements for data storage and retrieval, thus formalising expectations for both researcher and research participant. The second was to devise a semi-structured interview schedule for each different level of research, in each case consisting of a number of open-ended questions that focused on the different areas of workforce remodelling; we aimed at a loosely structured conversation in which an element of control was retained but in which participants were encouraged to raise issues that they believed salient or important. This allowed interviews to take unexpected directions while retaining focus on the main areas of investigation (Walford 1994: 35–36). The researchers then conducted the interviews in pairs, ensuring both consistency in interviewing approach and adherence to the interview schedule. Joint interviewing also had the advantages of giving each member of the team the opportunity to remain involved with the research process and facilitating ongoing informal discussion that often began on the way home from a day's interviews. This was an important aspect of the research in that these discussions offered an opportunity to test our understandings and interpretations at an early stage and allowed us to reflect more fully before feeding ideas and interpretations into the more formal meetings when all three were present.

The integrity of the research was further fostered by the Reference Group, convened early in the project's lifetime. The intention was that this would operate as a sounding board for the research and stimulate discussion both on methods and findings, meeting at critical points and communicating in between these meetings through email. We invited employers, Government and unions to nominate a senior representative but were aware of the sensitivity of the situation in which there may be a tension between the nominees' official and personal views. Given these potential difficulties, there was agreement that Reference Group names would remain undisclosed and that what was said in the meetings would remain confidential to those who were involved. At this stage, the members consisted of one person from each of the six teacher unions, a member of the Training and Development Agency for schools, a member of the Local Government Employers, a primary headteacher, a teacher and a remodelling adviser— a mix of union officials, employers, a civil servant and practitioners that would reflect the interests of all who were involved in the implementation of workforce remodelling. Suggestions from the Reference Group that support staff should be included in the project, on the grounds that workforce remodelling was part of a move to recognise the value of all staff involved in schools, meant that a member of Unison joined at a later date. Regular meetings throughout the lifetime of the project gave rise to lively debate that made a substantial contribution to our thinking and thus to the clarity of our analysis.

ACCESS, SAMPLING AND DATA COLLECTION

The first task in the process of data collection was to interview national-level trade unionists and national WAMG members. In such a situation access to the relevant groups and individuals can be difficult, and our experiences echoed some of those outlined in Walford's (1994) volume *Researching the Powerful in Education*. Very early on it was apparent that the Social Partnership consisted of a powerful network of people who had invested considerable resources into this model of working and were more than anxious that it should be seen as successful. This view was particularly understandable at the time because the Social Partnership was in a potentially critical position with two associations on the 'outside'—the National Union of Teachers (NUT) through refusing to sign the agreement in 2003 and the National Association of Head Teachers (NAHT) through withdrawing at a later date over disagreement about funding. In addition a leak to the *Times Educational Supplement* (Stewart 2003) about an idea for the more extensive use of teaching assistants expressed within WAMG had caused considerable consternation in the public arena, and had contributed to a sensitivity among partnership members regarding confidentiality and possible indiscretions. The immediate result was that officials from both the NUT and the NAHT agreed without hesitation to interviews, but access to the Social Partnership was less straightforward.

One of the key features of the Social Partnership is the unanimity of voice; members are expected to 'promote and promulgate' (DfES 2003: 15) the terms of the National Agreement and, as a consequence, to support the decisions made in the Partnership; as we learned during the course of the interviews, those who were perceived to show disloyalty to the Partnership could come under strong pressure to make good any seemingly unfavourable consequences. The dilemma for individual interviewees was therefore one, in the broadest sense, of corporate loyalty or individual freedom. Members were cautious about the research, and we found we were being tested by different parties within the group: we were invited by civil servants to discuss our research in a formal meeting at the DfES; one official rang up for informal conversations; and another official made it clear that his union was unhappy with certain phrasing in the initial research outline. And, as Fitz and Halpin (1994: 39) comment, individuals within such networks communicate with each other both about the project and the researchers, so passing these 'tests'—both within the Reference Group and in the wider context—was critical to accessing the type of interviews that we wanted—a narrative of each person's understanding of the process and outcome of workforce remodelling within the new industrial relations structures that were part and parcel of the reforms.

Suffice to say that after a presentation of the research to the national WAMG, we were able to assuage any concerns and thereafter to arrange interviews with WAMG members from the four remaining teacher unions and local government representatives. On the advice of the Reference Group we included Unison in the research in order to gain insight into a support staff perspective; Unison has the largest number of education members of the three support staff unions and is regarded by other members as the most active WAMG participant. Views from Unison members are thus included in the study, although the principal focus remains on the six teacher trade unions. Although professing to be supportive of the project, the DfES (now DCSF) refused our invitation to participate in the research on the grounds that it was 'not appropriate', but we were able to interview two senior members of the Training and Development Agency, a body which is closely involved with and reports to WAMG on a regular basis. At this stage of the research we spoke to 18 different people in a total of 12 interviews. Details of interview participants at all levels can be seen in the appendix.

The next stage of the research explored the details of the national agenda including the ways in which workforce reform was being interpreted in particular contexts, and how local industrial relations were affecting and being affected by national level changes in industrial relations. The most appropriate approach for this stage of the research was case study, as this would give insights into the dynamics of policy implementation in specific contexts. Accordingly, and after consultation with the Reference Group on the choice of one LA, we selected a London, a unitary and a rural LA using three criteria: they should be from different geographical regions, they should represent a range of different socio-economic conditions and they should have differing union membership profiles. Both the London Borough and the unitary Authorities had the problems of deprivation associated with inner cities alongside pockets of affluence, whereas the rural LA was relatively sparsely populated but had a more even spread of socio-economic conditions. In terms of the union representation, the London Borough Authority had a strong NUT membership, the rural Authority had an equally strong National Association of Schoolmasters Union of Women Teachers (NASUWT) membership, while the unitary Authority had a more even balance between these two largest unions. We believed that the combination of these three Authorities would enable us to access as wide a range of responses as possible. Throughout the research they are named London Borough, City and Shire Authorities to protect their identity.

Central to the process of workforce reform was the role of the local WAMG[1], the group set up in most Authorities arguably as a mirror image of the national Social Partnership. This body was the key focus for our research at LA level, for interviewing members of each of these groups would enable the exploration of both the impact of the National Agreement on local industrial relations and, in turn, the effect that unions were having on the ways in which policy was interpreted for local schools. We therefore interviewed the following people from each case study LA:

- the LA employee who chaired the local LSP sessions at the time of the interview, plus where possible other LA employee(s) who were involved with workforce remodelling;
- the remodelling adviser(s) employed by each LA;
- the representative(s) of each of the teacher union members. These are referred to in the data presentation by the generic term of 'branch secretary'. Although different union structures mean that this is not necessarily the correct term, it is used to indicate that this person represents his or her union at LA meetings and negotiations.
- the representative(s) of Unison.

Interviewees were invited to raise issues that they believed were of primary importance and to tell the story of workforce remodelling in their authority, their experience of the training, the function of the LSP, the issues that had arisen in the course of the remodelling programme and, in the case of union branch secretaries, the ways in which their own organisation had been involved with and/or affected by the agenda. An important focus in the latter interviews was the unionists' interpretations of the local WAMG's impact on existing bargaining structures and how existing industrial relations structures had been affected by the new body set up in response to the workforce remodelling agenda.

We interviewed representatives from all six teacher unions in City, but were unable to find a representative from Voice in either London Borough or Shire. As in the national level interviews, we included Unison in the research to provide a support staff perspective, again because this union was regarded as the one that attended the local meetings most consistently. In City Authority we also interviewed an elected councillor and an ex-headteacher who were not involved in the LSP but were nonetheless interested in the process as it was affecting their LA. As these were 'one-off' interviews we use them to inform our understanding but do not draw directly from them when presenting the evidence. Access was generously

---

1 Local WAMGs have now been rebranded local social partnerships (LSPs) but, as the research participants often refer to local WAMGs as such, we use the term interchangeably throughout the book.

granted at this level and in total we spoke to 35 people in 29 interviews. Details of these interviews can be seen in the appendix.

The final stage of the research was to interview key members of staff involved with remodelling from two primaries and two secondaries in each case study LA. At this stage, difficulties with access returned as we quickly discovered that mentioning trade unions in early approaches to schools was liable to result in a refusal to participate in the research. We believe there were several reasons that lay behind this. In the first place, the project could be seen as 'high stakes' research for schools in the sense that we were investigating a major plank of Government policy and, although we stressed that this was not an evaluation of remodelling within the school, it could have been interpreted as such and 'failure' in this sense could be damaging to staff morale. Secondly, schools operate in a highly competitive environment and, conscious that any research may throw up perceived inadequacies within the establishment, they are simply unwilling to take the risk of allowing researchers to reveal them to anyone else. Thirdly, industrial relations in schools can be a sensitive area, and there was evidence that it was not one with which some headteachers felt comfortable. This apparent discomfort may have been exacerbated by the recent introduction of teaching and learning responsibility points, which union officers had informed us had been responsible for considerable friction in some schools. There is also the not insubstantial consideration that many schools may receive a considerable number of requests for research and may genuinely not have the time to spare. The irony of adding to teachers' workload through this research was not lost on us—or, indeed, some of our respondents.

4 Setting the Agenda
The Emergence and Significance of 'Social Partnership' at the National Level

INTRODUCTION

Previous chapters have shown how the collapse of the post-war welfarist consensus presaged an attack on teacher unions as successive governments sought to diminish and marginalize their influence. This was most graphically illustrated by the removal of national negotiating rights in 1987 (Busher and Saran 1992), but has been buttressed by many other ways of progressively sidelining teachers and their unions. The election of New Labour in 1997 saw no obvious initial shift in this position, with teachers (explicitly), and their unions (implicitly), presented as resistant to the process of modernisation required to bring about the required transformation of the school system (DfEE 1998). The recent emergence of a national level Social Partnership in English school sector industrial relations is therefore a significant departure in policy. While elements of the school workforce remodelling agenda could be viewed as continuity with previous policy, the emergence of the Social Partnership highlights the need to see policy as both process and product, reflecting the way in which the mechanism of generating policy has become integral within the policy itself. There can be no artificial separation of means and ends; each is embedded in the other.

The significance of the Social Partnership is that it represents the first concerted attempt in 15 years to establish a formal relationship between central government, local authority employers and teacher unions at a national level. This chapter analyses the development of the Partnership. The aim is to establish a conceptual understanding of the Social Partnership model within industrial relations, while clearly recognising the contextual specificity of school sector industrial relations. Some of the key features of Social Partnership working are described—how the Social Partnership functions on an operational basis, how Social Partnership 'business' is determined and the processes by which the Social Partnership arrives at agreed outcomes. Finally, issues relating to the significance and implications of partnership working are assessed, in part from the perspectives of those inside and outside of the Social Partnership.

PARTNERSHIP IN PRACTICE

Chapter 2 described how the Social Partnership emerged, somewhat organically, from the discussions that led up to the signing of the National Workload Agreement, and during the period of the research the Social Partnership appeared to go through a period of consolidating its position in the policy development process. The Partnership grew initially out of the Workload Agreement Monitoring Group (WAMG), a body comprising representatives of the Department for Education and Skills, the Local Government Employers, the Welsh Assembly, five of the six main teacher unions and three unions representing support staff. The National Union of Teachers (NUT) refused to sign the National Workload Agreement and has remained outside of the Social Partnership ever since, whilst the National Association of Headteachers (NAHT) left the Social Partnership of its own volition in March 2005, before re-entering in Spring 2007. The Training and Development Agency for Schools is not a member of the Social Partnership, but works closely with it and reports to WAMG on a regular basis. Alongside WAMG the Social Partnership has grown to encompass the Rewards and Incentive Group (focusing largely on issues of teachers' pay and Performance Management (PM) issues but not making decisions on pay which remains the responsibility of the School Teachers' Review Body) and the Support Staff Review (dealing with those issues specifically related to support staff).

The Partnership itself meets weekly, usually at Department of Children, Schools and Families (DCSF) offices in London but sometimes at other venues such as the offices of other Partner members. Meetings often last a full day with WAMG business conducted first, followed by the Rewards and Incentive Group and Support Staff Review generally in the afternoon. At the time of the data collection the Partnership had no obvious constitution or written procedures for conducting its business. There were, for example, no rules regarding representation rights at Social Partnership meetings and those attending determine who will represent them. Whether a union was represented at meetings by one or four of its officers was determined more by the importance attached to the Partnership and by relative union resources than by any formal rules. All unions acknowledged that the regular weekly meetings and attendant business represented a significant increase in their workload and smaller unions struggled to keep up with the resource demands that were the corollary of this. However input from Social Partners on the project Reference Group did indicate that, as the group developed, protocols were becoming more explicit, suggesting that the lack of formality was partly style, but also partly a function of developmental stage.

The regular contact between members (the Social Partnership meets throughout the year) means that all those involved know each other well. There is also a considerable amount of contact between Partners that takes place outside formal meetings. One interviewee described times when a type of 24/7, virtual negotiating process took place, as important decisions were made via email exchanges:

> And, and you'll get days when the emails fly, when you sit there and you look at the computer and they're coming in from [General Secretary of another union] and they're coming in from [employer negotiator] and they're literally exchanging every couple of minutes and you have this flurry of negotiation that takes place not in a meeting but by computer because somebody's set a deadline because Ministers have to get this out by a certain time: 'we have to put this in front of the Minister so they can make an announcement on so and so'. 'Well why can't they just wait?' 'No, no' we're being told.
>
> (National Official 1, Voice)

Another added 'never a day goes by when you don't get several emails all with attachments, all wanting our comments' (National Official, ASCL). These descriptions give some idea of the intensity of the discussions but not of the origins of the issues discussed. Here the, albeit sometimes indirect, pressure of the demands of Government on the Partnership is of critical importance in the issues which appear (or do not) on the agenda.

SETTING THE AGENDA

Given the critical role of the Social Partnership, what framed the issues that it discussed, and how agenda items for formal business were determined, were of some importance. In examining these issues we distinguish between two 'levels' of agenda setting. One level might be referred to as the meta-agenda—the broad over-arching framework within which discussions take place. At a level below that, there is a concern with the practical issues of how items for discussion are decided and how formal Social Partnership business is organized and ordered.

In order to understand the meta-agenda it is important to reiterate the origins of the Workload Agreement as emerging from a coalescing of Government and union concerns about system sustainability. The Workload Agreement reflected both Government concerns about standards 'plateauing' and union concerns about teacher workload. In many ways what united these concerns was a shared anxiety about teacher recruitment and retention. The Workload Agreement, and the subsequent remodelling of the workforce, represents a coming together of union demands for improved working conditions and Government concerns for school reform, in which the former are subordinated to the latter. The primacy of the Government agenda is consummately expressed in the ordering of the title of the Workload Agreement itself—*Raising Standards and Tackling Workload* (Department for Education and Skills [DfES] 2003).

The corollary of this focus on standards is an understanding that Social Partnership business at a formal and practical level is conducted in a framework that does not seek to fundamentally challenge the overall trajectory of Government policy. Union gains are secured in so far as they can be aligned with the broader goals of school improvement. This may not be problematic where the goals and means of securing school improvement are not contested. However, where there are fundamental conflicts over the nature of policy then such conflicts must either be suppressed, or conducted elsewhere. This is not to argue that the Social Partnership crudely and obediently implements State policy—as we shall demonstrate, the reality is far more complex. However, it is to assert that the basis of Social Partnership is at minimum a tacit and/or pragmatic acceptance of the fundamental principles that frame and drive Government policy. This provides the context within which formal Social Partnership business is conducted.

Due to the Social Partnership's origins, and the fact that at the time of our research the Partnership was clearly still in its early stages, it appeared that the Partnership had few formal rules for determining its business. This lack of clarity ensured that what was appropriate Partnership business was often evolving and sometimes contested. At a technical level it was reported that it was possible for any member of the Partnership to table an agenda item for Partnership meetings, although 'the practice is that the DfES draws up the agenda' (National Official 1, Voice). This movement towards a Government agenda seemed to reflect the changing nature of the Social Partnership. The Partnership originated from very focussed discussions about tackling workload problems, and the Workload Agreement represented a clear and tangible output. Discussions that followed had a clear focus on implementation of the Workload Agreement (reflected in the titling of the Workload Agreement Monitoring Group). However, there was an emerging trend towards the Social Partnership becoming a body the Government wished to use to consult on a wide range of policies—'it's about much more than that [workforce reform] now' (National Official, ASCL). One union official described the Social Partnership as 'a general consultative and negotiating committee across a wide range of things' (National Official 1 Voice), and went on to argue that 'it was being used as a sort of clearing house for anything the Department wanted to run past the unions'. Another interviewee referred to the Social Partnership as 'the receptacle for all departmental policy in terms of consultation with the unions and the employers' (National Official 1, LGE). Areas that the Social Partnership was being drawn into included the Extended Schools agenda, 14–19 reform and initiatives associated with *Every Child Matters*. The same LGE representative asserted, 'I think 90% of it is Government agenda'.

At one level this may be seen as a coming together of industrial and educational concerns in a way that suggests English teacher unions might be starting to bargain over what Kerchner *et al.* (1998: 114) has called 'the other half of teaching', that is professional and pedagogical issues. In reality this was not clear-cut and the handling of professional issues within the Social Partnership was both more limited and more complex. For example, although the Partnership clearly had a broad agenda, its focus was on the implications of initiatives on workload, the merit or efficacy of individual policies themselves was not discussed. Although different teacher unions identified different priorities within the remodelling agenda, there was actually a clear consensus on the part of teacher unions to restrict Social Partnership discussions to what might be referred to as traditional industrial concerns related to workload. The motivations reflected the ideological approaches of different teacher unions, often blended with pragmatic tactical considerations of what was considered possible and desirable. The complexity emerged from the way in which apparent concessions on workload were secured through acceptance of a range of wider managerial issues, such as pay restructuring and revised PM regulations that clearly had a professional dimension.

The earlier characterisation of the National Association of Schoolmasters Union of Women Teachers (NASUWT) was of an organisation historically emphasizing concerns relating to pay and working conditions. The union has previously explicitly rejected campaigning on wider educational issues (see Vincent's (1993) analysis of the union boycott of standardized testing). NASUWT officials saw their union's participation in the Social Partnership as entirely consistent with this approach. The focus on workload emphasized the union's concern with 'bread and butter' issues:

I think because we have a very simple philosophy, we have no problem. We have no identity crisis in our union—we are a trade union representing the interests of teachers. We have a very simple slogan and philosophy of putting teachers first and we do that with no apology, on the basis that if we look after teachers and headteachers in our membership, they are then free to concentrate on their critically important job of looking after the pupils and making sure they're educated properly. And I think that's made us quite distinct from other unions because we've never had any schizophrenia about 'Are we an education union? Are we there for the pupils? Are we there for the teachers?' We've had a clear trade union philosophy—but we've managed, and I think we've demonstrated this particularly in the last three years, to demonstrate that the professional agenda and the industrial relations agenda are not separate. So we will engage in the issues around education but the baseline we always use is 'what will the impact be . . . on our members?' So for example we could all have very interesting . . . debates about educational philosophy, what should be in the curriculum, and we're very clear as a union the things that we need to engage on at that level and then the impact assessment we have to do for our members, because on many issues in education, teachers themselves have their own professional opinion, their own professional judgement. What they want us to do is to create a climate for them to be able to exercise those properly.

(National Official 1, NASUWT)

In many senses this response represents a classic statement of industrial unionism—the union is presented as agnostic in relation to wider education policy, a stance justified by the belief that this is a matter for individual members. Indeed it is the union's agnosticism that allows it to sit so comfortably in the Social Partnership—if the union does not have a view on the educational merits of policy, there can be no basis for a dispute with Government on these issues. The basis of any dispute emerges from the workload consequences that flow from policy. Perhaps significantly there is a recognition that the 'professional agenda and the industrial relations agenda' (National Official 1, NASUWT) are not separate, but the link is rationalized in a way that is both unproblematic and continues to give primacy to industrial issues. Solving conditions of service issues is seen as an essential precursor to addressing educational issues, on which the union deliberately avoids adopting a position.

This position contrasts sharply with that of the Association of Teachers and Lecturers (ATL), which explicitly describes itself as 'the education union' and which has sought to position itself as the union with clear policies on educational and professional issues. ATL therefore might be considered to be more supportive of the trend towards broadening the Social Partnership's agenda, as this would draw the Partnership into an area of relative strength for ATL. In reality, ATL was as keen as NASUWT to limit the focus of the Social Partnership to traditional areas of conditions of service, although for quite different reasons. ATL was not agnostic on Government education policy, quite the contrary. ATL officials argued that they had strong policies on a broad range of educational issues and these were often at odds with, indeed 'diametrically opposed' (National Official 1, ATL) to key elements of Government policy such as the role of the Inspectorate, and the specific uses of standardised testing. For ATL, the imperative to separate out educational issues from the Social Partnership agenda allowed it to assert its independence on issues where it felt the need to be more critical of policy—'we don't want to be tied in to the whole range of Government education policies' (National Official 2, ATL). Given ATL's apparent opposition to key elements of Government education policy, the focus on conditions of service issues allowed the union to make a tactical consideration to participate in the Social Partnership, whilst maintaining a more critical perspective on other areas of policy.

Officials from Voice made similar points, emphasizing that 'the political agenda' (National Official 1, Voice) including issues such as trust schools and academies are not generally discussed within the Social Partnership. These issues are seen as more contentious and therefore best placed outside of the Partnership. There is a recognition that it can be difficult to 'draw the line' between 'political' and 'practical' issues (National Official 1, Voice), but this distinction was presented as the yardstick for assessing whether issues were legitimate Social Partnership business or not. Interestingly, traditional industrial issues are presented as 'practical', whilst matters of education policy are 'political'. This was a common approach to presenting Partnership issues—as practical problems requiring technical solutions, stripped of their political background and context.

Framing issues as practical evaded the more general questions of how these practical questions emerged from political and ideological frameworks, allowing discussions and decisions to be seen as technical, practical and pragmatic. These stances, and the inter-personal relations that they fostered, are themselves informed by a more general political framework and it is this that is now examined.

DISCUSSING AND DECIDING

In 2003 one of the largest teacher unions in the US issued a publication (NEA 2003) in which the author, Sally Klingel, explored the concept of 'interest-based bargaining' and in particular its application in education. Klingel suggests that 'Public frustration with collective bargaining's inability to deal with intractable conflict and lack of progress in school improvement' had led to a search for 'alternative bargaining techniques' (NEA 2003: 5). The key features of interest-based bargaining were a rejection of 'adversarialism' and the adoption of new structures, processes and behaviours in bargaining. Klingel argued that 'interest-based bargaining' placed a strong emphasis on the re-framing of 'problems' as the focus of discussions from which agreed solutions might emerge:

> Instead of presenting proposals, parties develop problem statements and provide the respective interests underlying negotiating positions to be used as criteria in developing solutions. Multiple options are considered, rather than two opposing positions. Trading concessions and compromising toward a middle ground is discouraged in favor of a focus on a workable solution that maximizes the benefits for both parties.
>
> (NEA 2003: 2)

A central focus therefore is placed on defining the problem, 'problem-solving' and the achievement of consensual solutions in which each side can claim to have secured progress. As such interest-based bargaining can be said to have its roots in the concept of integrative bargaining developed by Walton and McKersie (1965) with its emphasis on 'win-win' outcomes, and a corresponding rejection of zero-sum approaches associated with distributive bargaining.

A very similar approach to bargaining was reflected in many of the discussions we had with members of the Social Partnership. A Training and Development Agency for Schools (TDA) official described the mutual framing of problems in the following terms:

> 'We've got a problem. We've not got enough teachers, or we need to reduce their [working] time so we retain them. We've got to make a better life for these people. How are we going to do it?' So what these people [the Social Partnership] do is painstakingly work through these things. The attention to detail is phenomenal, absolutely phenomenal . . . they look through every piece of paper, every piece of training material, everything that's done in minute detail until they are satisfied they all agree that that is the way it is going to go forward.
>
> (National Official 1, TDA)

Members of the Social Partnership concurred that outcomes were achieved by consensus, but it was recognized that consensus could be difficult to achieve. It was often a long and drawn-out process, with difficult discussions to be made.

> I mean it can only happen through give and take really at the end of the day and a lot is done around that table in terms of trust and working through what needs to be done and understanding of each others' agendas. So what people started to do was to put themselves in each others' shoes and think about 'I might win this one but I'll lose that one' and you know, it's all about how do you get there at the end of the day—so everybody benefits. And that's what Partnership has meant.
>
> (National Official 1, TDA)

Describing a similar process, a union official described the following situation.

> Teaching Standards . . . came back from the TDA after all the consultation conferences over 15,000 words long. We stayed there in a darkened room for three and a half weeks to reduce them to 7000 words, and we just stayed there, line by line by line negotiations.
>
> (National Official 1, ATL)

An analysis of the views of these Partners reveals a complex blurring of the distinction between 'consultation' and 'negotiation'. The language of both is used, but this often merges and the terms are used almost interchangeably. Within traditional industrial relations there is generally a clear distinction between negotiation and consultation, with unions jealously protecting those areas where they 'negotiate'—defined as issues where, following good-faith bargaining, a joint agreement is reached. Within the education sector, negotiation traditionally focused on industrial issues, whilst professional issues were the subject of consultation. The blurring of consultation and negotiation processes within the Social Partnership points to a parallel blurring of education and industrial issues in the work of the Partnership, although this is neither clear nor straightforward. For example, although unions were often adamant that the Social Partnership focused on workload and conditions of services issues, it was also the case that this agenda developed to include issues relating to, for example, PM and professional development. This blurring in part occurs because it is simply not possible to make a distinction between so-called industrial and educational or professional issues, highlighting the difficulty Social Partner unions had in 'containing' the agenda to issues of workload only.

Within traditional collective bargaining if negotiations break down, there is a 'failure to agree' and procedures for dealing with a failure to agree are usually themselves the product of a collective agreement. A continued inability to reach an agreement may ultimately result in a dispute in which either the employer or employee side withdraws from negotiations and presses their case through either a lock-out or industrial action. The Social Partnership has no such procedures for dealing with conflict and a 'failure to agree'. A strong emphasis was placed on 'working together', towards consensus, but achieving it was not always easy. As one TDA officer asserted, it was 'blood on the carpet sometimes' (National Official 1, TDA), although whose blood was not clear. Strong and open disagreement appears to have diminished and one union official described the normal process as 'consensus by attrition', expanding on this by suggesting that discussions continued until agreement was reached.

> Social Partnership doesn't work by votes, you sit there at the table and you negotiate until you've reached a compromise. No-one has a veto although there are key positions on which every Partner will say 'Well actually I can't move on this one'. Civil servants will say 'I can't move on this, it's a ministerial imperative', I will say 'Look my executive will not allow me to . . . But no-one has a veto.
>
> (National Official 1, ATL)

> There are flashes of temper occasionally but it's always controlled and it's always understood that at some point somebody has to give in, in order to reach the consensus, and my experience over [time] is that it's always been reached.
>
> (National Official 1, Voice)

This was a commonly presented view in the data, although two intervie-wees referred to two specific instances where there had been a failure to agree, and these issues had been referred to the Minister for a 'ruling'. This could suggest there is a ministerial veto, although this is not a claim we would wish to assert confidently. These two cases appeared to be dealt with on an *ad hoc* basis, and the suggestion from all Partners that the Minister be allowed to arbitrate suggests that although agreement could not be reached, teacher unions felt that in these cases they could live with a ministerial decision that went against them.

The assertion by one interviewee earlier, and echoed by others, that 'no-one has a veto' is significant and points to an important principle within the Partnership—that of formal equity between parties. In several inter-views a picture was presented that rejected votes according to member-ship strength, caucuses and intra-organizational bargaining—trappings of traditional collective bargaining and certainly a feature of the Burnham model in which advantageous voting rights were jealously guarded and intra-organizational bargaining between teacher unions and employers was the order of the day. One union official's view of this earlier period was stated in the following terms:

> When we did that traditional way [collective bargaining] with the local authority we came in with an agreed position of the unions. Whoever was chairing the union side would put the union position. We don't do that now. All the Social Partners have the opportunity to contribute equally and it doesn't matter whether you've got 200,000 members or whether you've got 30,000 members, or whether you've got 11,000 members, you have equal time at that table if you want it. And equal opportunity to contribute.
>
> (National Official 1, Voice)

Within the Partnership interviews there were frequent references to 'a teamwork approach' (National Official 1, TDA) and the notion of equity between parties. In reality the position of equity described by the Voice official earlier appeared to be more complex with evidence from within the same interview that power was not distributed uniformly across the Partners and that at times the union had had to assert stridently their right to equal status. This was arguably in part due to the embryonic nature of the Partnership and there is a case to be made that in time, as 'conventions' settle, these issues may be resolved. However, the suggestion that power imbalances will in time disappear seems at best naïve. For example, the local government employers clearly saw themselves in a subsidiary role rela-tive to the DCSF. This is perhaps not surprising but graphically illustrates the re-balancing of local-central relations in education policy following the ERA 1988 (Whitty 2002). For many years in the Burnham Committee the local authority employers dominated the central government department

(Ironside and Seifert 1995), whereas within the Social Partnership, as across the whole of education policy, that situation is now almost completely reversed.

Similarly, amongst the unions, there was some correlation between membership size and influence in the Partnership. The NASUWT is the largest teachers' organization in the Partnership and they were perceived to assert a very significant, arguably disproportionate, influence on its workings. As a large organization they were not only able to assert numerical superiority (in union terms, members matter as numbers are a proxy for relative strength), but they were also able to devote more resources to supporting Partnership business. In contrast, smaller unions struggled to keep up with the demands of weekly meetings and a growing business agenda. This was an issue highlighted by Voice, but also by the headteacher unions. The dominance of the NASUWT was sometimes perceived as excessive and problematic by representatives of both the employers and other unions, and the view was expressed from representatives from both sides that the inclusion of the NUT in the Partnership would provide a useful counter-weight to the disproportionate influence of the NASUWT.

This imbalance between unions was also evident in the relations between the teaching and support staff unions, with a perception that support staff unions 'don't feel on a par with the teacher unions' (National Official 2, LGE). Hierarchies within the workplace appeared to be mirrored in the Social Partnership, although here again there was evidence that in time these issues were being re-ordered. Certainly there was significant evidence over the course of the research of Unison's increasing presence in school sector industrial relations and its emergence as a key player in both the Social Partnership and school sector unionism more generally. Prior to the Social Partnership, Unison had 'never been part of any discussions in the DfES regarding schools . . . it was never on their radar' (National Official, Unison). This situation was clearly beginning to shift, and was in part evidenced by the unions' industrial action in schools in 2008 (Barker 2008). There was also evidence of informal coalitions between Trades Union Congress (TUC) affiliated unions, and those outside the TUC. Where this was the case Unison and the larger teacher unions became the 'in-group', with non-TUC affiliates such as voice and the headteachers' unions on the outside. This coalescence was perceived as important when it became necessary to lobby ministers as TUC unions had access to the Government in a way that non-TUC unions did not. Indeed, this issue was particularly significant for Unison whose relationship with the Labour Party (Labour Party affiliated and a major donor to the party) gave it better ministerial access than the TUC teacher unions, who are not Labour Party affiliated.

Despite the issues identified previously, the principle of equity within the Partnership was presented, at a rhetorical level at least, as an important principle of Partnership working. It was consonant with the notion, often identified in the literature, on alternative forms of bargaining, of rejecting 'us and them' approaches to bargaining and instead adopting a form of joint problem-solving (NEA 2003, Streshley and DeMitchell 1994). Throughout the interviews members of the national Social Partnership made it clear that they saw the process described as underwritten by 'trust'. The notion of trust emerged as a recurring theme throughout the interviews, both as a central feature of Partnership working, but also as a source of tension for Partner unions. Given its centrality we give some consideration to discussing this issue in its own right.

PARTNERSHIP AS 'TRUST'

As demonstrated, partnership working emphasizes a problem-solving approach to industrial relations, from which it is hoped to generate 'win-win' solutions. This approach rejects the idea of polarized positions that result in an unsatisfactory compromise depending on the relative bargaining strengths of participants, and instead promotes the notion of innovative, radical but consensual solutions. However, within the highly politicized environment of a bargaining context, and education policy more generally, it may be argued that the pressure is towards the *status quo*, rather than innovation (Stevenson and Carter 2007). For these reasons it was argued that the Partnership needed to create ground rules through which discussions could take place that would encourage radical thought, and this necessitated an environment of 'trust'.

> . . . if you're going to actually be quite radical and move things forward, you've got to be able to almost think the unthinkable and then pull back from it. You've at least got to be able in comfort to put it on the table, even though you may not necessarily sign up to it, and say, 'Well, what about that?'

> (National Official 1, NASUWT)

This conception of 'trust' suggested an acceptance of other people's positions, a willingness to explore potentially radical proposals and a commitment to contain discussions of these issues within the Partnership. Discussions within the Partnership were described as 'confidential'—a protocol accepted by all participants. The trust, however, went beyond this and embraced the notion of 'collective responsibility'. This was in part formalized in the National Agreement, which placed a responsibility on all parties to 'promulgate' the agreement to members and 'all parts of the education service' (DfES 2003: 15). The commitment to promote and 'promulgate' the Agreement and its subsequent impact are clearly articulated by a union official in the Partnership:

Once we've agreed it in that room, when I go outside, I say 'This is what has been procured in Social Partnership—this is what the Partners have come up with' and I don't say 'Had it not been for ASCL or had it not been for the employers we would have got this, this and this'. I say 'We've done this, we've gone through all the arguments, this is what we've come with, this is where I believe it's better than what we've got'. You take ownership—but more than take ownership you promote it. So we go out there and we promote, anything we agree with Government we promote.

(National Official 1, NASUWT)

Given the Partnership's pronounced way of working it becomes possible to understand the emphasis that is placed on confidentiality and the trust required to underwrite this. Confidentiality and trust are not requirements in their own right, but facilitating conditions to support the Partnership's preferred approach to working. However, these requirements also begin to fundamentally re-order relationships—not only within the Partnership, but also between, for example, Partner unions and their own members and between unions inside and outside of the Social Partnership. At this point the concept of trust becomes potentially problematic.

In the context of Social Partnership the key development is that trust is located *within* the Partnership and a new loyalty is created between the Social Partners. Implicit in this trust is dissolution of the 'us and them' relations that underpin traditional models of industrial relations. Loyalties cross the divide between employers and unions and suggest that partnership becomes possible only when disappearance of more fundamental antagonisms is assumed. This trust may be necessary to create the conditions in which Partnership discussions of the type described can take place but they also severely restrict the ability of a union to communicate openly with its membership. Perhaps most importantly, it severely undermines unions' ability to mobilize their membership in support of the unions' negotiating aims. Indeed, the relationship between union officers and the rank and file is re-cast as one in which union officials sometimes have the role of lowering members' expectations, not raising them. This is perhaps best illustrated by the requirement on Social Partners to promote the Partnership-endorsed pay restructuring that in some cases resulted in teachers' receiving significant pay and pension cuts.

... when you have come up with the agreed settlement, then you have to go out and defend it. I, for example, spent quite a lot of last year in the Autumn term going round to branch meetings, having to defend the position on teaching and learning responsibility points [pay restructuring] to members who were losing money. And that's hard ... that's not your usual job as union official. So you know, you have to do that as well. So there is a tension between working in Social Partnership and keeping your members informed and keeping them on board but I think we've managed to do that successfully.

(National Official 1, ATL)

Another union official described how he had made a public statement that was considered inappropriate and that he had received a reprimand from other members of the Partnership in which he was told:

. . . what we should and shouldn't say in public. We understand that— we do understand that—but it does present us sometimes with problems with our membership, where our membership say 'Well, why aren't you out there saying this?'. 'We never hear you saying, you know, fighting our cause'. Well. 'We're actually fighting your cause within the Social Partnership but I'm sorry, we can't go public on that' and that is a difficulty for us, I have to say.

(National Official 1, Voice)

There can be little doubt that these sensitivities are heightened by the location of the NUT outside the Social Partnership and the likelihood that it would exploit divisions and tensions within the Social Partnership.

INSIDE OR OUT? THE CALCULATION OF RISK

The Social Partnership functions in key ways that represent a new phenomenon in school sector industrial relations, or indeed public sector industrial relations more widely. For the teacher unions this development is not only very different to the years of union exclusion following the abolition of negotiating rights, but very different to the more traditional form of collective bargaining that was characteristic of the Burnham era. This analysis has attempted to convey the complexity of the issues facing teacher unions as they calculated, and continue to calculate, whether they should participate, or not, in the Social Partnership. The NUT has always remained outside, although periodically questions arise as to whether it might join. As has been indicated, the NAHT was a member, left, and has since rejoined. For other unions inside the Social Partnership initial membership was not automatic, but was sometimes agreed after considerable internal union debate and in these cases continued membership periodically arose as a topic of debate. There is agreement that the emergence of the Social Partnership is a significant, but high-risk, development—with serious potential consequences flowing from either being on the inside or outside. This section examines how different unions have evaluated these risks, including the consequences of membership of a Social Partnership that does not include the largest teachers union.

For unions inside the Social Partnership the principal benefits of partnership were presented as access to Government and the ability to influence policy. There was a clear belief that membership of the Partnership gave the teacher unions a voice.

> I was 30 years in teacher trade unionism . . . for education unions for most of my life they've had absolutely no clout whatsoever. Their achievements in terms of persuading the Government to recognise its agenda have been nil. Now I don't want to overplay the degree of contrast but there is a contrast. We now have considerable say . . . in a way it's like the UN, we all know that it's difficult for the UN to get decisions that the USA doesn't agree with, because . . . that's the realities of power and global power. And the same applies in the Social Partnership. The realities are that the Government have got more cards than anybody else, but we have got some cards, which we never had.
>
> (National Official 2, ATL)

A recurring theme was that partnership provided a voice in policy, and that being 'in the tent' (National Official 2, LGE) gave unions a level of access to Government officials that was unprecedented. The view expressed by members of the Partnership was that this had generated significant benefits— 'the gains are absolutely immense'. The same official went on to assert:

> I can show tangible things we've achieved and I can say to them [members] 'Look, we're not complacent, it's by no means nirvana that we've reached, there's an awful lot still to do' but I'm showing them that we're actually making a difference and we're also in a position to influence.
>
> (National Official 2, ATL)

There was a view therefore that on balance the benefits of membership had been positive—sometimes in the forms of important gains and new contractual entitlements, and in other cases in the form of 'damage limitation'. In areas such as pay restructuring and PM, for instance, it was argued that initial proposals from the DfES had been 'draconian' (National Official 1, NASUWT) and significantly worse for teachers than those eventually presented on behalf of the Social Partnership. Underpinning this analysis was that these gains or the limitation of damage could only be achieved by a willingness to engage constructively with Government, and that unions' ability to press their demands through industrial action was not a realistic option.

> Unions have a certain amount of influence, but governments are powerful. And governments have a directly elected mandate and in the end your only recourse as a union is to industrial action, and teachers are highly reluctant to take industrial action.
>
> (National Official 1, ATL)

The NASUWT presented a different view, asserting its continuing history of militancy: 'we're quite clear that we will take industrial action to support our members' (National Official 1, NASUWT). However, there was a view that relying on industrial action was costly and difficult to sustain.

> . . . you'll remember in the 80s, you were rolling from one period of industrial action to another and even coming into the 90s it was every two years there was going to be some major industrial action. Whilst occasionally you would make some gains—and I would never in any way underestimate the achievements we got at that time, because I think they were extremely good for the time that we were in—the fact of the matter was that they weren't sustained. There was either a change of Minister or there was a change of emphasis from the Government and things you'd fought hard for, and your members had often fought hard for, were just eroded away. And we'd had an ambition as a union that there must be a better way of working.
>
> (National Official 1, NASUWT)

Against these perceived benefits, unions in the Social Partnership were acutely aware that they could give the impression of having forfeited their independence. The reconfiguring of relationships within the Social Partnership, and the apparent rejection of 'us and them' adversarialism, required a commitment to working with the Government that could be problematic, especially when unpalatable decisions were the outcome. Partner unions were of the view that partnership working required a willingness to compromise, but that it did not involve surrendering independence, especially on issues outside of the 'Partnership agenda':

> . . . there are areas like academies, trust schools, even Building Schools for the Future and Private Finance Initiative where we absolutely disagree with Government. And we say to them in public and the Social Partners always said . . . the unions have the right to criticise those parts of Government agenda that they can't agree with. And that, we never signed up to and were never consulted on. . . . . So we haven't lost that ability to, to criticise those areas that we feel we haven't been consulted and we have no input.
>
> (National Official, Unison)

Whilst asserting this independent role, there was also a clear recognition that union involvement in the reform agenda had considerable benefits for Government:

> it takes quite a bit of DfES resource to keep it going—but bloody hell, don't they get a lot out of it . . . They say the TDA is the delivery arm of the DFES, actually we're the bloody delivery arm. We bust a gut.
>
> (National Official 1, ATL)

It was recognised that the DfES had been able to secure major structural change without experiencing resistance through industrial action on a scale sufficient to derail it. The view that teacher unions had been 'incorporated' by the Social Partnership, was not one universally shared, but it was acknowledged by some members. One member argued that 'I don't think any of us honestly anticipated when we signed the National Agreement that what we would become is a branch of the DfES. But in many ways we are' (National Official 1, NAHT). In another case an official accepted an element of incorporation, but argued that benefits continued to outweigh costs. At the point when that balance tipped the wrong way then Social Partnership membership would need to be reviewed:

> the fact is we're talking about incorporation and only a fool would try to deny it. I mean that, but it's a calculated acceptance from the union point of view. From my point of view, on the part of ATL it's a calculated acceptance of incorporation because of the benefits it brings. If the disadvantages ever got to outweigh the advantages then we would walk away.
>
> (National Official 2, ATL)

In this instance the calculation of costs and benefits is made explicit, as is the Social Partnership's only clear means for dealing with fundamental disagreement—exit. The NUT stance is less about calculation and more about principle. The NUT's fundamental opposition to the use of staff without qualified teacher status to undertake whole class teaching meant a steadfast decision to remain outside the Partnership. This position, moreover, was reinforced by the union being at odds with the central thrust of much Government policy and the NUT's unwillingness to support a much wider range of Government policies (see Chapter 2). The NUT has had to consider that being 'outside the tent' (LGE Officer 1) substantially reduces its access to Government and thus its influence. One NUT official referred to the union as being 'out on the tundra' (National Official 1, NUT). The union's stance could also affect its relationship with some members as it has also failed to receive any credit for securing PPA (planning, preparation and assessment) time for primary school teachers—a policy the NUT has probably campaigned for longer and harder than any other union. The absence of credit for success here has ramifications for membership support, reflected in another official questioning whether members would continue to support a union that appeared to be excluded from the key levers of influence on policy.

Yet the damage to the NUT of not being inside the Partnership is far from obvious. Indeed, opposition to the Social Partnership confers some advantages to the union, prime amongst which is its ability to campaign vigorously against unpopular policies, some of which are the outcome of the Social Partnership itself. The union has taken up a number of issues with varying degrees of success. The union's opposition to the use of support staff to provide whole class teaching has been partially successful (see Chapters 6 and 7), but has been difficult to pursue through industrial action. The union had more success using industrial action to challenge the pay restructuring (in its December 07 Executive Committee Report, the union reported 319 indicative ballots, 112 formal disputes—106 resolved and 6 ongoing—and 3115 strike days in regard to this issue), although successes were measured in terms of resolving implementation issues at the level of individual schools, rather than an ability to challenge the fundamental tenets of policy.

Within the Social Partnership, attitudes to the NUT's absence differed significantly. A common view was that the NUT had cut itself off from the centre of the policy processes. Its attitude towards policy, and partnership working, was presented as 'Luddite' by more than one interviewee. It was common to present its stance as grounded in the belief in some mythical golden age, a stance unsuited to the new times and the contemporary policy environment. Despite these attitudes towards the union there was still a widely shared view that the Social Partnership would benefit from NUT membership, and a number of different arguments were presented to support this position. There was a view that the Partnership without the largest union lacked a degree of legitimacy. It was also asserted that the NUT's strength in the primary sector, and its absence from the Partnership, had resulted in decisions having a clear secondary school emphasis. In some cases this had resulted in decisions that were inappropriate and particularly difficult to implement in a primary school context, such as the pay restructuring. Finally, as has been argued, some Partner members felt the NUT's inclusion would help to 'balance' the Partnership and to some extent neutralize the domination of the NASUWT.

One member of the Social Partnership suggested that the NUT's decision to remain outside of the Partnership had been 'catastrophic' (National Official 2, ATL) for the NUT, but this argument is difficult to sustain. The most obvious manifestation of 'catastrophe' would present itself in haemorrhaging membership and during this time NUT membership increased by 50,000 according to official statistics (see Table 2.1). Indeed, despite all these controversial changes, the relative memberships of different unions continue to be stable. Although it may be possible to suggest the NUT has lost 'influence' through its self-imposed exile from the Social Partnership, this argument is also difficult to sustain. Some Partners viewed the NUT's ability to assert an independent position with some jealousy. This was particularly evident on the pay restructuring issue, but also related to issues beyond the remit of the Social Partnership. For example the NUT's campaign of industrial action against the 2008 pay award points to a room for manoeuvre in relation to Government policy that Social Partner unions might lack. However, the NUT's inability to sustain this campaign also points to the weaknesses that arise from its isolation.

It is also important to recognise that even from without the Social Partnership the NUT was able to assert an influence within. This derives in part from the situation in which all teacher unions may be considered to be in competition with each other for members, but the principal rivalry is between NASUWT and the NUT. There was a view that this had intensified as the NASUWT had become the 'lead union' within the Partnership (the role the NUT had traditionally played in Burnham), whilst the NUT was the Social Partnership's most vocal critic. Although national NASUWT interviewees made no explicit reference to the NUT (itself perhaps significant), other interviewees (representing both employers and other unions) expressed the view that the NASUWT was particularly sensitive to issues that would make it vulnerable to criticism from the NUT. Although the extent of the NUT's 'arms-length' influence is obviously impossible to gauge accurately it is nevertheless important to acknowledge that despite the union remaining outside the Social Partnership, the need for Social Partner unions, and in particular the influential NASUWT, to take account of the NUT policy does give the NUT some indirect but potentially significant influence *within* the Social Partnership.

CONCLUSION

The Social Partnership represents a new and significant development in English industrial relations, with particular significance for both public sector unionism generally and teacher unionism in particular. At the same time, it is important to recognize however that the model of Social Partnership described is peculiar to the school sector in England. The Social Partnership in this study shares a name, but little else, with the European model of social partnership, promoted at various times by the TUC. Moreover, within England it remains rooted in the school sector and there is little evidence of it being exported to other areas of the public such as health or the civil service. The significance of the development of the Partnership rests therefore both with its novelty within the public sector and its strategic importance within education.

Participants in the Partnership, and specifically the unions, emphasise the extent to which the Partnership provides them with a voice in decision-making and the development of policy. At one level this is unquestionably the case—the Social Partnership involves engagement with policy that has been unprecedented in recent years for teacher unions. However, the price for this access to decision-making is broad acceptance of a much wider policy agenda and one that requires tacit acceptance of key elements of the neo-liberal restructuring of State education. In this sense the Social Partnership model described may be considered as a form of *rapprochement* between unions and the State in which unions trade support for a workforce reform agenda that dovetails into policies of school improvement and intensified teacher accountability in return for promised improvements in working conditions (a promise that does not appear to have been realised). Although in their different ways the unions involved often argued that the focus of Partnership discussions and decisions was limited to a narrow range of issues, specifically those relating to workload and conditions of service, the Partnership agenda does seek to make an explicit connection between workload issues and the particular form of school improvement the Government seeks to promote. It also highlighted the difficulty of being able to make a neat and tidy distinction between industrial and professional issues. Whilst Social Partner unions sought to argue that educational and professional issues were outside of the remodelling agenda, the inclusion, on the one hand, of issues such as PM and professional development, and, on the other, the exclusion of the effects of Ofsted (Office for Standards in Education, Children's Services and Skills) inspections on workload, highlight the complex relationship between all of these elements.

Unions in the Social Partnership point to significant gains in terms of a collective agreement aimed at reducing teachers' workload and improvements in access to continuing professional development. However, substantive gains in the form of falling workloads are still problematic, and marginal gains have only been accompanied at the costs of pay cuts for some and acceptance of labour substitution. When these costs are combined with a new and changed relationship with union members they run the risk of tying unions into a wider reform agenda that may be deeply unpopular with members, a situation likely to become even more acute in less favourable economic conditions.

In contrast, the NUT's approach might best be described as one of resistance: it has consistently opposed key elements of the remodelling agenda, and therefore set itself against the grain of the Government reform agenda. There is little evidence to date that this has penalized the union to any significant extent, although its isolation has made it difficult to secure its wider policy objectives on issues such as opposition to performance-related pay or standardised testing. The union had some success in resisting some features (such as pay restructuring) but there is less evidence of it achieving significant and tangible gains. Its campaign of resistance has been largely reactive and focused on damage limitation, with its isolation making it difficult to adopt a more proactive approach to secure policy objectives. A worsening economic climate may favour the union and bring into sharper focus many of the contradictions that underpin the Social Partnership model. However, the extent to which the union is able to capitalize on these conditions remains to be seen.

5 Industrial Relations in Transition
The Changing Role of Local Authorities

INTRODUCTION

This chapter is concerned with different ways in which the National Agreement was implemented within three case study local authorities (LAs). As the previous chapters have indicated, the National Agreement marked significant changes to the way teacher workforce industrial relations were organised at national level. However, although interviewees from the national Workforce Agreement Monitoring Group (WAMG) were keen to show the increased influence that unions had on Government policy, they also spoke about the difficulties that the Social Partnership was generating with the membership. The aim at this next stage of the research was therefore to explore the ways in which workforce reform was being interpreted and mediated in specific contexts and how local industrial relations were affecting and being affected by the National Agreement. A key variable was the nature of relations within the LAs, organisations that stand between national policies and industrial relations at school level.

LOCAL AUTHORITY CONTEXT

There is general agreement that the role of LAs has undergone significant change since their inception (for example, Brighouse 2002, Lowe 2002). Created in 1902, they were a key part of the 'national system, locally administered' that involved a tripartite relationship between Government, local education authorities (LEAs) and schools, and provided a series of checks and balances so that, theoretically at least, no one participant would have a monopoly over the decision-making process (Chitty 2002: 262). This accord came under increasing pressure during the economic instability of the 1970s (Brighouse 2002), when neo-liberalism emerged to challenge the post-war welfare consensus—the period of organic crisis described in Chapter 1 as central to understanding contemporary developments in education policy. In particular the tensions between local autonomy and the imperative from the central State for control (principally of public expenditure) began to generate a series of local-central conflicts. These tensions became acute in the 1980s as the Thatcher administration found itself in almost perpetual conflict with a radical and effective New Left based in the major urban authorities (Boddy and Fudge 1984). The reaction of the Conservative administration was to legislate to abolish the Greater London Council in 1986 and to curb the powers of LAs (Lansley *et al.* 1989), which inevitably impacted on LEAs' capacity to provide education services. At the same time, during the period of teachers' industrial action in 1984–1986, LAs continually found their role undermined by central government (Ironside and Seifert 1995). Ultimately, the Government's unilateral abandonment of Burnham and the abolition of negotiating rights was as much an attack on local authorities as it was on the teacher unions. The decisive moment came in 1988 when the Thatcher Government delivered what Chitty (2002: 266) describes as the LEAs' '*coup de grace*' with the Education Reform Act (ERA). This Act centralised much of the decision-making process by giving the Secretary of State 451 new powers (Tomlinson 2001: 46), introduced the notion of parental choice and established local management of schools (LMS); schools were also given the option to become grant maintained and remove themselves altogether from LEA management. The effect was drastically to reduce LEA power and independence (Fitz *et al.* 2002, Hannon 1999, Tipple 1998).

Under the current Labour Government the LA role has been evolving in different ways. On the one hand, they have been weakened by increasing privatisation, with Ball (2007: 53), for instance, making reference to 'virtual authorities' in the light of increasing contracting-out of services, but, on the other, have had their role strengthened in areas such as monitoring of standards. Fletcher-Campbell and Lee's evaluative research argues that LAs are now seen as 'central to the local implementation of national policies' (Fletcher-Campbell and Lee 2003: iii), a position substantiated by Dhillon (2006: 6) who suggests that their role is concerned with 'leadership, influence, challenge and co-ordination'. Less optimistic assessments see the LA role as one where it operates under 'direction, licence and scrutiny' (Hannon 1999: 210) and Sharp, for instance, argues that 'the only players that really count' are the Government, who make the decisions, and the individual schools, who put them into operation. He suggests that the LEA role is intermediate, in that they mediate some aspects of policy, and provisional, in the sense that they need to be able to show that they are discharging their duties adequately (Sharp 2002: 212–213). Indeed LA performance is regulated by increasingly complex inspections that are reinforced by initiatives such as the Beacon Scheme that is aimed, among other things, to recognise the 'best' performers (Hartley *et al.* 2008: 6) in terms of specific policy initiatives; four LEAs, for example, were awarded specialist status with regard to their role in workforce reform (Morton 2005).

Changes notwithstanding, one of the enduring LA roles has been to provide stable local industrial relations, and at the time of the ERA, LEAs and unions had long-established procedures for negotiation and consultation. Although the changes wrought by LMS and the corresponding weakening of the LEAs were seen in some quarters as a development in industrial relations that would drive union activity away from the LEA structures towards the school (Ironside and Seifert 1995), LA structures seem to have continued in much the same pattern as before. Drawing on localised research into the National Union of Teachers (NUT) in a Midlands LEA, Carter (2004) illustrates how relationships between this union and the LEA have continued in the pre-LMS pattern of negotiation and discussion. Similarly Stevenson and Carter (2004) argue that industrial relations in three authorities could be characterised as 'business as usual', with a strong desire on the part of LEAs, headteachers and union activists to maintain a local industrial relations structure. More broadly authorities have continued with a variety of Teachers' Negotiating Committees and Teachers' Consultative Groups, and to fund facilities time for union representatives. Similarly schools have often appeared reluctant to negotiate, for example, their own grievance and disciplinary procedures and seem to have been more than happy to accept policies promoted by LEAs that have been negotiated with the unions (Ironside *et al.* 1997: 126). Together these different bodies of research point to the continuing existence of many of the pre-LMS structures and relationships, which suggests that the results may be applicable to a greater or lesser degree within many authorities. An established pattern of working relations covering a range of issues has continued to suit the LA, unions and schools.

Currently, however, a number of changes are impacting upon these arrangements. One is the growth of academies that operate outside the remit of local authority, a development with implications for both unions and LA structures. Secondly, LA reorganisation has followed from the Every Child Matters agenda (HM Government 2004), which aims to provide multi-agency service provision for children and young people. Education is at the core of this integrated approach to services, with extended schools seen as 'key sites' of their delivery (Cummings *et al.* 2006: 2), and it is envisaged that every school will be able to offer (or signpost) services ranging from specialist therapies to childcare by 2010 (HM Government 2007). This has implications for existing industrial relations structures, as different groups of professionals and support workers are drawn into schools and the composition and profile of the school workforce becomes even more complex. The third change stems from the remodelling agenda in the shape of pressure from the national WAMG (2004, 2007, 2008) and the National Remodelling Team (NRT 2004) for each LA to set up a local WAMG to oversee local workforce reform in schools. The implementation of workforce remodelling, the pressures arising from it, and the ways in which the three case study LAs have reacted at local level is the focus of the next section.

LOCAL AUTHORITIES AND REMODELLING

The high level of expectation concerning LA remodelling responsibilities can be seen in the following extract sent to Chief Education Officers in England by Stephen Kershaw, Director of the School Workforce Unit and at one point chair of national WAMG:

> We expect LEAs to play a central role in ensuring that these changes [arising from the remodelling agenda] are implemented as smoothly as possible. This will mean promoting the changes, building a clear sense of momentum and dealing quickly and effectively with those schools that . . . have not completed implementation to the timescales required . . . It is essential that LEAs, as the school workforce employers and strategic leaders in school improvement, get to grips with the national agreement and help schools translate it into powerful reform.
>
> (Kershaw 2004: n.p.)

This leaves no doubt that the LAs' role was to implement (rather than mediate or facilitate) an important part of Government policy and that there were high expectations concerning their ability to do so. This responsibility resulted in two particular pressures from the Government, described here by a remodelling adviser:

> One was . . . to try and get as many schools as possible through . . . our training events . . . There was a lot of pressure . . . put on us to get every school to take part in that. In the event we didn't get every school and no LA managed to do it, I don't think. There's no compulsion on schools to attend them . . . But then the bigger pressure I suppose was to make sure that every school had actually implemented each stage of the regulations.
>
> (Remodelling Adviser 1, City)

The adviser is referring to the two parts of workforce remodelling that are distinct and separable. Implementation of remodelling regulations was an unambiguous requirement on all schools and thus at one level was unproblematic; the statutory changes had to be implemented according to the schedule set out in the National Agreement. However the training events to which he refers were a different matter. These events were partly to explain the terms of the agreement and to set out the conditions that had to be fulfilled by required dates, again a relatively straightforward process. More controversial, however, was the 'how'. Training involved support for the particular form of change management, comprising the 'five-stage process of M4D (mobilise, discover, deepen, develop, deliver)' developed by the private consultants (Spooner 2006). This originated from the National Remodelling Team (NRT), a private-public partnership that, according to its director, offered a dynamic, team-working approach to change, which schools needed to embrace if they were to develop a sustainable model of change management. How the NRT operated was a model that schools were expected to embed in their own culture and working practices:

> . . . this team is not blocked by existing 'assumptions', is able to introduce practices and tools often untried in the education sector, is experienced with working in large organisations and dealing with change, brings a wide range of new skills and experience to the task and is designed to meet the demands of the task. Members of the team are used to working in teams and, perhaps of most value, radiate a 'can do' attitude, no matter how major the task.
>
> (Collarbone 2005d: 77)

As the remodelling adviser cited previously suggests, this 'cultural revolution', promoted by the NRT, presented the LAs with some difficulties. While there was some considerable pressure brought upon LAs to promote it through the training, even where schools sent representatives to training events, no school could be forced to employ the change management process.

Each of the three case study LAs mitigated the pressures of implementing the agreement and managing the training in two ways. The first was to employ remodelling advisers who were either former or serving headteachers. These were regarded as critical appointments by all three authorities, for the advisers were well-known in the area and gave the whole remodelling team what one interviewee described as 'street cred' (Remodelling Adviser, London Borough) having an ability to 'sell' the package to other, possibly sceptical, headteachers that other LA employees lacked. Two LA employees described the importance of the advisers:

> WAMG Chair: . . . this is important, [we employed] remodelling advisers who weren't employees of the County Council . . .
> LA Officer: . . . And I personally think that's why it did work so well . . . because we did have three headteachers who saw it . . . from the school perspective and . . . they were actually really keen, enthusiastic, signed up to it. So I think that was half the battle, them being able to go out and, not sell this, but basically, they could explain to heads why it was necessary to do this, the benefits they were going to get from doing it . . . And coming from a headteacher, it's definitely different to coming from an LA officer.
>
> (WAMG Chair and LA Officer, Shire)

Equally important, and significant in terms of demonstrating the importance of remodelling, was the Government funding for these posts: 'I think that the success of remodelling was the DfES actually ring-fencing money for LAs to employ specialist staff to do the work. If we hadn't had that resource, it [remodelling] would not have happened' (WAMG Chair, City).

The remodelling advisers were seen, variously, to have three key functions: to update the local WAMG on developments on workforce reform in schools, to smooth out problems in individual schools, and to deliver the remodelling/change management training to headteachers and governors (sometimes with LA employees and at other times without). In contrast to Easton *et al.*'s (2005) research, remodelling advisers' reaction to their own training from the NRT was mixed. One remodelling adviser was uncritically enthusiastic about what he saw as the private sector approach, explaining how his team strove to reproduce its ethos when they in turn trained headteachers and governors:

> . . . that NRT approach was something we'd never seen before. That very, very slick, very focused, very industry . . . style and doing it in a professional way, treating us as professionals [with] top class facilities . . . We hadn't come across that. And . . . we brought that attitude and that way of treating people into the way that we did the remodelling. And whenever we brought people to training, it was very well organised in, in luxury, and [we] treated them as professionals. And I think, it is only a small point, but it really helped the whole feeling towards the way we worked.
>
> (Remodelling Adviser, Shire)

Some LA employees and advisers were, however, less impressed and viewed the prescriptive format of the PowerPoint slides and their scripted delivery as constricting rather than enabling. One, for instance, complained about the lack of flexibility in local interpretation:

> The prescriptive nature of it was . . . some of the issue that we had at a local level . . . because we had to be so precise and were monitored on that . . . I think it took away some of the spontaneity of . . . the discussion . . . Some of the prescription made it, because we couldn't adapt it to a local context, meant we were setting ourselves up for arguments that we mainly could have avoided if we'd have had some degree of ownership over it.
>
> (WAMG Chair, Shire)

Others, such as the two remodelling advisers and the LA Officer cited next, were also highly critical of both the training and the assumptions underlying the change management model:

> LA Officer: When it started there was all this business about . . . one size doesn't fit all . . . But in actual fact
> Remodelling Adviser (RA) 1: It was a one-size model

LA Officer: And then you got all this jargon which in [this authority] . . . goes down like a lead balloon, doesn't it? The mobilisation stage and things like that

RA1: Oh, god . . . embarrassing . . .

RA2: . . . I worked a lot on . . . Fullan's work on change . . . And I was just thinking, this is an absolute nonsense. All his work shows that it's utterly fluid . . . why are they using such a limited research base as him to establish their change model? I feel it's a nonsense

RA1: . . . I just feel all along in my career that there hasn't been enough listening to what the professionals know well . . .

RA2: Oh, some of those training sessions were weird, the trainers that need to be trained. Just excruciating, weren't they . . .

RA1: Yeah, dead embarrassing

RA2: Yeah. Just being treated like children. And the, the amount of money that has been poured in to the whole thing

LA Officer: Hear, hear

RA2: I feel really strongly that a bit more of that should have been put into schools.

(Remodelling Adviser 1 and 2 and
LA Officer, London Borough)

These different criticisms are not new. The absence of Government trust in experienced teaching professionals has long been a source of unhappiness (for example, Brighouse 2001, Troman 2000). Conversely, Ball (2007: 138) notes how the 'products' of private sector companies do not receive unqualified enthusiasm from those who are in receipt of them, and it is unsurprising in this context that these interviewees believed the resources dedicated to training would have been better spent in schools. Despite their trenchant criticisms, however, these LA employees remained committed to the remodelling agenda and faithful to the LA's remit of implementation:

RA2: So we just go along . . . we do what we know works and, and pay homage slightly, watching over our shoulder, to what we're being told now to do. But the clever ones amongst us who have managed to develop the skills to do this . . . learn how to speak the speak but to do what we want to do to get things done (laughs).

(Remodelling Adviser 2, London Borough)

The second way in which the three case study LAs dissipated the responsibility for remodelling was to set up a local WAMG. As noted, their establishment was encouraged by the national WAMG and the NRT who argued that there needed to be a local monitoring group in the same way that there was a national body. Local bodies could help build Kershaw's sense of momentum by gathering intelligence on the way the remodelling was progressing, providing information to schools, disseminating what was seen as best practice and giving support where needed to ensure compliance to the regulations. Many LAs did set up a local group and ran it alongside established industrial relations structures, although groups could be given a variety of different names and there were local variations in the structure, membership and functioning. These variations and the influence they had on the process of workforce remodelling and the development of industrial relations over the three years of the research project are apparent in the workings of the local WAMGs established in the three case study LAs.

LOCAL INDUSTRIAL RELATIONS

The three case studies highlight the context-specific nature of industrial relations in each of the different LAs and for this reason the case studies are discussed in turn. In particular, the focus is on the creation and functioning of the local WAMG as the most obvious manifestation of the impact of the remodelling agenda on LA industrial relations.

Shire WAMG

Shire WAMG can be regarded as a model body for a variety of reasons: it has marked similarity to the national WAMG in terms of relationships and members' attitudes, it has been highly proactive within the Authority and it is continuing to function as extended services and measures towards an integrated Children's Workforce are beginning to take shape. Shire has a history of collaborative relationships between the LA and the unions and during the course of the research regular mention was made of the inclusive 'Shire way' of doing things. 'We all get on very well here' was a constant refrain. This history of collaboration meant that the LA set up the local WAMG relatively quickly, seeing it as a 'natural thing' (WAMG Chair, Shire) in view of the significance of the remodelling project. Chaired for the first three years by the assistant director of education and subsequently by another LA employee, the group consisted of LA HR officials, branch secretaries from five of the six teacher trade unions (in the absence of a local branch, Voice was not represented), two support staff unions, governors and two extra headteachers. The latter were included 'because we wanted buy-in . . . we wanted them to feel that they had a voice' (WAMG Chair, Shire), a recognition that headteachers were key delivery agents who needed to be brought onside. At the same time there was no question of the NUT Branch Secretary being left out:

> It was taken as read that I would be on that [WAMG]. You know, there was no sort of discussion or debate about it, it was just 'Right, you are on this aren't you?' . . . this is the sort of all-inclusive way in which Shire works.
>
> (NUT Branch Secretary, Shire)

There was disappointment, referred to by both teacher union and LA interviewees, that Unison had, despite membership of the group, shown a reluctance to participate, although they had lately become more involved. The union's somewhat ambivalent attitude towards the WAMG was rooted largely in its frequent but irregular demands for attendance:

> So . . . when the schools' remodelling thing came along . . . they set up these WAMGs . . . the meetings here. We've attended as many of those as possible but again, they started having the meetings one after the other at very short notice and we just couldn't get to them all. You know, when you've got disciplinaries on, you can't just drop a disciplinary to go to a meeting. So, so it was very difficult to keep a track of it.
>
> (Unison Branch Secretary, Shire)

However the WAMG's remit was seen by the LA officials as straightforward: ' . . . we were very clear what our role was going to be . . . monitoring, policy development . . . negotiation, support . . . We have created new policies and guidance' (LA Officer, Shire).

There was also agreement among interviewees that the nature of relationships within the group was collaborative, and in the following extract an LA employee speaks about the way in which she believes the Social Partnership has improved the industrial relations climate:

> You had the old . . . 70s style of union approach because teaching unions still are the last bastion of trade unionism as it existed. They've just developed Social Partnership to do it in a different way. And I think we all benefit from that because there is less confrontation . . . so I think the way of working . . . nationally for schoolteachers has . . . evolved into the Social Partnership through RIG, through the role of the employers, and that filters through into how we then are able to again build the trust and build the relationships to enable the social dialogue to come to some kind of agreement. There are some things on both sides that are not negotiable. There are some things that you cannot give and that they will not give . . . But having said that, the majority of the time we are able to come, through dialogue, to some kind of . . . decision or . . . agreement.
>
> (WAMG Chair, Shire)

Here again are the familiar concepts of trust and dialogue encountered in the national level interviews in Chapter 4, and the passage has strong echoes of national WAMG interviews. But another, arguably greater, parallel with the national WAMG is the dominance of the National Association of Schoolmasters Union of Women Teachers (NASUWT) within the group, despite the presence of the NUT. Shire's NASUWT Branch Secretary brushed aside any difficulties that the NUT branch secretary might produce, explaining that its membership of the group:

> . . . didn't make any difference. I mean as long as they agree with us, I'm happy with it (laughs). I mean if, if the NUT . . . said, 'Well you know' . . . I'd say, 'Hang on . . . Social Partners have said this' and point out to the LA that they're as much Social Partners as we are [and say], 'This is what we're going to have' . . . And so I was quick to jump on the NUT.
>
> (NASUWT Branch Secretary, Shire)

As the previous passage suggests, the Shire NASUWT Branch Secretary is a powerful personality, and he is respected as one who knows the pay and conditions document 'inside out' (Headteacher, Shire Secondary 2). His position, however, is reinforced by institutional factors. His ability to assert the influence presented in the interview also derives from relative membership strength with NASUWT being by far the dominant union in this LA. In addition, he has a well-coordinated network of active school representatives and his position is further buttressed by strong links with the national leadership. He therefore brings insider knowledge from the union leadership to the local WAMG which, in turn, ensures that WAMG business retains some prominence within the LA agenda:

> . . . not that I want to give [the NASUWT Branch Secretary] more credit than he's entitled to, but . . . because there is that link . . . to RIG and the national agenda, it makes it [workforce remodelling] higher on our agenda to make sure that we know about it, that we're up on it.
>
> (WAMG Chair, Shire)

However, the LA employees in this interview were aware of the possible effect of the NASUWT Branch Secretary's impending retirement. At present:

> . . . if NASUWT brings something to WAMG you know that it's set out and almost pinned down. But that doesn't mean to say that we don't have some incredible debates and it doesn't mean to say that actually sometimes we're on the same side . . . When we have a new NASUWT rep in place . . . it will be interesting to see NUT's take on that . . . [The NASUWT representative] won't have the same kind of link [with the national leadership] that [the current branch secretary] has and the way in which we deal with it will be very different. So the challenge will come from a different place.
>
> (WAMG Chair, Shire)

This interviewee also talked about how the influence of the Social Partnership model of working was filtering through to another forum in which unions and authority employees meet:

... I think it, it potentially has made the association secretaries' meeting more of a Social Partnership and less of a confrontation in that particular group . . . Less of a 'unions say this, management say this' and a stand off position because I think the unions particularly are more used to working in Social Partnership.

(WAMG Chair, Shire)

There was also a claim that another effect of the remodelling agenda has been to encourage the kind of culture change envisaged by the NRT through the change management process. In some schools:

... people are thinking outside the box now . . . It's not like it used to be where . . . the headteacher makes that decision. Now it's . . . groups of staff coming together, talking about it, discussing it, coming up with ideas you know, looking at options. And that's certainly what I've sort of been picking up and certainly what I've been seeing as well. So you know, coming from the private sector HR, I was used to that . . . In the private sector . . . it was all about quality circles, change management, having groups, having discussions and so to come here in education for me was a massive culture change and quite a culture shock, it was like going back 20, 30 years . . . What I'm seeing now is mirroring . . . what is happening in the private sector.

(LA Officer, Shire)

This WAMG is regarded as successful; interviewees were proud of its achievements and believed in its usefulness as a body that had a distinct focus, encouraged collaborative working and had some standing with schools in the authority. In this respect the data from this LA show the continuing importance of a local industrial relations structure at local level, but they also suggest a shift in the dynamics of the relationships within it. The dominance of the NASUWT Branch Secretary is not new, but is now underpinned by the authority of the Social Partnership, which he clearly uses to his advantage to silence NUT opposition and, at times, to steer the LA agenda. At the same time it is important to note his influence was exercised in a context of LA commitment to the remodelling agenda and to a more collaborative form of working to achieve its implementation: the NASUWT Branch Secretary's knowledge and pressure works with the grain of LA policy. Thus, rather than a dramatic change in industrial relations, there are subtle shifts. At one level things are very much the same—'we all get on very well here'—but these relationships have deepened towards a Social Partnership model of working that has the potential to spread to other fora within the authority. However, and again mirroring the national position, there is recognition of the provisional nature of any agreement, for the industrial relations landscape could shift again as new personnel are brought in to replace those who are retiring.

City WAMG

City, too, has a history of collaborative relationships but in this case they are most notably between the teaching unions, all of which have close links through meeting regularly over many years in different educational fora within the Authority. These relationships can be seen as having strength and continuity that is lacking within the City LA itself, for the authority has had a turbulent time in recent years with a high turnover of senior education personnel, changes in political control of the council and little investment in Human Resources (HR). In contrast with Shire, in City there is a more even balance between the NASUWT and the NUT in terms of membership strength, although the NUT in City has a higher profile in the LA in that it leads on wider issues, for instance building a local alliance against the expansion of academies.

City WAMG was set up in a similar manner to that of Shire and included LA employees, all six teacher unions, the support staff unions GMB, Unison, Transport and General Workers, and governor representatives. Once again there was no question of excluding the NUT, as the WAMG chair explained:

> My view from the very beginning was okay, they didn't sign up to the agreement . . . but actually . . . their staff that they're representing will be affected whether or not they like it because the National Agreement is a statutory requirement. So there was never, ever any consideration for excluding them from the meetings. And to be honest . . . they've been very helpful.
>
> (WAMG Chair, City)

However this WAMG had neither the central commitment in terms of time and resources evident in Shire, nor its status, reflected in the fact that the chair of the group was employed at a lower grade than assistant director of education. In part this lack of institutional support reflected the circumstances of the LA. The WAMG chair explained that the difficulties of juggling multiple demands has the effect of pushing workforce remodelling down the list of priorities:

> . . . the department's going through a reorganisation at the moment and there's also a corporate . . . HR review going on at the moment which aims to save £1.2m a year on HR . . . So that is a pressure. But [there are] the added pressures if you like of, for instance, the Children's . . . Workforce Development Council . . . and the requirement to produce a [City] Children and Young People's strategic partnership workforce strategy, which is another pressure on me . . . so we've got that pressure and the pressure of working with partners across the city to produce a workforce strategy for the children's workforce across all partner organisations, the private, voluntary and independent sector as well, and that is a huge, huge job. We've got then the added pressure of we have to produce a departmental workforce strategy, and that obviously

ties in with what's happening at the strategic partnership level, but it also ties in with what's happening at the corporate level, because corporately we will require a workforce strategy. So [there are] all these tensions pulling, pulling me in every direction if you like. Then there's the continuation of the remodelling agenda.

(WAMG Chair, City).

The remit for the WAMG was seen as monitoring compliance with workforce remodelling regulations and, unlike in Shire, it was not seen as a place for negotiation. Again in contrast to the Shire interviews, in which WAMG members emphasised the collaborative ethos of the meetings, there are differing views on the dynamics of the meetings that are conditioned by the different levels of union strength:

Because of certain animosities around the table, which are nothing to do with the LA and are much more to do with union disagreement, it [the atmosphere in meetings] was quite tense at times because you would literally get the union members arguing with each other across the table . . . Ultimately of course everybody's come to accept that this National Agreement is in place, that's it . . . you cannot waver outside it . . . As a way of kind of softening some of those arguments and debates, I would occasionally say, 'Well, why don't we offer some local guidance on . . . how you might cover PPA [planning, preparation and assessment], for instance?' And some people would almost, well metaphorically bang the table and say, 'There will be no local guidance, it is a national agreement', you know. And we went 'Ah, right, okay' (laughter) . . . Gradually . . . we just got to know each other better really, we got to trust each other a bit more . . . So yeah, the relationship has changed I suppose, simply out of starting to build up trust and understand each other's positions.

(Remodelling Adviser, City)

The extent of the trust generated is, however, problematic, as is the level of consensus. The NUT Branch Secretary's view, for instance, was that:

I'm tolerated in a . . . professional sort of way. Because most of the people of course on the local WAMG I know but they just think that we've got these crazy old-fashioned ideas of having teachers teaching and support workers supporting . . . so I don't think I've had very much effect really at all . . . but the legislation is the legislation and the NASUWT have been particularly strong. The local secretary . . . he's doing exactly what he should be doing which is promulgating all this because that's what they have to do . . . it's been quite difficult I have to say, from my point of view.

(NUT Branch Secretary, City)

The impression of exclusion and slight despair evident here is different again to the NASUWT Branch Secretary's confident interpretation of how the local WAMG operates:

> With this remodelling . . . it was very clear that it wasn't open to local negotiation, that it was a national agreement and as such it had to be implemented as a national agreement. We didn't have any problem with that. I mean some of my colleagues did at times but they knew there was no way we would go down the line of trying to . . . renegotiate a national agreement so they didn't really push it too much . . . it's important that you know that.
>
> (NASUWT Branch Secretary, City)

Nonetheless other union members of the City WAMG spoke of the group being 'relatively harmonious' (ASCL Local Officer, City) or, more critically, 'a bit slow' (NAHT Local Officer, City) and no interviewee made reference to any lasting tension between the teaching unions. But these differing perceptions of the relationships within the local WAMG highlight the tension that is apparent between the NASUWT and the NUT nationally, and in the following extract the NUT Branch Secretary explains how the national situation has impacted on City WAMG:

> . . . there has been a rift, I think . . . the association secretaries work very closely together . . . and we do have a very good working relationship . . . This has I think caused a rift and we try to rise above it. And I try to not lower myself to sort of make snidey comments all the time. But I have to say that there are snipes, not from me but from other parties. They just can't bear not to say that there are benefits. And we admit that there are benefits, we're not saying that the whole remodelling agenda has not been beneficial.
>
> (NUT Branch Secretary, City)

A deeper friction has been more apparent with the local Unison branch, which disengaged itself from the group for a while. Reflecting their frustration with the WAMG processes, local officers identified both its focus and functioning as sources of concern:

> Unison Officer 1: . . . when a particular issue is, is raised . . . for discussion it always primarily starts off with how this will affect teaching staff.
> Unison Officer 2: . . . the reason we pulled out of it was that it was toothless, absolutely toothless . . . Nothing happened. You'd go in there, sit there for two hours and it's called . . . the Workforce Agreement Monitoring Group isn't it, that's what WAMG means . . . and we say, 'What's the point in monitoring if you can't do anything? . . .

You've monitored what's going on but you can't do anything'. And we say, 'Well what's the point of it? I mean there's absolutely no point in us sitting round the table with you lot, monitoring what's going on in schools'. We might as well be going up there, going in to schools, trying to do something.

(Unison Officer 1, Unison Officer 2, City)

City Unison have subsequently returned to the WAMG, believing they should follow the national lead and 'monitor it and make sure it's managed right' (Unison Officer, City), suggesting either a re-evaluation of the judgement that the body was 'toothless' or, as was argued by Social Partnership members in the national interviews, that inclusion into this particular body, even if limited and unsatisfactory, is better than exclusion. Equally Unison's return to the local WAMG may signal the union's growing significance on the stage of school workforce industrial relations.

A notable point about this WAMG, reflected in the less than enthusiastic attitude of the NUT and the reluctant attendance of Unison, is that it lacked the dynamism of its Shire counterpart. The absence of both a 'key local leader' (Fosh 1993: 581) and strong LA leadership seemed to mean that members tended to be reactive rather than proactive. As indicated, in this LA the NUT was arguably the lead union on many issues, and its key personnel were well-known, and well-regarded, figures. However, given the institutional support for the National Agreement, the NUT lacked the membership strength needed to challenge on remodelling issues, and its influence was muted. The result was that the WAMG came across as a fairly workaday group. As one member commented: 'We know one another, there's not any histrionics between us and as a result you, you just pootle along' (Voice Branch Secretary, City).

Thus in many ways the union relationships in City can be seen as carrying on much the same as before, with continuity between teacher union personnel who have worked together for many years and who are, to a greater or lesser degree, trying to 'rise above' the national tensions, with or without the co-operation of the support staff unions. In a broad sense this WAMG is seen as being a success by most of its members: having monitored the implementation of workforce remodelling, it reconsidered its remit at the end of the three-year project and continued to operate as a forum for discussing and monitoring developments in continuing professional development and extended schools. However, despite continuity of the body and relative harmony among its members, the national agenda has helped re-align relations of power. Tensions have been introduced between local NASUWT and NUT officials as they attempt to influence local proceedings in accord with their union positions, and the strong influence of the NUT outside the group has been, if anything, reversed within the WAMG where the NASUWT holds centre stage. Nevertheless, the NASUWT still lacked the strength, dynamism and will to drive the partnership model forward in the manner of the Shire Branch Secretary, while the NUT undertook a defensive, watching brief that was unable to block, and unwilling to enhance, the workings of the WAMG.

London Borough WAMG

The London Borough Authority has a different union history and configuration to that of either Shire or City, with the chief difference being the high levels of NUT density and organisation, a feature of many London boroughs. The NUT Branch Secretary described the historical strength of the union being based on:

> . . . reputation and a tradition. And once you've got it, it goes on. As long as you don't mess it up . . . so we are absolutely systematic about recruitment, we're absolutely systematic about . . . materials going out to our reps, we've been at the forefront of most innovations in the union in terms of communication whether it's setting up a website, or . . . using email more to communicate . . . we have a reputation for solving case work sensitively . . . But we're also not frightened of going into a school, if there is a collective problem and . . . balloting the members or holding a meeting, telling the headteacher that you mustn't do this or else . . . and that's just been done consistently.
>
> (NUT Branch Secretary, London Borough)

In this Authority the local WAMG was called a working party. Its chair who, as in City, was employed by the LA at a lower grade than assistant director of education, described its set-up as follows:

> We established the various groups that were required including the working party and that was a key group for us . . . The trade unions are very active in [this LA] and . . . the working group was also a key way of engaging with the workforce unions, primarily the NUT and Unison.
>
> (WAMG Chair, London Borough).

This extract confirms both our own experience and the view of the NUT Branch Secretary that the NUT and Unison played key roles within the Authority. Despite our intention to interview all union members of the local WAMG, we were able to interview only the branch secretaries from the NUT and Unison. We were unable to locate a member from Voice, both the NASUWT and Association of School and College Leaders (ASCL) branch secretaries were unaware that the group existed, and the Association of Teachers and Lecturers (ATL) Branch Secretary believed that it was part of the Teachers' Negotiating Group. The chair of WAMG's reference to 'active' trade unions can thus be seen as code for active NUT unionism within schools.

Unlike its counterparts in Shire and City, the WAMG had been disbanded by its chair by the time the fieldwork was begun:

> I decided that we, we weren't going to continue unless there was a definite need to continue . . . We don't carry on meeting, we aren't a social . . . club. And it seemed to me that the work primarily towards the end of the last two terms it was more about CPD [continuing professional development] and it was less about the remodelling and it was also more about the extended offer . . . I told them all . . . that we probably needed to carry on meeting until the summer . . . and I said after that date I didn't really feel that we needed to carry on . . . meeting in this way.
>
> (WAMG Chair, London Borough)

This bland explanation of the body's demise was not corroborated by interviewees from the NUT and Unison, both of whom argued that the LA had been intransigent in its handling of the remodelling agenda, that the unions had tried to seek agreement over different issues and that they had effectively been stonewalled by other members of the working group:

> . . . we did try in those discussions at an earlier stage, to try to come up with some local agreements and principles . . . that we could apply . . . we spent hours and hours and hours as a negotiating body writing documents about principles and [the LA] kept saying 'Oh we'll respond next time, next time, next time', dragged it on, never, never did . . . and we were just told that . . . there was not going to be any agreement. End of story.
>
> (NUT Branch Secretary, London Borough)

And Unison:

> So it was . . . in a sense, it was very frustrating . . . we had good relations with the NUT . . . We spent a very long time negotiating, trying to negotiate with the LA to have a joint position, like a sort of a statement of intent about how it [remodelling] should be dealt with . . . And that in the end went into the sand really, it didn't happen and . . . I think a lot of time was wasted on that . . . because we couldn't reach agreement with the LA.
>
> (Unison Branch Secretary, London Borough)

This impasse between unions and LA almost certainly reflected the latter's reluctance to see the local strength of the NUT and its close relations with Unison used to breach the national agenda, and it may have been easier from its point of view to procrastinate rather than face an argument over substantive changes to the National Agreement with powerful unions.

Yet another account came from the interview with two remodelling advisers and an LA officer who saw the local WAMG as helpful although not as inclusive as they would have wished—'our Deputy Director would love other unions to be involved' (Remodelling Adviser 2, London Borough)—although possibly because they regarded the NUT officials just as obstructive as the NUT regarded the LA. When asked if the NUT's refusal to sign the National Agreement caused any problem, the answer was immediate and unequivocal:

> LA Officer: Yes
>
> Remodelling Adviser (RA)1: Yes
>
> RA 2: Yes, undoubtedly, massive problems . . .
>
> RA 1: And I think some heads were almost, felt that they couldn't act as they wanted to act
>
> RA 2: Absolutely
>
> RA 1: Because of the threat of the unions, yeah . . .
>
> RA 2: Very definitely . . . I would agree totally with that
>
> RA 1: Even the very experienced heads . . . are always cautious here, they have to be . . . And mindful of the fact that . . . the NUT is has got a very, very strong voice.
>
> (Remodelling Advisers 1
> and 2 and LA Officer)

Evidently, the disagreements in approach to workforce remodelling have not been resolved to arrive at a joint position as they have in the other two authorities. The powerful, historical position of the NUT was unable to overcome the LA's 'central role' in promoting workforce remodelling (Kershaw 2004), while the LA has equally been unable to engender enough support from other sources to resist the NUT's position. Once again a critical influence has been the 'key local leader' (Fosh 1993), in this case from the NUT. As in Shire, the individual concerned might be considered exceptional—he was a national executive member (significant in London Borough where these posts are often hard fought for), had held national office in the union and had many years experience as a local officer and negotiator. Combined with overwhelming membership dominance these factors made this person a dominant figure. Again, as in Shire, LA personnel and local headteachers saw securing this individual's endorsement as central in any significant change issue.

However, while neither the NUT officials nor the LA appeared to have much interest in re-forming the local WAMG, Unison regretted that it had not been more productive and the Branch Secretary argued that they had wanted the meetings to continue:

> We were, I think, upset because we didn't get to that clear position where very authoritatively, the local authority saying, 'We've reached agreement with the trade unions on this and this is what we recommend

to you', which is what the sort of model that we always looked to do . . .
We wanted it [the working party] to carry on because it was one of the
few opportunities we had to sort of raise issues . . . I think the meetings
were always a bit of a conflict because there was us trying to push our
. . . issues and the NUT trying to push their issues and they [LA] were
trying to deal with [that]. And I remember we spent ages talking about
work/life balance for headteachers and . . . stuff they could just sort of
get people in to speak about and we'd all fall asleep and we'd want to
[say] (bangs table), 'And this isn't happening'. We wanted to use this as
like a monitoring process and say you know, 'These schools are doing
these outrageous things and what are you going to do about it?'

(Unison Official, London Borough)

Three particular points arise from these interview extracts. The first is
that, as with the other two authorities, they point to shifts in the nature of
local industrial relations despite things remaining ostensibly the same. This
time the dominant union is fundamentally opposed to key aspects of the
National Agreement and the NUT has, in its own terms, been far more successful at resistance to the national agenda than in the two other case study
LAs. This leads to the second point: the major support staff union Unison
has substantial areas of agreement with the NUT but, nevertheless, saw
the local WAMG as offering an opportunity to engage more meaningfully
with local policy, or, to put it another way, to increase its own influence
within the authority. Thirdly, the interviews illustrate how little room there
is for serious local negotiations on aspects of the remodelling agenda. Once
policy has been agreed by the Social Partnership, implementation seemed to
allow little of the innovation or free thinking foreseen in the culture change
promoted by the NRT.

More generally, the data presented in this chapter suggest that there is
little sign of change in relations leading to new forms of membership participation and hence union renewal in these three LAs. What we see, broadly
speaking, is *rapprochement* in Shire, resistance in London Borough and
an intermediate position in City, where both the larger teacher unions are
aware of subtle shifts in position but neither is able or willing to turn the
situation to their union's advantage. The uneven development of these local
WAMGs, and their various responses to the conditions created by workforce
remodelling, can in part be explained by the existing structures for dialogue
between LA officers and union representatives. Whatever the variations,
however, there was no industrial relations gap that needed to be filled as
there was at the national level. The local WAMG in all three case study LAs
was additional and ran parallel to existing arrangements, albeit offering a
wider union representation (although one not always received with unqualified enthusiasm) through the inclusion of Unison, GMB and T&G.

However both positions of *rapprochement* and resistance are problematic. In the first place it could be argued that membership participation is
being dampened down in the case of the (perceived) successful functioning

of the Shire WAMG, the closest of the three case study models to the *rapprochement* of the Social Partnership. The expectation that remodelling advisers should sort out problems in schools once they have been brought to the group's attention expands the role of the LA officers at the expense of union representatives and suggests a possible dilution of the union role within the LA. *In extremis* the unions could become supplicants, raising problems inside the WAMG for LA officers to take up with headteachers while union officials wait on the sidelines. This approach may be attractive to weaker unions such as ATL, which lack school-based representatives, and may encourage them to feel that they operate within the WAMG on more equal conditions with the stronger and more powerful NUT and NASUWT. However it may also bring the danger that all union activity becomes undermined as LA officials assume greater importance in fulfilling a role that has been largely performed by union representatives. This then brings into question the effectiveness of the *rapprochement* approach as a long-term strategy for maintaining union influence in LAs.

Another interpretation, however, is that LA officials have always performed the function of conflict resolution in schools, particularly in small primaries where (as we demonstrate in the following chapter) union representatives are not always welcome or where union representation is thin on the ground. Union acceptance of this role can be seen as a pragmatic response to demands placed on local union officials (who often have insufficient capacity to attend to all problems within, for instance, the relatively large number of primary schools) rather than a desire to work hand in glove with management. The issue in this case is the way in which the status and power of the local WAMG develops as new demands are brought to the LA through the pressures of developing a Children's Workforce, expanding the number of extended schools and overseeing the transformation of an increasing number of maintained schools into academies.

The dismantling of the local WAMG in London Borough shows the difficulty of eclipsing the NUT, but at the same time illustrates the problems of isolated resistance. While the NUT's stance may have slowed down the implementation of workforce remodelling, the interview data presented in this chapter suggests that the controversial measures to which the NUT were opposed have eventually been adopted rather than abandoned by school managers as unachievable. The NUT have slowly retreated from their position of total opposition, citing the intransigence of the LA personnel, but the union has been unable to generate sufficient support from other teacher unions on a national scale to present a significant challenge either to the direction or to the content of workforce remodelling reforms. This national weakness undermines confidence of local members and encourages managers to pursue the reform agenda. The question of the ability of the union nationally to mobilise members to act at workplace level makes it timely now to consider the changes within schools and their effect on membership confidence and industrial relations.

6   Transforming the Primary
       School Workforce

INTRODUCTION

This chapter is concerned with the response of the case study primary schools to workforce remodelling. Workforce remodelling, for a number of reasons, has impacted upon primary in a different way to secondary schools. Primary schools tend to be smaller, with correspondingly smaller budgets and fewer staff, which gives less room for manoeuvre in terms of staff deployment. Secondly responsibility for a class of children has remained 'at the core' of the primary teacher's role (Pollard and Bourne 1994: 2), which tends to lead to a more intimate type of relationship between class and teacher as each spends a larger proportion of time in each other's company (Passy 2003). These factors, in turn, mean that arrangements for covering planning, preparation and assessment (PPA), for instance, have presented different problems to those in secondary schools. It is also the case that the industrial relations context tends to be different in smaller schools with a concomitant impact on union workplace organisation. The smaller workforce, spread across several unions, results in individual unions often having only small numbers of members in each school with the consequence that industrial relations structures in primary schools tend to be quite informal. Union culture and organisation is often poorly developed and there is a tendency to depend on external union support when union intervention is required (Stevenson 2003).

This chapter is divided into three sections. The first is concerned with the general response to workforce remodelling from headteachers, deputies and bursars within the case study schools. The second section examines the ways in which the teacher labour process has been affected by the reforms, drawing on interviews with teaching staff. The third section draws on interviews with headteachers and union representatives to consider the nature of the industrial relations within these schools.

INSTITUTIONAL IMPLEMENTATION: RESPONDING TO REMODELLING

The case study primary schools differed markedly in terms of location, size and leadership style, although the urban schools had a number of common features. All of the urban schools were located in areas of high socio-economic deprivation, and all placed a strong emphasis on children's social and emotional development. City Primary 1 and City Primary 2 were both medium-sized schools that took pride in their approach to inclusion in which all pupils in the community were welcomed onto the roll. London Borough 1 was a large school, had been judged by Ofsted to have had difficulties in the past, but had shown substantial improvement in the latest report. London Borough Primary 2, also a large school, had high pupil turbulence and had suffered staff recruitment problems in the past, but the (relatively) new headteacher's priority of raising staff quality and stability was having a positive impact. The challenges in these schools contrasted with those faced by the two smaller, rural Shire schools, both of which were located in fairly prosperous areas and had a stable staff but were in a region that was suffering from falling rolls.

None of these headteachers claimed to have been surprised by the remodelling agenda but presented it as part of an ongoing process of change: new Government initiatives, differing pupil needs, staff changes and budget changes/constraints all impinge on the running of the school, which means that, when taken in the context of what one headteacher described as being 'endlessly told . . . to drive up standards' (Shire Primary 2), all six head-teachers were constantly reviewing issues around budget and staff deployment. At the same time particular situations or projects were provoking four of the schools into further changes in school management: building work in City Primary 1 and London Borough Primary 2 following amalgamation of two schools, the response to an unfavourable Ofsted report in London Borough Primary 1 and the necessity in Shire Primary 2 of making staff redundant provided extra stimulus for reflection and re-organisation. Thus for one headteacher, remodelling was 'endorsing' what was already happening in the school, three other headteachers pointed out that they were 'ahead of the game' and the remaining two gave examples of the ways in which they had started to move administrative tasks away from teachers before the reforms officially began.

Nonetheless the headteachers' response to workforce remodelling ranged from calm acceptance to unrestrained anger about the manner in which the changes were brought in. The former response is exemplified by the relaxed attitude of Shire Primary 1 headteacher:

> I have to say this was just one more initiative alongside many others . . . we found as we do with a lot of initiatives in that, because we are a Shire county where there are not huge recruitment problems, there are certainly no retention of staff problems . . . it feels as it does with a lot of things . . . that these are national strategies being imposed on schools where actually teachers here were not worried about photocopying, they were not worried about putting up displays, they were not worried about . . . stress and workload. I mean yes, it is a demanding job

but we're well paid and we get good holidays . . . And of course the children here are very different to [those] in some schools where I've worked, where you are literally just hanging on in there by the skin of your teeth.

(Headteacher, Shire Primary 1)

The other Shire headteacher, however, was incensed by what he saw as an over-complicated process that insulted his intelligence and failed to appreciate the realities of headship in a small, rural primary school:

Every initiative we have, you get this panel of people and that's all they're doing. And I'm sure their brief is [to] make this as complicated, as difficult, as time consuming and as pointlessly futile as you can to achieve the objective . . . I look back on it now . . . We had the lovely glossy literature which I sat in here and read. They made me so angry I just hurled it in the bin because I thought . . . I don't need this . . . I don't need to be told . . . the obvious. If I had the money in my school budget I'd be doing all of this now. I haven't . . . It would take me five minutes to come up with this plan of how I could run it. I don't need this.

(Headteacher, Shire Primary 2)

Part of this head's anger was related to headteacher workload problems, with a number of headteachers having left the Authority in the recent past through stress, provoking resentment among some local interviewees at what was regarded as undue pressure on headteachers of rural schools. This headteacher was also in the process of making a teacher redundant, which may well have fuelled his anger and frustration at the time of the fieldwork. Nonetheless his attitude is indicative of the resentment that can be caused by what one report has called 'initiativitis' (PwC/DfES 2007, p. vii)—the sheer number of initiatives being implemented at any one time.

Although no other headteacher reacted quite as strongly, the difficulty of funding the remodelling agenda, in particular PPA time, was a common theme in the headteachers' interviews. It also was the catalyst for the National Association of Head Teachers'—albeit temporary—withdrawal from the Social Partnership in 2005. One headteacher interviewee referred to workforce remodelling as 'a fantastic idea—totally and utterly ridiculously underfunded' (Headteacher, London Borough Primary 2), and others talked about the 'creativity' needed to manage the budget while trying at the same time to safeguard quality of cover while teachers were absent. All had experienced difficulty in this respect and regarded the organisation of PPA as an ongoing, time-consuming and difficult process. In the words of the business manager (London Borough Primary 2): 'it's been a huge nightmare'. Only one school had found a system that was considered satisfactory and of the other five, one was not happy with the quality of the lessons, saying that the higher level teaching assistants (HLTAs) who covered PPA were 'not perfect' but were 'getting there', two were substantially reviewing procedures for the next academic year and the remaining two were reverting to the more expensive route of using qualified teachers for PPA cover. After negative experiences with instructors, teaching assistants (TAs) and contract language teachers, they believed that this was the only way to cover PPA so that pupils could receive the quality of education to which the headteachers believed they were entitled.

Funding was also relevant to headteachers' responses to the introduction of teaching and learning responsibility points (TLRs). The key to the restructuring was that it was perceived as a form of rationing. As one headteacher put it: 'there were fewer TLRs to be handed out than there were management points. I mean this was the whole issue behind it, wasn't it?' (Headteacher, City Primary 1). Implementation of the TLRs can be seen as part of the process of focussing teaching staff on teaching and learning through ending payment for responsibilities that were seen as peripheral to the learning process. They also had the effect of removing from management those who were unwilling to take on this type of responsibility (in two case study primary schools, different members of staff did not take up a TLR post) and obliging schools to make choices on which areas of the curriculum to prioritise through a calculation of how many TLRs the school could afford. It was a potentially difficult process as it involved consultation with governors, unions and staff in each school, and evidence presented throughout the project suggested that in many cases it was a difficult process because teachers could—and did—lose salary and pension rights. Of the six case study primary schools, City Primary 1 and 2 both had teachers who were net losers: City Primary 2 used TLRs as an opportunity to restructure leadership and management, while in City 1 it was part of an ongoing process of leadership reorganization within the school. The two Shire schools were relatively unaffected: it was a 'five-minute conversation' (Headteacher, Shire Primary 1) as staff were shifted into new posts with their responsibilities apparently unchanged, while Shire 2 was unable to fund a TLR post due to the small number of teaching staff. The two London Borough schools described the process as 'assimilation' in which existing responsibilities were reconfigured into nominally new posts.

The other general response to remodelling concerns support staff. There was a general feeling expressed by headteachers that support staff had been well served by the reforms through greater opportunities for training, the chance to take on further responsibility and the capacity to have improved status within the school. The exception to this was the case of nursery nurses, who were seen by City Primary 2 headteacher as losing both status and pay in the City Authority, a judgement strongly reiterated by the local Voice official. Notwithstanding the caveat concerning nursery nurses, all shared the following headteacher's views that:

... for the support staff and for the school I think it's [remodelling] good because it's a means of promoting yourself. And I think our HL-TAs, their own self-esteem and their own confidence and ... their own stature in the school has risen as a result of becoming this person ... *who's in charge of a class* [our emphasis]. All that is good.

(Headteacher, London Borough Primary 1)

The reference to HLTAs being 'in charge of a class' highlights the extent to which support staff are clearly taking on a teaching-type role, with a view expressed by headteachers that this was offering enhanced status and esteem in the school. It was not a view shared by several Unison officials we interviewed, who believed that increases in the responsibilities of support staff were not being recognized by a commensurate increase in remuneration; pay levels for many support staff on the lower grades remain low—in the words of the Shire Primary 2 headteacher, support staff are 'incredibly poorly paid'.

However, the reforms were seen as only partly responsible for the changes in support staff roles, largely for the reasons outlined earlier: each school was in a continuous process of adaptation in the face of changing circumstances. Thus four schools had a full-time bursar (or business manager) by the time of the project interviews, but three of these had been full-time secretaries or administrators before the reforms began and had taken on many of the responsibilities in such a way that upgrading to bursar seemed to be part of a longer-term evolution. Similarly TAs had been involved with literacy and numeracy schemes before remodelling, so to train them in other aspects of the curriculum and to give them greater responsibility in the classroom was not a dramatic change in itself. A Shire bursar describes the process:

I think lots of aspects of remodelling we were already ... in the process, we were naturally getting there under our own steam ... For example the TAs, when I first came here they were ancillary helpers, then they became classroom helpers, then they became classroom assistants and now they're TAs ... and yes, there have been changes in the expectations as well as the title ... But it's been just a gently, gradually evolving process rather than someone sitting down and saying Right, this is what's happening, it needs to be this, woomph!

(Bursar, Shire Primary 2)

The Shire bursar's comments reflect the earlier argument that workforce remodelling is not a decisive shift in the work of teachers and support staff, but is a new phase, in which sometimes long-established processes are given new impetus and accelerated.

In sum, the experience of primary schools points to a differential impact across the phases of implementation of the reforms. All schools cited PPA as the aspect that is continuing to cause problems. Limited budgets, restricted opportunities to deploy a small staff flexibly and some concerns about the quality of provision from TAs all served to present problems. Against this must be set a clear acknowledgement of teachers' appreciation of the benefits of PPA. For largely the same budget-based reasons TLR restructuring had caused relatively few problems, presenting short-term difficulties in two schools. The limited opportunities for teachers in primary schools to receive promoted posts, especially in smaller primary schools, made the TLR restructuring a virtual non-issue in four of the schools. The change in support staff status was recognised, and interviewees from all six schools commented favourably on how support staff were generally more valued. However, these reforms have a long fuse: the changes wrought through the remodelling process, although apparently relatively small and part of a process already begun in these schools, are having a significant effect on the teacher labour process. We analyse these issues further in the following section.

RESTRUCTURING PRIMARY TEACHERS' WORK

The aims of remodelling were encapsulated in the full title of the National Agreement *Raising Standards and Tackling Workload* (DfES 2003), and the rhetoric that has surrounded the agreement is deceptively simple: teachers have been overburdened by too many tasks that have not only distracted them from their 'core task' of improving teaching and learning (Rewards and Incentives Group 2005) but also led to problems with recruitment and retention. If those tasks can be shifted to others (preferably at lower cost), then not only will teachers be able to focus more clearly on raising standards, but the problems with recruitment and retention will be dissolved as the stress caused by overwork disappears. However, and as perhaps may be expected, the reality is rather more complex. Schools are coping with the impact of a number of different initiatives at the same time as they are absorbing and implementing others, and it is difficult to separate cause and effect in the current environment of continuous change in the education sector.

Nonetheless the evidence presented in this section suggests three trends have been intensified through workforce remodelling. The first is increased pressure to perform (Ball 2003, Jeffrey 2002). In a system that is driven by Ofsted and assessment results, schools are, as one headteacher remarked, 'fairly scary places to be at the moment' (Headteacher, Shire Primary 1), something described in more detail by a teacher in another school:

> . . . [the head] gets pressure from somebody and then pressurises us and then we think, oh you know, SATs, SATs, SATs [Standard Assessment Tests]. . . we were talking about this the other day, they were saying

that the current Year 5s, the SATs probably aren't going to be that good . . . obviously we will have people in here going, 'Why aren't your SATs good? What, aren't they this good?' You know. And we're already thinking that it's probably two years away. But we know somebody's going to be in there and, 'Well when Ofsted come . . . ' and you just think oh my. And it is that, you have got that always looming over you now, 'Have you got evidence for this?' or, 'Have you got evidence for that?' . . . It's a pressured society really and I think that . . . [teachers] particularly are very, very pressured.

(Key Sage 2 Teacher (KS2), Shire Primary 2)

This pressure on staff is passed on in different ways through the case study schools, but it is clear that there is a focus on maximizing the use of resources through careful allocation of people and tasks. In Shire Primary 1, the head-teacher describes how he assigns the TAs to teachers in his school:

So first of all I do my SEN [Special Educational Needs] and that goes in first . . . because you've got a moral responsibility for those children and . . . money's being put in the budget specifically for those children . . . And then after that we're looking at class size, we're looking at the dif-ficulties that the children are having . . . My timetabling is a nightmare because . . . it would be much easier just to put a TA into every classroom . . . Because every hour you put a TA into a classroom, that's £450 a year . . . And it's just a figure that I carry with me all the while. So you prune a little, you gain £2,000 or £3,000, oh, that's another three hours. But where are you going to put that? Well . . . I know a group of boys in Year 4 who were really struggling with writing and three hours a week can make a difference. So many of the TAs . . . are in there to do specific tasks, partly decided by me . . . There's hardly any kind of, 'You're going to get a general TA and it's your decision to [decide] what they're doing'. And . . . the staff know that, as I'm walking through school every day, popping in, I don't mind what the TA is doing but she'd better be doing something with children, as in raising standards.

(Headteacher, Shire Primary 1)

The views expressed by this headteacher clearly highlight the calculations that inform decisions in the search for 'efficiency'. Teachers, with their pro-fessional knowledge of the children they teach, are not given discretion to deploy TAs, but rather the decision is a cost-benefit calculation made by the headteacher. The work of teachers and support staff is reduced to a mon-etary value—a 'figure that I carry with me all the while'—to be deployed wherever it will add most 'value'. Here there is a clear emphasis on deploy-ing TAs on specific tasks where it is perceived impact will be maximized. Teachers retain an overall responsibility for making sure that TAs are employed to maximum effect whilst the headteacher's role is supervision at a distance—'popping in' to check. It is significant that the role of the TA is framed in terms of raising standards, not tackling teacher workload—'she'd better be doing something with children, as in raising standards'. In these circumstances it is questionable as to whether the TA will impact positively on teacher workload as this is not how the TA's contribution is being evaluated. This not only diminishes the potential benefit for teachers, but also draws TAs into the web of performativity culture, as a teacher in the same school describes:

> I think they're fantastic to have in a class. And there's a lot expected of them, they've got a small group and you are expecting them to feed back to you to say, 'They [the pupils] could do that, they couldn't do that, we need to do some more of this'. And they're assessing all the time as well, you know, they are like your right hand person, aren't they, in a class. And I do think more and more is expected of them.
>
> (KS2 Teacher, Shire Primary 1)

Raised expectations are not confined, however, to TAs, and in City Primary 1 the focus is clearly on the teachers. Here the headteacher describes how staff meetings are run as a form of continuing professional development (CPD) that ensures each teacher takes some kind of responsibility for school development:

> It's distributed leadership I think in the extreme . . . but it's intensely monitored by [the deputy] and myself and our governing body . . . All the staff feel so part of what's going on in the school . . . [In] our staff meetings . . . we gave them six areas that . . . needed developing in this school, that had come up from our own monitoring the previous year. The usual school improvement sort of work. So we gave them the six areas . . . and said, 'Right you're going to work in twos on these six areas for us all to lead the development' . . . And the six areas were things like presentation . . . marking . . . differentiation, extended writing, real down, grassroots stuff that came out of all the subjects . . . So then you were in different teams so . . . you'd be given time to investigate and promote and then you would come in our professional learning community staff meetings, which were every three weeks, and you'd say 'Right, we feel for presentation, guys, we should be doing this, can we follow it for three weeks? We're going to come in and do some work scrutiny'. And then in three weeks they would have to feed back to the professional learning community. So what we're doing is CPD but I think we're also training up future leaders because monitoring . . . and evaluation synthesis, and application of that monitoring afterwards . . . to me is really the big chunk of what leadership is about.
>
> (Headteacher, City Primary 1)

This way of working is seen as benefiting all as it reduces the workload of senior managers, helps more junior staff to develop leadership skills and can be part of generating an enthusiastic, collaborative working environment. The teachers we interviewed spoke approvingly of the system and seemed to value the challenges they were given. However the headteacher's comments are informative in that she talks about 'intense monitoring' of her staff and about 'monitoring and evaluation synthesis' as 'the big chunk' of leadership.

This extract is also informative in that it introduces the two other trends evident in the data; increased use of data to monitor children's progress and its corollary, an enhanced managerialism in which these data are used at differing levels to monitor teachers' performance and then, as the headteacher quoted in the previous extract puts it, for the 'application of that monitoring'. Here two Key Stage (KS) managers from London Borough Primary 2 provide an example of how using the data in this way might work:

> KS1 Manager: . . . when we first did it, [the teachers asked], 'What are you doing?'
>
> KS2 Manager: 'You're judging me'.
>
> KS1 Manager: Yeah . . . And you did feel that way . . . But as it's moved on, there are so many other people involved and it's saying, 'Right, actually this child needs help' . . . Also in this, in teaching you don't get 'Well dones' very often and . . . it's something which is really missed out because you could always do more, there's always more to do. But . . . when you have got children who are making progress, it jumps out [from the data] and it's like . . . how has that been successful? Then you're tuning in to . . . constraints that teachers have because . . . there are teachers that I know who are very good, you know, very strong [at] literacy and getting children moving on writing, so again that's then targeting somebody else. So it opens up quite a lot and I think people welcome it now, it's not something that people go, 'Oh my god, I've got to do this programme'.
>
> KS2 Manager: And . . . they know it's not part of performance management, they're never going to be asked to have a target to get so many to this level by the end of the year . . . and that's been made quite explicit . . . And the same for you know, the Key Stage SATs results.
>
> (KS 1 Manager and KS 2 Manager,
> London Borough Primary 2).

These middle managers, as those involved in operationalising this process, interpret the use of the data as benign, but they also acknowledge that teachers' strengths and weaknesses become more exposed and recognised. When this is taken in the context of their own role of 'having an overview of where standards are across the board and if they're not where they should be' (KS2 Manager, London Borough Primary 2), there can be no doubt that so-called weaker teachers will be under pressure to improve their performance despite the assurances that unreasonable targets will not be set, or that such targets will not be linked to performance management (PM). When, in turn, this monitoring is combined with the new PM regulations (Rewards and Incentives Group 2007), which are used to judge suitability for pay and career progression, tightening Ofsted criteria for lesson delivery (Ofsted 2008) and the latest teachers' standards framework (TDA 2007), this data management can be seen to be part of the process of increasing pressure on teachers to perform more successfully in clearly defined ways, with increased pay going to those who are able to fulfil the prescribed conditions. Certainly, anecdotal evidence from a union official on the project Reference Group indicated that concerns were growing about the use of crude quantifiable targets for student test scores as the basis for PM objectives. Furthermore, as noted, monitoring becomes more systematic and extensive with responsibility for it cascaded down to middle managers, a process that is then reinforced by their involvement in PM of teachers and support staff who are lower in the hierarchy.

On a more positive note, all the teachers interviewed welcomed the advent of PPA, with one expressing a general sentiment that it gave her 'more of a life outside of school' (KS2 Teacher, Primary Shire 2). However, PPA has also played a role in ratcheting up the expectations of teachers' performance. As a consequence, much of PPA time is spent strengthening the process of data collection and its use for a more intensive monitoring of pupils' progress. This then encourages a more systematic approach to lesson planning, as this teacher explains:

> I'm doing a lot more assessment of the children, [I] have more time to assess the children's work and things like that . . . I think PPA has brought that back round really, it's always . . . starting with assessing what the children know [and you think], 'Right, where are we taking them now?' It's not just thinking, 'Oh what am I doing this week? Oh, I haven't done those objectives' . . . I think it's making teachers realise, well, me realise more . . . where children are and moving them on.
>
> (KS2 Teacher, Primary Shire 2)

Intervention programmes, such as Speakeasy and Reading Recovery, each of which requires careful monitoring in order to assess the impact on children, further reinforce this process of assessment. Once again the middle managers from London Borough 1 describe how these initiatives produce a wealth of data:

> KS1 manager: . . . [this programme] is quite data heavy as you're showing the impact . . . of the programme on the children so you're then recording their PSE levels, scale points and their . . . literacy and

you target that each term . . . You are looking at the effects and seeing how the children move on and as part of the ISP we are a data rich school . . .

Interviewer: ISP?

KS1 manager: . . . Intensive Support Programme . . . So with that you, when you do your assessment it's . . . putting all your children where they are for their levels at reading, writing and maths. And . . . you meet . . . the standards team . . . And you talk through the progress of children in your class and look at children who've made good progress, children who have not moved on and it, it happens every term. And so we then have all the data from reception to Year 6 and again there's lots of data there

KS2 manager: And you pick up all sorts, the amount of progress . . . ethnicity, just a range of things.

(KS1 Manager and KS2 Manager,
London Borough Primary 2)

But the monitoring is not just the product of internal school policies: it is a response to the gaze of Ofsted. One headteacher spoke about Ofsted's favourable comments on their 'clinical statistics' (Headteacher, London Borough Primary 1), while another came from a different direction, highlighting the perceived threat of Ofsted should the data not be satisfactory:

. . . if Ofsted look at the external data [and] they see that there's an issue here, if you haven't been tracking these children with teacher assessment all the way through you lay yourself open to [accusations of] 'You're not doing your job properly, you don't know where they are'.

(Headteacher, Shire Primary 2)

These data suggest that the benefit of PPA can be weighed against the increased expectations surrounding teachers' work, with higher levels of performance, greater use of data, and a trend towards enhanced managerialism appearing to have brought a shift in emphasis rather than a reduction in workload. The following comments from one teacher effectively summarise the views of all the primary teachers interviewed in the project concerning the effects of workforce remodelling:

I know we're supposed to not be doing all those administrative tasks but the amount of other things that we're requested to do (laughs) . . . is phenomenal . . . the amount of assessment, the amount of planning . . . You have a literacy plan, a numeracy plan, you have half-termly plans for art, history, geography, PE, RE, music you know, the week's literacy. And then you've just got plans and plans and plans. Then you've got individual children's profiles, assessments for individual children.

(KS1 Teacher, London Borough Primary 2)

RESTRUCTURING PRIMARY SCHOOL TEACHERS' WORK——THE IMPACT OF TEACHER UNIONS

Clearly, whatever the benefits to teachers of workforce remodelling, issues arose that were ripe for union representation. Support for union activity, however, varied considerably between the six case study primary schools, and depended in part on the level of union activism in the LA. Both London Borough schools had strong National Union of Teachers (NUT) allegiance, claiming approximately 80% of the teachers in those schools, and both had an NUT representative. Shire Primary 2 and City Primary 2 also had NUT representatives, with the NUT being the strongest union in City Primary 2, but membership spread out between different unions in Shire Primary 2: neither City Primary 1 nor Shire Primary 1 had school-based representatives among the staff, who again had no particular allegiance to any one union. There was no evidence of any formal representation from any other teaching union in any of these schools. Whilst this would not necessarily be typical, it does highlight the traditional strength of the NUT in the primary sector. Interviews were conducted with the two NUT representatives in the London Borough schools, but not in the others: City Primary 2 had had difficulty with the previous NUT representative over a matter unrelated to workforce remodelling and, in view of the sensitivity of the situation and the fact that there was a new person in post, the headteacher was unwilling to grant access in this respect. In Shire Primary 2 the headteacher denied knowledge of any representative, although we later discovered that there was an NUT representative in the school who was absent on the day of the fieldwork.

Union activity can broadly be divided into three levels among these case study schools, largely reflecting the nature of the schools' cultures and the strength and role of the NUT in the LA. Unions featured little in the consciousness of the staff of the two Shire schools where such comments were made as, 'I'm not particularly union minded' (KS2 teacher, Shire Primary 1). The suggestion of school-based union meetings was often considered inappropriate with such a small number of staff and where informal exchanges of information are the norm, as illustrated by the KS2 teacher in Shire Primary 2, who said:

> [Name] is the school rep but well, it's so small, isn't it . . . I mean all the post comes to you and she just shares it round and if there are issues that the union's bringing up she'll, we'll just have an informal chat about it.
>
> (KS2 Teacher, Shire Primary 2)

This attitude was broadly similar to that of the two Shire headteachers, although perhaps for different reasons. Both said they encouraged staff to join unions and both professed to be open to union representation within the school, but neither had consulted specifically with unions during the remodelling process. In Shire Primary 2 this was partly because the head-teacher believed that he had the ultimate responsibility for the quality of education provided in the school and partly because having a small number of staff did not lend itself to formal consultation. Talking of the process leading up to the introduction of PPA, he stated:

> I talked to the teachers and I talked to the TAs separately about it. If we . . . had the TAs and the teachers together, the TAs would be swamped . . . by the teachers' views and I wanted the TAs' views . . . The bottom line is whatever system of PPA cover . . . we get to the real big issue is I've got to be happy it's adequate . . . So me as a head, [it's] my decision. I do talk to the other staff about it, we're changing what we're doing now because we're all not happy with it, but ultimately it's my decision. I've asked them informally about the place. I haven't called together . . . a meeting of everyone but just [asked], 'How's it gone today?' Because it's a small school and it just works in a different way. It doesn't need to be formalised.
>
> (Headteacher, Shire Primary 2)

In Shire Primary 1 the headteacher regarded himself as having an 'invitational leadership style', and saw his role as working out practical solutions to problems as they arose:

> . . . no-one is paid here for managing a subject and we all co-ordinate at least one subject . . . I did say to teachers, you know, 'You do not have to do this anymore, you know, I've been told in the workforce remodelling you don't have to co-ordinate subjects'. At which the staff said 'Who's going to do it?'. Well, I haven't got a clue really, I have no idea what's going to happen. But people want to co-ordinate subjects. But I think part of it . . . is helped for example when we get a, a teacher training day in September, half of that day is given over to people monitoring work from the previous year . . . And the English curriculum, which is a massive one, we've got two co-ordinators and when a course comes up they both go. So I would like to feel that people felt valued in what they were doing and it wasn't always being done in their own time. So they were keen to carry on really.
>
> (Headteacher, Shire Primary 1)

Several issues arise from these extracts, among which are the close control that each headteacher has over the school (albeit with different leadership styles), the sense of a small community in which each staff member needs to pull his/her weight and is valued for so doing, the willingness of staff to contribute to the school in ways perceived to be necessary, the management of potential conflict by Shire Primary 1 headteacher's tacit appeal to altruism and his own justification of asking teachers to do more than they contractually should. None of this is conducive to union activism within the school.

Headteachers in the City schools were less inclined to ignore union influence and both had had formal consultations with staff over the introduction of TLRs. However, as with the Shire schools, unions were operating in a difficult environment. There was, for instance, a tendency for the headteachers to pre-empt resistance to proposed changes by presenting staff with a plan that was difficult to amend and offered little room for objection. The headteacher of City Primary 1 illustrates the point:

> We had one representation [during the TLR restructuring] from one teacher feeling that PSHE needed, because of the school we are, needed a real representation. We respected that and we actually went along with it. We really did listen to what the staff were saying. We didn't get to union level. But I feel for us . . . if you've got a damn good plan, and showing what the needs of the school are, then, then how can a member of staff [object]?
>
> (Headteacher, City Primary 1)

City Primary 2's headteacher used a similar tactic with the introduction of PPA by presenting the options to staff as a simple choice between larger classes or greater responsibility for the TAs. But in City Primary 1 the form of distributed leadership cited earlier in the chapter also precluded the rehearsal and collective formation of grievances and hence any strong union activity. Staff meetings focused on professional development: ' . . . they don't have any clutter in them like . . . We're all going on a trip on 5th November, or anything like that. That doesn't exist in our meetings, it is really CPD' (Headteacher, City Primary 1).

In such a system, where staff are focused on school and their own development and in which general meetings are not a common occurrence, there is little room for union business. Interviewed teachers in this school, too, had very little time for union business or activism: ' . . . we don't talk really about union things in school that much actually. Our leaders give us information, just a booklet but you know . . . you don't read it (laughs). You don't read it because you just haven't got time' (KS2 teacher, City Primary 1).

The pressure to perform not only increased workload pressures, but also effectively squeezed out any union activity that might help address these issues. Neither was union business encouraged among the staff: ' . . . we wouldn't mind any union involvement, we're very open, it wouldn't frighten me or stop me doing anything. We'd just hope to take them with us' (Headteacher, City Primary 1). It seems fair to say that both City headteachers recognised their schools as being loosely unionised but were conscious of the indirect influence of the unions through the presence of local officials. They were inclined therefore to prepare their position carefully before presenting changes to staff. Staff, for their part, seemed to have limited involvement in formal union activism as represented, for example, through attendance at local association meetings.

The London Borough schools were qualitatively different to the other four in that both headteachers regarded the NUT as 'strong'. Both were members of the NUT and both regarded consultation with the NUT as an important part of managing change within the schools but, just as their styles of school management differed, so did their styles of dealing with the unions. Their attitudes can be seen contributing to the very different responses of the two school-based NUT representatives, as well as high-lighting more general issues surrounding teacher union activism. The NUT representative in London Borough 1 was regarded by the headteacher as a key member of the school management team:

> We welcome the union without reservation where the union representa-
> tive would say, 'Well, maybe we shouldn't monitor that much', for ex-
> ample . . . And what that does is it that . . . you sort of develop policies
> and procedures and so on . . . Once the guidance is on the table we're
> saying, 'Well that might be the guidance from the union but actually
> we're in this position . . . and we need to be doing things here . . . which
> is outside perhaps of the union guidance' . . . And once you sort of get
> a policy in place which is agreed by the staff and the unions can . . . see
> . . . you're in a position so you need to be doing this, then that really
> does become a bit more helpful in moving the thing forward. And I
> think that's what we have because we have that . . . union representa-
> tion within the senior management team.
>
> (Headteacher, London Borough Primary 1)

This interpretation of the relationship is not entirely reflected in the NUT representative's interview, in which there was a confident assertion of his own and his union's influence:

> I find it a lot better me being on the management team because any
> issues . . . relating to agreements or guidelines from the union, they
> say, 'What do you think about the union's position on such and such?'
> 'Look, if it's wrong, if what you're going to be doing is not within the
> union's guidelines, you don't do it'. And that's how we've gone for-
> ward. That's the best way.
>
> (NUT Representative, London
> Borough Primary 1)

Thus during the TLR restructuring the headteacher 'followed the union's guidelines to the very full stop' and 'everybody was quite happy with the way in which they were then moved over into the TLR points' (NUT rep-resentative, London Borough Primary 1). Both headteacher and NUT representative agreed that the process had been uncomplicated. In this case there is a strong representative, supported by a small committee within the school, who has been able to 'create a voice' (NUT representative, London Borough Primary 1) for the union in such a way that it has become an integral part of school leadership and management.

This in-house arrangement provides a sharp contrast with the industrial relations situation in London Borough Primary 2, where the headteacher deals with the local branch secretary rather then the school representative. Here he describes how the TLRs were introduced in his school:

> I'd already involved my union [the NUT] prior to [the TLR] assimilation . . . We had a meeting with the NUT so the local branch secretary came [to the school meeting] and said, 'You've just heard what [your headteacher] has said, I'm delighted to hear that, we're working hand in hand'. Therefore as an association member you listen, you hear your branch secretary [and] your headteacher talking hand in hand, talking at the same meeting together, and you think, 'Well great. Therefore if . . . the headteacher is going to do this or the governing body wants to do this, I'm going to understand where it's coming from' . . . It [TLR assimilation] wasn't a problem for us.
>
> (Headteacher, London Borough Primary 2)

In this school, the NUT representative was disillusioned with levels of trade union consciousness and action, both generally and specifically, arguing that 'people are less and less engaged in union activity' and giving three reasons why this may be the case. The first was that protesting has little impact in the current political climate of increasing centralisation, and the 'huge protest' against the war in Iraq was used as a general example. More specifically she drew on the case of the NUT petition on pay levels, saying that 'people look at you like you're an idiot when you say, "Sign a petition". Who's going to listen to that?' The second reason concerned school management systems, which she argued militate against people feeling they can have an impact on school organisation because the different hierarchies effectively divide staff into different groups. In this context she also mentioned differentiated school salary structures, that mean: ' . . . instead of the whole mass of teachers being together it's now, "Oh you can go up that scale . . . but you've got to prove you're good at that" . . . and it mitigates against people feeling collective' (NUT Representative, London Borough Primary 2).

The third reason concerned the NUT membership of the headteacher, which she believed made members less inclined to speak out when they thought something was amiss:

> . . . there was one instance when one member of staff felt she was being bullied so I called a union meeting . . . to discuss bullying within the school, just in general terms. And nobody would say anything . . .

because the headteacher was there, he's an NUT member. People will not take things up, you see, they won't take things up . . .

(NUT Representative, London
Borough Primary 2)

In this interview there is little of the other NUT representative's confidence of being at the centre of developments within the school but rather a sense of a hard struggle against a variety of factors that depress union activity. A feeling that the NUT was betraying its principles over PPA cover perhaps also exacerbated low morale:

> I'm quite annoyed with [the union]. The NUT's sort of backtracked a bit I think and now seems to be taking the line that it's okay for TAs or nursery nurses to take classes . . . I just think to myself it's the thin end of the wedge really.

(NUT Representative, London
Borough Primary 2)

This was the only time in these interviews that the NUT position was described in these pointed terms. In the other London Borough school, the NUT representative reflected the general response from teachers in the other primary schools, seeing the process as relatively uncomplicated. Nevertheless, underlying anxieties still persisted:

> . . . we didn't really have any issue . . . surrounding that [PPA cover] . . . although some teachers did feel that if in the long run support staff was going to be allowed to take classes, what was the need for qualified teachers as such. It was raised but not to an extent where it caused serious concern within our school . . . As far as I know I don't think there was any real resistance to that.

(NUT Representative, London
Borough Primary 1)

This degree of resigned acceptance concerning the use of TAs suggests that these teachers' attitude towards PPA cover is not straightforward. They have been glad of their PPA and are supportive of the greater opportunities that workforce remodelling has offered support staff, but, at the same time, there is a sense that the principle of a graduate profession is being undermined, and the two positions are difficult to reconcile (Edwards 2008). As the previous quotation suggests, the whole adds up to a feeling that things cannot be changed and the best strategy is perhaps to make the best of an imperfect situation. Where such demoralisation exists, the likelihood is that union responses focus more on *rapprochement* rather than resistance; accepting and going with the grain of reform rather than challenging the trajectory of policy. There is little evidence, with the possible exception of the situation in London Borough Primary 1, of union renewal in these schools.

These findings point to a workplace union culture in primary schools where workplace organization is often limited. Individual school-based representatives tended not to be significantly involved in school-based decision-making. In many cases, the key union personality was not in the school, but outside it. Certainly the evidence highlighted the significant role of the branch secretary, cited as important by both union representatives and headteachers. Factors operating against more general union activity within these primary schools include, variously, the headteacher's ability to control workforce conditions, an increasingly differentiated workforce, a focus on teachers' individual development and the feeling among some teachers, particularly in small primary schools, that unions are only necessary when things go wrong, a safety net rather than a positive part of working life. It is also worth noting that the size of primary schools and the number of classroom teacher unions are both unhelpful in this respect, for it is possible that all four classroom unions may be represented, further diminishing any possible sense of collectivity. It may also be significant that the majority of teachers in primary schools are women, who for a number of complex social reasons have a history of being less involved than men as union activists. However, union activism has historically been greater in secondary schools than in primary and it is to these that we now turn.

7 Workforce Remodelling in Secondary Schools
Towards Extended, Accountable Management

INTRODUCTION

If, as Gunter and Butt (2007: 5) argue, New Labour felt the need to 'break the dominance of teachers as providers of education', workforce reform did not appear to offer the means to do so within secondary schools. Within this sector, the impact of a number of aspects of workforce remodelling promised to be less than dramatic and certainly less so than in the primary sector. The transfer of routine tasks to support workers was the least controversial element of the reforms, and the size of secondary schools already offered the possibility of moves towards greater potential divisions of labour. The separation of pastoral work was not unproblematic but again the organisation of teaching rotating classes in secondary schools, where teachers are subject specialists, resulted in weaker emotional ties with students, so was likewise not perceived as a great threat. Moreover, the major benefit of the reforms for primary teachers, the guaranteed 10% planning, preparation and assessment (PPA) time, was already in place in many secondary schools: indeed we have examples of schools already having more non-contact time than the reforms stipulated. The reduction in cover was a definite gain and was welcomed with less ambivalence than in the primary sector, where teachers felt uneasy sometimes about the quality of staff taking 'their' class. The reforms were very much with the grain therefore.

Where Gunter and Butt's observation does have purchase, however, is in the way the reforms ushered in a further restructuring and refocusing of management within secondary schools that has extended the reach and intensity of management and accountability. The mechanism for change was the abolition of management allowances (MAs) and their replacement by much more prescriptive teaching and learning responsibilities (TLRs). Schools being larger and more complex organisations than their primary equivalents, many more staff within them had MAs for responsibilities that were not directly tied to teaching and learning. Concerns were expressed about the process of implementation of TLRs and the consequent loss of pay and its impact on pension entitlements, and unions tried as far as possible to have members with MAs assimilated into posts that carried TLRs.

This transition was largely successfully achieved with staff moving across to the new posts and successfully retaining their pay and status levels. In gaining this apparent victory, however, less attention has been paid to the fact that the moves also signalled a significant change in work roles: it was not just the nomenclature of the posts that changed but also their substance. The emphasis on teaching and learning and the loss, for many, of pastoral responsibilities has meant that TLR holders have a much more managerial role monitoring the performance of the staff beneath them, a role with which many are uncomfortable. This movement towards greater line management and more extensive control has significant implications for teachers' work and casts further doubt on Bach *et al.*'s (2006) simplistic dismissal of the relevance of workforce reform from a labour process perspective.

WORKFORCE REMODELLING: SCHOOL LEVEL RECEPTION

The six secondary schools that provide the case studies are not collectively untypical of English secondary schools (although there was no failing school to enable examination of the particular problems and pressures associated with this category). The size of the schools varied from 800 pupils to over 1400 in the largest. Five out of the six schools were mixed and one was an all-girls school: three out of the six had sixth forms. The locations of the schools obviously affected their make-ups. One of the rural schools, a largely white specialist sports school, had an intake with low levels of social deprivation and was oversubscribed. Ofsted had rated it as satisfactory, even though its results were above average, because in its judgement the school failed to stretch pupils. The second rural school had been awarded specialist technology status and had a catchment area that contained pockets of deprivation as well as affluence. Again, its students were largely white, and like its counterpart in the Shire the school was rated satisfactory in its last Ofsted inspection. Both City schools had large numbers of students from different ethnic backgrounds with one in particular having high numbers from an Indian heritage. The first one was a specialist science school in which standards of attainment were below the national average but in which students made good progress from their starting points. Moreover it was improving its provision and was graded good by Ofsted. The second had become a specialist sports and science college in which, despite the social factors, students made outstanding progress. This judgement was reflected in Ofsted, awarding it outstanding status in its last inspection. The first London Borough school was located in a prosperous area but also took students from different ethnic groups from deprived wards. It had been awarded specialist performing arts status and, because of its ethos and improving provision, was judged by Ofsted to be a good school. The other London Borough school was an all-girls school that served an area of great ethnic mix. This is reflected in the school's intake, with over 50% of students speaking English as a second language. Again the school has specialist performing arts status but the grading by Ofsted this time was outstanding.

As with the primary sector schools there was a strong feeling amongst headteachers and senior staff that the process of remodelling had started well before the official Government initiatives and the National Agreement in 2003. Headteachers in particular were keen on emphasising that they supported reforms and restructuring at school level and that much of the credit for change belongs to them and not to the central perspectives. One stated: 'my own experience of workforce remodelling and my involvement in it predates any kind of official agreement' (Headteacher, City Secondary 4). Changes were, moreover, not Government driven, but frequently linked to wider educational values: to 'build a workforce that could deliver the kind of vision that I wanted' (Headteacher, City Secondary 3). The ability to achieve changes was in this instance premised on negotiating good conditions of service with the teacher unions at school level and ensuring that people enjoyed coming to work. The process of change also included persuading some staff to leave, but persuasion was made easier at the time by the ability of teachers to take early retirement at age 50 and by a willingness to re-employ teachers on temporary or part-time contracts. This willingness to re-hire also highlighted the tensions between the need to build a school responsive to the increasingly monitored demands of central government and the recognition that staff who were not good leaders or managers 'were still good teachers' (Headteacher, City Secondary 3), a judgement reflected by other headteachers.

Internally generated perspectives ensured that schools' routines and habits were critically scrutinised. Teachers' industrial action to pressure schools to reduce workload in 2001—particularly the refusal to attend more than one after-school meeting per week—did not cause schools to implode, illustrating that many meetings were inefficient or unnecessary. Some meetings were of course important and continued to happen, but there was a large degree of discretion attached to the potential participants: 'people, if they felt it was important, would meet. No one required them to do so' (Headteacher City Secondary 3).

RESENTMENT AND AMBIVALENCE

The progress made in some of the areas of remodelling reinforced resentment towards further Government imposition: 'I absolutely object to somebody telling me, and we all did . . . we know what we're doing really' (Headteacher, City Secondary 4). At the same time there was recognition of the usefulness of being pushed, particularly over certain issues such as examination invigilation, where the same headteacher stated: 'that needed to happen statutorily in order to get schools to move' (Headteacher, City Secondary 4). This ambivalence was reflected elsewhere:

what's been fascinating is how we now have a number of posts in operation, which we just didn't think would work before, like for example cover, which has always been one of the most horrible jobs in schools, is now run by a cover manager . . . She's not a teacher, she's an administrator in the office. She does a good job and we've had fewer problems since we've had her than we had when the deputy was doing it.

(Headteacher, City Secondary 3)

The headteachers were well aware of the statutory requirements but in addition support and encouragement were also available elsewhere. The local authorities (LAs) had appointed consultants to advise and guide on implementation, although these were largely ignored by secondary headteachers in two of the LAs. Secondary headteachers in City LA, for instance, took advice from outside bodies but held the LA in scant regard. City LA was viewed as slow to develop policies, conservative and risk averse. The headteachers would have preferred no nonsense advice in contrast to the way in which the LA tried to encourage implementation of remodelling using elements of the change management strategies laid out by the National Remodelling Team: 'It was the law, but in a sense they tried to pretty it up by getting people to do loads of bean bag type chairs, you know, sitting around and touchy-feely kind of stuff' (Headteacher, City Secondary 3). Resistance to enforced change extended to refusal to set up change teams (CTs). In only one school (City Secondary 3) was a CT established and then with a restricted membership and narrow brief. CTs were largely dismissed: 'I just thought it was a nonsensical concept . . . we couldn't think of what a CT would actually do' (Headteacher, City Secondary 4). Schools in all three LAs tended to use already existing mechanisms of consultation and, occasionally, bargained with trade unions. The position in one Shire school was: 'the change team if anything was myself and [the NASUWT rep]' (Headteacher, Shire Secondary 4).

LAs' involvement tended to reflect the pressure for change that undoubtedly came directly from Government. However, these reforms were also the result of the National Agreement with the unions and the unions themselves became a conduit for the changes. The role of the National Association of Schoolmasters Union of Women Teachers (NASUWT) as a major proponent of the reforms has already been highlighted, but active support was not restricted to this union alone. One headteacher described the role of the Association of School and College Leaders (ASCL):

I'm in Secondary Heads Association (SHA), now ASCL, and I remember having quite a big to do with the General Secretary . . . SHA was so keen upon making this thing work, as were all the other unions apart from NUT . . . that they were bending over backwards, almost to be the Government's agents . . . I said that actually SHA could have started acting a bit more like a trade union and they'd actually got to start supporting the members.

(Headteacher, City Secondary 3)

LABOUR PROCESS AND CHANGES TO TEACHERS' WORK

Secondary School Teachers' Work and the '25 Tasks'

One of the observations made by Adam Smith (1776) and reinforced by Braverman (1974) was that a greater division of labour and the substitution of skilled labour by less skilled labour cheapened costs within production. The shedding of teachers' routine tasks and their migration to support staff appears to fit this pattern and to pave the way for the possible employment of fewer qualified teachers. Moreover, because of the standards agenda, remodelling reforms have increased pressure on teachers to concentrate on teaching and preparation, while not necessarily addressing the question of overall workload.

These larger concerns were not widely reflected in the immediate responses we encountered. Secondary schools, on the whole, had few problems with either the idea of teachers shedding the more routine aspects of their jobs or with the possible long-term consequences. There was some minor resistance in Shire Secondary 4, for instance, with teachers continuing to mount displays, believing they did it better than support staff and that it saved them having to supervise and correct work afterwards. The shedding of routine work also closed some avenues of accidental and incidental sources of knowledge. Some teachers in the same school were reluctant to stop collecting money from students because they 'always want to know exactly who's paid and who hasn't and why' (Headteacher, Shire Secondary 4). Changes to examination invigilation and the administration and management of student absence also generated some concerns. There was some feeling amongst teachers that it was necessary for them to continue to invigilate, especially in schools that were associated with difficult catchments. Some problems also arose around student absenteeism and the mechanisms for dealing with it. Before systems were adequately in place, form tutors in London Borough Secondary 3 were refusing to chase up student absences and this had a detrimental affect on their figures. When responsibility for getting and collating information on students was subsequently centralised, however, form tutors were not always complimentary about the extent to which they were informed. In City Secondary 3 two clerical staff dealt with the absence issues relating to 1200 students, leading to concern that lack of communication with tutors weakened their continuing pastoral role.

The reluctance of teachers for both educational and practical reasons to cede tasks to support workers was mirrored by the responses of some headteachers and others in senior management roles. The Personal Assistant (PA) to the headteacher in City Secondary 4 referring to the willingness of the senior leadership team (SLT) to delegate said: 'I think they've become so used to doing them, it's not that they don't want to [delegate], they've just forgotten how to delegate'. According to a business manager in same school: 'It was the same with all of the SLT because they had admin roles . . . They feel threatened because if they let go, what are they going to do?' (Business Manager, City Secondary 4). She complained that, although her post was intended to be strategic, for far too much of the time she was performing operational, administrative work. Headteachers' reluctance to delegate roles to business managers is also related to clashes of perspectives and values. Part of the reforms has been to encourage more entrepreneurship in schools and for schools to adopt more private sector practices. Recruiting expertise from outside of education is one way of promoting this direction. There is evidence that this is far from unproblematic for schools:

> Since I've been here the head's been saying to me I don't want the school to be run like a business . . . but actually we are a business . . . Teachers . . . have been brought up in a different way and throughout their career it's all about teaching and learning, teaching and learning, not about management . . . they don't really understand that side of things.
>
> (Business Manager, City Secondary 4)

The argument for changes in staff roles reflected in the National Remodelling Team model assumes that, with innovation within the staff structure, capacity to cope with new demands will increase. The introduction of staff not tied to demarcations and traditional notions of professionalism will develop new ways of thinking about problems and new frameworks to solve them. Again the business manager in City 4 represented this tendency on the ground:

> if the grades are down, it's all about teaching, teaching, teaching . . . it's 'Okay we've got a bit of money, we need a teacher, let's get the teacher in', and that's what they do. They don't think 'Well actually, let's see if we can do something else and be more creative. Can we have a different type of support staff that could actually help support and raise achievement through working in a different way?' (laughs)
>
> (Business Manager, City Secondary 4)

As yet the desire to increase more radical modes of thought seems to have made limited headway.

Teaching Assistants, Cover Supervisors and Substitution

Teaching assistants (TAs) were used in secondary schools both before and throughout the period of reform but the scope of their work is much less than in primary schools. Because of the subject specialist nature of teaching in the secondary sector, TAs are not normally used to teach whole classes. Although the impact has been small, the professionalisation of TAs does hold out the possibility of some significant changes. With the development of higher level teaching assistants in City 4, for instance, they take groups of 12 or 13 low ability students and teach them within a separate curriculum structure (Assistant Principal, City Secondary 4). This teaching has given rise to some concern with the boundaries of work and their capacity to do it:

> That TAs can be told what to do and go off and do it with children . . . doesn't sit well . . . because of their qualifications and it's not just the paper qualifications, it's experience and understanding what their role is . . . to actually give them a class of students and to say I want you to teach . . . and then leave it to them, you've somehow gone too far away from the principle of the teacher being in control.
>
> (Staff Development Co-ordinator,
> City Secondary 3)

Teachers in secondary schools already had non-contact time, the amount of which sometimes exceeded the subsequent provisions for PPA. However, prior to the National Agreement it was rare for such non-contact time to be 'protected', and therefore it was the norm that at least some of this time would be required to cover for absent colleagues. The National Agreement placed a statutory maximum hourly limit on the requirement to cover, with an expectation that in time schools would progressively reduce the cover of teachers to levels significantly below the statutory maximum. The actual extent of reduction varies, with teachers in City Secondary 2 still doing up to a maximum 30 hours in the last full year. In the case of City Secondary 3, it has come down from about 36 per year to 7 or 8, but this was no means the most dramatic drop. In Shire Secondary 2, before the workforce agreement, cover was needed on over 2000 occasions and this has been reduced to 530, over a quarter of which are now covered by members of the senior management team. Because of the cover supervisor arrangements main scale teachers 'end up doing hardly any cover' (Headteacher, Shire Secondary 4).

Headteachers were generally supportive of a move towards no cover and unsurprisingly secondary teachers have few problems with this in principle or in the practice for achieving it—the use of cover supervisors rather than supply teachers. London Borough Secondary 1 was an exception to this with the NUT resisting the use of cover supervisors:

> The NUT's position has been to say that nobody except a qualified teacher should be allowed to stand in front of the children and teach them . . . so cover supervisors, until relatively recently, have been a concept that hasn't been supported by the NUT.
>
> (Headteacher, London Borough Secondary 3)

The significance of the phrase 'until relatively recently' is that the NUT, faced with their members continuing to cover, have now out of pragmatism accepted their use. The school, in which over 90% of teachers were NUT members, was 'one of the last to compromise on the whole idea' (Business Manager, London Borough Secondary 3).

Opposition to cover supervision was present elsewhere, but it never rose above the level of verbal objection, leading in practice to an acceptance of the arrangement. NUT officials were realistic about the situation over cover, recognising that teachers need respite:

> I've worked in primary and secondary school and I know that if you've got a class sitting on its own . . . and someone puts their head round the door and says '19 haven't got a teacher. Can you go and take them?', I don't care who takes 19. They can, they can (laughing) send Crippen in [an infamous murderer] . . . as far as I'm concerned (laughs). I've got something else I want to get on with.

> (NUT Assistant Branch
> Secretary, London Borough)

If there was union pressure at all, it was much more likely to focus on pressure to lower the level of cover demands on teachers, rather than on the mechanisms for enabling this. The NASUWT in Shire was particularly notable for this stance. In part, teachers' acceptance of arrangements was a pragmatic reflection of self-interest: but it is also recognition that supply teachers, and indeed teachers covering, have been less than effective in the past. Cover is widely and pejoratively (but not universally) regarded as babysitting rather than active teaching, and this view undermines any concerted opposition. It is not necessarily the case, however, that cover can be so characterised. In City Secondary 4, the organiser of cover, the PA to the headteacher, stated:

> I think actually with the, the two [cover supervisors] we've got on board, they teach. I do think they teach . . . I don't want babysitters, I want teachers, and this is what we said about cover supervisors . . . I think they do a really good job at teaching.

> (Cover Organiser, City Secondary 4)

Even if cover were to be largely 'babysitting', the role would require certain competences, and the employment of poorly trained cover supervisors could have repercussions on whole school behaviour. The solution sometimes is to employ staff who were previously TAs in the school and were therefore known and familiar with the school procedures and mores. Familiarity does not solve all problems, however. In Shire 3, two cover supervisors replaced the regular use of the supply teachers, prompting the following:

> They're very good, but it's still not the same as having a teacher. The children know they are not teachers and we get little confrontations.

You get 'I don't have to do what you're saying—you're not a proper teacher'. You hear the children say that, it's in their psyche.

(Headteacher, Shire Secondary 3)

When cover supervisors are already occupied, schools again resort to external help. In Shire 4, however, the less frequent use of supply teachers has had the consequence that the pool of reliable teachers has dried up and the better supply teachers have moved on. In Shire Secondary 3 the problem is more acute than using less able supply teachers: it calls in what are effectively supply cover supervisors who have very little training. The combined effects of these changes have impacted upon general behaviour in the school and 'very high standards here have declined' (Headteacher, Shire Secondary 3). Headteachers are well aware of the limitations of cover arrangements and their, sometimes, financial necessity. One expressed a judgement on the use of cover supervisors that many teachers would acknowledge: 'It's not ideal . . . often they would not be as good in a cover situation as a really good teacher but . . . it's a compromise that's worth it' (Headteacher, City Secondary 4).

Increasing the Division of Labour: Pastoral Work

The system of teachers' responsibilities for pastoral work was in many schools not regarded as satisfactory before the new emphasis on the core work of teaching and learning. Senior teachers with substantial responsibility for pastoral work had little time to do it effectively or did it at the expense of other demands, such as lesson preparation. Describing the pastoral role of five Heads of Year under the old system, one headteacher stated: 'They just tended to do crisis management all the time . . . You're actually asking people who aren't necessarily qualified social workers to take on that kind of role of bereavement counsellors or whatever they ended up becoming' (Headteacher, City Secondary 3).

Consequently, the shedding of pastoral work to non-teachers gave rise to comparatively little organised opposition. Non-teaching staff, unlike teachers, are always available to deal with issues. Seeing the logic of the movement towards non-teacher responsibility, however, is not enough to give confidence in particular changes. Breaking teacher links with students is one of the reasons why there is concern about the move. In Shire 4, while there has been pressure on middle managers' tutorial time, the pastoral involvement of senior staff is still highly regarded and retained without the pay cuts associated with the transition to TLRs. Even here, however, where teachers still retain residual responsibilities for pastoral issues, the increased concentration on teaching and learning can mean teachers' emotional relationships with students suffer:

you're looking at the whole child and it's all about building that relationship which has been the ethos of [this] school, which is very hard to do when I'm also expected to . . . be looking at data, moving the department forward.

(Head of English, Shire Secondary 4)

Whatever the effect on the quality of pastoral work, and the weakening of emotional relations between teachers and students, shifting the work to non-teachers has certainly added to the growing complexity of the social structure of schools. In City Secondary 3, the Heads of Year became Key Stage leaders and their pastoral roles were taken up by a whole range of different people from non-teaching backgrounds organised in hierarchical fashion: a student support manager, on a level equivalent to a registrar; two behaviour support workers, dealing with day-to-day issues; four learning mentors, also dealing with issues of the day; and beneath these TAs who will also pick up student problems. Growth in these staff has contributed towards a situation in which teachers are a minority in many secondary schools. In City School Secondary 3, out of approximately 200 staff, only 85 are teachers and the rest are support staff, including cleaners and others.

The encroachment of support staff on tasks that were the province of relatively senior teachers has extended as far at Heads of Year. City Secondary 4 is moving to this from a structure that includes non-teacher Assistant Heads of Year, recruited internally from existing support staff. Again the logic follows from remodelling: 'We . . . want teachers to be more involved in tracking progress, in monitoring and intervening positively with students' learning' (Headteacher, City Secondary 4). But it is also the case that taking responsibility for pastoral, and particularly for behavioural problems, can lead to support staff impacting on teachers' status and performance. In London Borough Secondary 3, the business manager, as part of the leadership team, was involved in classroom observations:

> going round to different teachers, doing a review of behaviour in the class . . . The priority was behaviour, how the kids were interacting themselves . . . but it was also about how the teacher was teaching the lesson.

(Business Manager, London
Borough Secondary 3)

TLRs: Assimilation and New Accountability

The abolition of MAs and the introduction of TLRs were expected to cause schools significant problems, as the accompanying staffing structures threatened a number of senior staff with future loss of earnings and reductions in their final salary pension levels. The response of the classroom teacher unions was to favour assimilation—the holders of MAs simply became the holders of posts that carried TLRs. The reactions of headteachers were not so uniform. Some headteachers were hostile to enforced changes that took away their discretion and caused acrimony:

> There were a number of people who worked here for a long time and had, rightly I think, been rewarded under the old system where you did a good job . . . we had to tell them that that worthwhile reward . . . is no longer valid.
>
> (Headteacher, Shire Secondary 3)

In this case the headteacher illustrated the problems arising by the reactions of a particular member of staff: 'He was professionally insulted . . . We had a long exchange of letters. We had long meetings. We had representations to the governors. He is now still a very, very angry man' (Headteacher, Shire Secondary 3). The emotional and practical consequences were high, leaving the headteacher with 'an immense amount of personal damage': 'every time there is any sort of initiative . . . he is totally, not just anti, but aggressively anti and . . . He's a very bitter man and I did not want that' (Headteacher, Shire Secondary 3).

In some schools the reception was less hostile and the opportunity was taken to restructure the management system, including, as noted earlier, the appointment of non-teachers as Heads of Year. In Shire Secondary 4, the headteacher was adamant that, because of the cost implications of moving staff to higher paid TLR posts, it was not an assimilation exercise. As a consequence, the new structure involved long and detailed discussions. Staff submitted over 100 written responses to the first draft proposals and the final governors' meeting on the subject lasted 4.5 hours. The headteacher reported some staff reaction: 'You are proposing that so and so is going to lose £4000. It's appalling and how can you do that to that person?' (Headteacher, Shire Secondary 4). In the face of such opposition, compromises were inevitable: 'There are compromises in there . . . There are posts in there that I wouldn't have wanted' (Headteacher, Shire Secondary 4).

On the whole, from evidence of the case study secondary schools, however, the implementation of TLRs caused many fewer problems than envisaged and it was not uncommon for headteachers and unions to share the characterisation of the transition to the new structures as an assimilation exercise. In posing the transition thus, and in implementing structures that tended to increase expenditure, schools made changes that were palatable to the unions. Acceptance was not restricted to the Social Partnership unions but also included the NUT, whose advice to members explicitly advocated an assimilation approach. Some headteachers again argued that the enforced processes and changes were not necessary, as progress in the desired direction was already under way:

> I was actually quite pissed off really because it was one reform too far . . . my view was that you didn't actually need a TLR thing . . . people

seemed to be saying that . . . people had money locked into whole MAs and they weren't actually doing anything to do with teaching and learning. Well that wasn't the case here.

(Headteacher, City Secondary 3)

There was recognition that the allocations of MAs in many schools had been *ad hoc* and unfair with Heads of Year on different scales with no justi-fication. Not only was the allocation of rewards arbitrary, the construction of staff jobs and responsibilities was also incoherent, with staff being given a series of disjointed roles rather than a focused and manageable job. Even where poor management practices were occurring, however, this was not seen as a justification for the new structures:

There were some schools which had chaotic MA structures and it wasn't like someone was given a job. They were given a point for this, a point for that, a point for other things, you know . . . [but] you could have cleared that up without TLRs. What you needed to do was actu-ally to think through what the jobs were.

(Headteacher, City Secondary 3)

Claims of the minimal impact of the transition or its unnecessary nature, however, tend to under-estimate its significance in a number of respects. Firstly, as indicated in the title of the awards—TLRs—the new posts car-rying these aimed at being more coherent by insisting that the focus is on teaching and learning, and, in accepting new TLR posts, many holders of the old MAs lost pastoral responsibilities in the process. Secondly, the introduction of TLRs was an integral part of a wider process, a logical outcome of the remodelling rather than, as seen by some headteachers, another incursion into their autonomy. More significantly, the new posts were not just stripped of pastoral duties, and thus narrower, to allow greater emphasis on teaching and learning. The emphasis on improving test and examination results was not new: the significance of the changes was that management structures within schools were being developed that were more closely aligned to secure improvements (or alternatively to expose failures), and a new level of accountability was born.

Performance Management and Accountability

Workforce remodelling is not taking place in a vacuum, but dovetails into a number of other changes which in turn impact upon it. The positions of headteachers and leaders are particularly exposed by school results and inspections. Reflecting on the new Ofsted inspection framework with its emphasis on school self-evaluation, one headteacher stated:

The pressure on headteachers and on leadership teams [has] abso-lutely intensified in all kinds of ways because a big part of the new relationship with schools is about supposedly, intelligent accountability. Actually it's not an intelligent accountability . . . It's a much more intensive accountability.

(Headteacher, City Secondary 4)

Accountability in turn reinforces the demands for performance management (PM). PM is not new in schools, but changes associated with workforce remodelling, and particularly TLRs, have changed its emphasis and increased its intensity:

We've improved teaching and learning; we've improved behaviour and we've got an outstanding Ofsted and so on but we now really need to pin individuals down and increase accountability, increase the seriousness with which they take training and so on and performance management will help us do all that.

(Headteacher, London Borough Secondary 3)

In particular, PM has increased the responsibilities of the holders of TLRs, the middle managers, for the performance of those they manage. Whether those being managed are performing well is increasingly determined by examining the data on students' performance. Moreover, weaknesses within their departments are in turn a commentary on middle managers' own performance. These changes are of some significance:

Heads of Year . . . on the third Management Allowance didn't line manage anybody except their deputy. So we agreed with the union that [the new] Directors of Learning line managed their tutors. They don't just look after them; they don't just chair meetings . . . they now do performance management.

(Headteacher, London Borough Secondary 3)

Another headteacher approached staff on the basis that: 'This is the TLR. It's no longer about the admin, it's no longer the capitation and your stock-taking—it's actually about monitoring your staff, monitoring your kids and trying to make them more accountable for their departments' (Headteacher, Shire Secondary 4).

Line management and PM also carry with them responsibility for recommending pay progression. Nor was pay progression necessarily just about pay:

What I have just made clear is that if somebody isn't progressing to the upper pay scale then it's because there are capability issues . . . So there isn't a limbo bit in which you are not good enough to move up but you're not bad enough to go in to capability—that's when you get ambiguity. So you're either good enough to move forward or there's concern and then we'll do it formally, by the book.

(Headteacher, London Borough Secondary 3)

The focus of monitoring the performance and results of teachers is central to the changes that have been engineered. Most headteachers raised the issue of capability but few had many instances of its use, the part reason for this gap being that schools have become largely uninhabitable for poorly performing teachers. As one headteacher reflected on poorly performing teachers:

> They just thought I can see where this is going and changed jobs or changed professions . . . Most people have just decided that it's not going to be the place to work if they know their results are so poor, because we're quite data-rich now: it's very difficult to hide.
>
> (Headteacher, Shire Secondary 4)

The informal process of self-selection for exit already largely worked, and this fact caused some hostility to the level of monitoring associated with TLRs and the new PM arrangements. Some middle managers, for instance, were clearly uncomfortable about having to engage in this overt monitoring as noted by one headteacher: 'I think there's huge resistance against that. I think most of us would not want to put those people in that position' (Headteacher, City Secondary 3). This judgement was echoed by another: 'I can't just delegate the lesson observation and the setting of objectives, I also have to delegate the recommendation of pay progression . . . that's a deeply uncomfortable position for some middle leaders to be in' (Headteacher, City Secondary 4). In response to the unease, one headteacher tried to downplay the extent of the change: 'I had to be very clear that ultimate decisions about pay will continue to be made by me' (Headteacher, London Borough Secondary 3). If some middle managers were not happy with the new role, it was equally the case that some teachers were unhappy about their middle managers. One headteacher, having stated his support for a system that places central importance on staff development, described the dynamic thus:

> I think it's tragic that it's being linked to pay . . . the impact of that is significant because . . . people now view it as a process that they are forced into and that ultimately has become a threatening process . . . the number of people who raised an objection to the person who was their team leader went up this year.
>
> (Headteacher, London Borough Secondary 4)

Some headteachers sympathised with the position of their managers, but nevertheless, saw advantages in the added responsibilities:

> In a school there's always been 'them' and 'us': 'management don't do that; management don't do this'; 'they're in charge of behaviour management—behaviour's bad because management don't do stuff'.

Actually that's rubbish . . . TLRs in my view were really helpful [in] formalising the idea of responsibilities.

(Headteacher, City Secondary 4)

The new national PM scheme requires that teachers are measured against certain objectives and this gives rise to another potential tension:

The major contentious area for us will be that the NUT are saying there should only be three objectives . . . We're saying that if you've got a TLR1, particularly if you are a Head of Faculty, that it is reasonable to expect that part of your student progress objective be around areas for which you are responsible . . . How can you not be responsible for the performance of that team?

(Headteacher, City Secondary 4)

The result of the increased accountability of managers is that they and the people they line manage further lose autonomy. Any notional space that is opened up by the migration of tasks to support staff is for classroom teachers closed by the monitoring and intervention of their managers. Having listed in minute detail the shedding of tasks to support workers, one NASUWT representative reflected on a question as to whether this had improved the job of teachers: 'I've been teaching 25 years. I honestly think it's worse and the reason I think it's worse is . . . the amount of interference from above now is a lot more than it was' (NASUWT School Representative, London Borough Secondary 3).

It may also be the case that we are witnessing a transformation of internal relations between teachers because of the changes in accountability and the greater prominence of line management:

In a sense what people are doing is creating mini-headteachers all over the school . . . One of the biggest things that I found changed my role from being a deputy [to Head] was things like sickness and absence and money . . . having to make decisions about are you giving that person leave of absence or not? Is that person getting a pay rise or not? Now that's really critical stuff when you're working with people on a day-to-day basis . . . sometimes the right decision is an unpopular one but you've got to be prepared to make it . . . It's pushed that lower down the school.

(Headteacher, London Borough Secondary 4)

Workload and Intensity

Even headteachers that had little difficulty in implementing reforms were sceptical of the motives of the Government and cast doubts on whether the purpose of, for instance, the removal of routine tasks, was really about reducing workload:

I wondered as well whether or not it was partly the Government . . . actually wanted teachers to do more. It wanted to take off certain things, like the 25 tasks, but in return was 'Well you haven't got to do all of those, but we want you to do more of the kind of normal professional stuff'.

(Headteacher, City Secondary 3)

Another headteacher stated that the removal of routine tasks from teachers 'can only be a good thing' but also remarked: 'I'm not entirely convinced that it's had the desired impact because we don't seem to be working any less hard than we were before it came in' (Headteacher, London Borough Secondary 3). All teachers, indeed all staff, are now more accountable and this has pressured and intensified their work:

Levels of accountability have just shot up . . . that's a much more acute kind of pressure than having to do your own photocopying . . . we've taken away a lot . . . of comfort activities . . . Shifting results, helping students with all kinds of barriers to their learning . . . that's infinitely harder.

(Headteacher, City Secondary 4)

Moreover, the professionalisation of support staff increases the demands on them, but it has also simultaneously meant more demands on teachers as managers of these staff.

Whatever the motives of those implementing the reforms at workplace level, one of the consequences has been to raise the expectations of teachers' performance. In making additional demands on staff, in establishing what are effectively more managerial schools, increased work and accountability are also demanded of senior managers. Moreover, as gaps open up in organisations, which now have more prescriptive rules about who does what, managers frequently fill them, even to the extent of doing cover supervision and routine, as opposed to managerial, tasks. Standing at the apex of schools, ultimately accountable for the implementation of change, performance and results, are headteachers that have seen pressure on themselves and their own workload enormously increase. With none of the headteachers in the case study schools taking the dedicated headship time to which reforms entitled them, the extent to which they have handled the pressures well could be questioned. One headteacher reflected:

Even though they're supposed to be powerful people, they don't seem to be able to organise their own lives . . . They are supposed to be powerful people. Well if powerful people can't control their lives, how can everyone else do it?

(Headteacher, City Secondary 3)

The detachment of this headteacher may have been influenced by the fact of his imminent retirement and was not typical. Even where headteachers are conscious of the need to control their workload, the reforms have made it difficult:

> I've been a headteacher for 11 years. I'd just got my workload under control and I'd managed to bring it down to just around 50 hours . . . It went out of the window with this [workforce remodelling] and I'm currently running on about 65 hours.
>
> (Headteacher, Shire Secondary 3)

UNION PRESENCE AND WORKPLACE INDUSTRIAL RELATIONS

The presence of teacher unions was tangible in all conversations about the changes but in practice the focus was on either or both the NUT and the NASUWT, with the ATL and Voice, whatever their roles nationally and locally, having little presence at school level. The NAHT is largely a primary sector union and therefore did not figure here. Headteachers tended to belong to ASCL and/or the NUT. Where ASCL was mentioned there was some criticism (as noted earlier) of their lack of union, as opposed to managerial or professional, orientation. The union has expanded to include support staff members of senior management teams, but the idea of representing such members against their immediate line managers and employers does not appear to be prominent. One member described her introduction to ASCL at a business managers' forum:

> We were all asked to be part of ASCL . . . they [City Council Finance Officers] . . . recommended that it would be in our benefit that we actually became members, and the heads all said 'Yes'. So. I'm quite lucky because the school here pays for my membership (laughs).
>
> (Business Manager, City Secondary 4)

NUT was strongest union in the London Borough schools and NASUWT in Shire, with a much more even balance in City. In all schools there were union representatives who did much more than open the post from their unions. When asked if changes were discussed with the NUT, one headteacher responded: 'We've even discussed the cakes in the staffroom on Friday' (Headteacher, London Borough Secondary 3). Here there were regular formal meetings once a month between the union representative and the headteacher and there was a workplace NUT committee. Where the NASUWT was strong, it was equally influential in the workplace. In contrast, where unions were weaker, meetings tended to be less regular and occur when issues arose. At City Secondary 3, where the NUT has only about 30% of teachers in membership, despite relations with the NUT headteacher being good, the NUT representative complained that she was not always in the loop: 'things will come up perhaps at Head of Faculty level that I'm not privy to and that grates a bit' (NUT School Representative, City Secondary 3). The position of unions when they are in a small minority can also difficult. In Shire County the weakness of the NUT and its nominal opposition to the workplace agreement placed it in a difficult position. One headteacher told the NUT representative in the school:

> 'You need to stop doing that [the representative role]. You need to join the NAS [UWT] if you want my view' . . . [The NUT] were quite frankly useless. There were a couple of occasions where they said, 'Well we just don't agree with this restructuring. We're not party to that'. I said, 'It's the law, so it does not matter'.
>
> (Headteacher, Shire Secondary 4)

In most schools, the divisions at national levels between the unions did not cause problems, with union representatives cooperating with each other and presenting a common front. Often the dominant union spoke on behalf of all staff.

Union Influence on the Reforms

As indicated, headteachers were not enthusiastic users of CTs and preferred instead to use their normal patterns of negotiation and consultation with staff representatives and union officers. Typically, the process would involve discussions at senior management team level followed by involvement of the unions and then wider consultation with staff. Meetings with the unions were frequently formal and minuted, but informal contact was also extensive. There is evidence that union presence has impacted on the shape of the reforms and their implementation at workplace level, with the transition to TLRs being a case in point. One headteacher offered an example:

> we started off with a really good idea about what we wanted our ideal shadow structure to be . . . you do all the stuff about trying to make it manageable financially and so on and so forth and then you get into all of the discussions with the unions and so on and the unions want it to be an assimilation process and they're saying 'No, there's no reason to start from a blank page. You start with what you've got' and all the rest of it. In the end we ended up with something which effectively was an assimilation. We got clawed back and clawed back and clawed back . . . the governing body were very mindful of the ethos and the mood of staff. So there was a lot of pressure that was being put on the leadership

team to make sure that whatever happened at the outcome of the process, that we weren't going to get massive staff unrest.

(Headteacher, London Borough Secondary 4)

The unions' aim generally to secure no loss of income to members on the MAs was understandable. With this focus, however, there appeared to be little recognition or resistance to the transformation of the new posts into more accounting and accountable ones. In welcoming uncritically the earlier shedding of routine tasks and the narrowing definition of teachers' work, they accepted a logic that would inform the restructuring and the implementation of TLRs and thus the potential for intensification of work through greater pressure and accountability.

Failure to arrest changes that have potentially malign effects on teachers' work is never absolute, however, and there are elements of the new arrangements that provide points around which new defences are built (Bates and Carter 2007). Already it is possible to see new rigidities being constructed. The increased complexity of the school staffing structure has led to a greater division of labour and a heightened consciousness about the particular tasks allocated to different grades with a consequent breakdown in collegiality. In particular, one interviewee saw division developing between SLTs and teachers who are on contracts that specify 1265 hours a year of directed work: 'Before, a member of staff would support the senior member in their post . . . whereas now because there's such a distinction they might say to themselves, "Well hang on, they're getting paid for that, I'm not" (NASUWT School Representative, London Borough Secondary 3).

This loss of cooperation across the school hierarchy has if anything been reinforced by national NASUWT policy. The NASUWT tendency to regard the Workload Agreement as a legal, fixed edict means that in places it dovetails into its previous characterisation as a craft union more narrowly concerned with terms and conditions than with wider educational policy debates and social justice (Ironside and Seifert 1995). The London Borough NASUWT representative reflected this approach:

I think that's a very important thing the unions can still stick to resistance to extra duties . . . for TLRs. . . . So there'd be things that [senior managers] would say 'Well because you're now on this top tier . . . you should go and do this'. And we said 'No. This is just to do with responsibility of the number of staff who are underneath you in terms of your actual post. It's nothing to do with extra jobs'. So for example . . . when . . . a group of staff are out at break time . . . one person will oversee [them] . . . and the talk was these people on TLRs would do that. I said from my union 'No'. Teachers were saying 'No I'm not going to do that. SLT can do that'.

(NASUWT School Representative,
London Borough Secondary 3)

It may also be that a new generation of teachers takes the idea of new professional boundaries more seriously: 'There's less of an idea of it [teaching]
being a vocation . . . It's more of a job and people do treat it as a 9–5 a little
bit more' (Staff Development Co-ordinator, City Secondary 3). Another
member of staff in the same school reinforced this view:

> It's interesting . . . with the youngsters coming into the profession, you
> find that they are now less willing to do anything extra on top of their
> teaching which is sometimes difficult. They want to know what they're
> going to get paid for it . . . and that certainly wasn't the case 10 years
> ago. But that has been an unwanted side effect of everything else that's
> come in.
>
> (Assistant Principal, City Secondary 3)

Non-cooperation is particularly the case where relations are more conflictual, giving added impetus to organise resentments around the new regulation of teaching. Headteachers' attempts to lubricate relations by offering
extra money to encourage additional work also threaten to further limit
goodwill:

> So many staff do extra things and want to . . . I think there are real
> benefits to that but also a bit of caution there. I do a mock trial citizen-
> ship competition . . . and I found out yesterday that another member of
> staff was doing a debating club but he was getting paid . . . if there is
> money for extended school . . . I think it should be used.
>
> (NUT School Representative,
> City Secondary 3)

TLRs have both to be permanent and to be allocated for coherent jobs.
There is no opportunity for assembling a job that is made up of uncon-
nected elements. One response is for schools to introduce bursaries for
specific tasks and responsibilities that fall outside the TLR posts. The
ostensible reason for bursaries is to encourage staff development and to
give people internal opportunities so as to discourage them from seeking
moves elsewhere. There is the possibility, however, that a pattern grows
up whereby staff taking on new developments will expect a bursary
and refuse the responsibility if it is not forthcoming. There was also
some evidence that the inevitable formalisation of responsibilities in the
National Agreement opened up the legitimacy to be less flexible than in
the past. Rather than increasing the capacity of the workforce by making it focus on problem-solving and fluid boundaries, the opposite was
taking place:

> It has placed more obstructions in the way [of school development] . . .
> We've got residentials out at the moment. Now the only way we can do
> residentials is by people volunteering to cover and there are a number

of people saying 'Well, I'd really like to but actually my union says I shouldn't be'. You get that answer all the time.

(Headteacher, Shire Secondary 3)

Similar examples could be found elsewhere. In one London Borough school the headteacher complained:

You'll say to someone 'Right, could you put that on to a spreadsheet for me and send it to me', and they'll say, 'But that's data entry twice isn't it?' And you just think (laughs) I'm not asking you to do something that's going to take you the next 4 hours or 5 weeks. But you get little niggly things like that, that does make a difference.

(Headteacher, London Borough Secondary 4)

As indicated in Chapter 4, at national level there appeared to be a tacit assumption amongst the Social Partners that by reducing workload, standards would rise. Not only does it appear that the standards agenda invaded the space created by shedding routine tasks to intensify work, it also seems that the reaction to this could now rebound on quality and standards. In Shire Secondary 3, the NASUWT used the professed purposes of reducing workload to challenge initiatives. In response to plans to implement monitoring of progress through half-termly meetings of Heads of Departments with individual staff (looking at planning, assessment, teaching groups and students) the headteacher reported that, despite the fact that there is ample time in the school timetable for this, the NASUWT representative stated in a staff meeting that 'I can't agree with this—the national agenda is to drive down workload' (Headteacher, Shire Secondary 3).

School Relations with Local Union Secretaries

School's consultations with the unions take place at a number of levels. Previous studies have commented upon the, if not weak, then uneven presence of union organisation at school level (Carter 2004, Stevenson 2003). There is little evidence that the growing number of issues generated at school level is increasing the involvement of unions' members in secondary schools and this could be a cause of union concern. The reasons for lack of involvement within the unions are complex. There is no doubt that, where individual unions were dominant within an authority, branch/divisional secretaries wield a great deal of power. In Shire, for instance, when asked whether the workforce changes had led to strikes, the local official stated:

We've threatened it because I've gone into a number of schools and said on cover particularly. What I'll do is we'll say a maximum of 12 this year, hours of cover, and zero from September. And if you don't we'll ballot our members on it . . . usually the threat has been sufficient.

(NASUWT Branch Secretary, Shire)

In some instances headteachers managed to use the centralised power of the unions to secure the process of school reorganisation. Speaking of plans for the new staffing structure that arose through the transition to TLRs, one headteacher stated:

> The first thing I did before I even went anywhere near the staff with our final-ish draft was brought in the City union representative . . . I negotiated [with the NUT] before I even went to consultation with our staff . . . So he almost did my work for me in the sense that he had a meeting and he said he'd seen the structure and in his view it was perfectly legitimate.
>
> (Headteacher, City Secondary 4)

The attempt by headteachers to gain support from union officers was also apparent in London Borough 3. Here there was a two-part response to NUT strength. Firstly, the headteacher joined the union because he felt 'somewhat uneasy about large staff meetings at which I wasn't present'. Secondly, membership also meant that 'local NUT officers would have to support me instead of fighting me . . . headteacher members are quite rare in the NUT, particularly secondary, quite a valued commodity' (Headteacher, London Borough Secondary 3). This strategy was also replicated in the other London Borough secondary school:

> Whenever there's been a potential issue, and either of those two [NUT divisional officers] have been pulled in, I've held a separate meeting and I've said 'Okay, I'm part of the NUT: so as my representative what would you advise me to be doing in this situation? . . . I know that the NUT doesn't want to lose its headteachers to other unions, so what's the advice?'
>
> (Headteacher, London Borough Secondary 4)

There was therefore in place a strategy of bypassing or undermining the effectiveness of workplace representatives, a strategy with which the NUT, on occasion, appeared complicit. Speaking of some representatives who see union activity as part of their wider politics, the Assistant Branch Secretary said:

> We'll say to reps, if you have a meeting and you need to tell the headteacher something, you can go in and tell them. But if you make loads of comments about it then we'll come in and do it instead. I'm afraid we've deliberately infantilised a couple of our more um (laughter). They were creating more problems than they solved really . . . The whole way that all the teaching unions work now I guess is a top down thing.
>
> (NUT Assistant Divisional
> Secretary, London Borough)

There is evidence from secondary schools that despite the national acceptance of workforce remodelling, there are a number of issues that are contentious at school level and that rather than the reforms increasing capacity beyond the extra resources that are being invested, they are in danger of creating new rigidities. Resistance is, however, occurring without any seeming guidance and support from coordinated and coherent national strategies. Actions and initiatives are not integrated into any LA-wide strategies *let alone* national ones and it is hard to see, given the uneven level of workplace organisation, how this would be a realistic possibility.

8 Workforce Remodelling
Transforming Teaching?

INTRODUCTION

One of the principal aims of this volume is to explore the link between teachers' experience of their work and the wider industrial relations environment in which that work takes place. Previous chapters have presented and discussed data that describes how workforce remodelling has brought about changes in teachers' work and the way that it is organised. This was done through separate chapters on both primary and secondary school contexts, reflecting qualitative differences between the two sectors and the ways in which workforce remodelling played out differently in the two sectors. This chapter seeks to draw this material together and explore, at a more analytical level, the wider developments that are shaping teachers' work under the broad heading of workforce remodelling and 'transforming the school workforce'. This analysis of teachers' work continues to draw on a framework provided by labour process analysis, which treats teaching as work, teachers as workers and schools as workplaces (Connell 1985, Ingersoll 2003). The chapter aims to draw on one of the major strengths of a labour process approach within education writings, namely its focus on the work of teachers coupled with an ability to connect this to wider institutional and macro-policy contexts.

The concern with the individual teacher leads, at its most basic level, to an interest in what teachers do. What does teaching 'look like' in a remodelled environment? How is it changing and what do teachers now do differently as a result of workforce remodelling? However, interest in what teachers do also raises questions about how teachers' work is organised and managed, and this focuses attention on institutional questions of management and control. What is the balance that exists between autonomy and control in the organisation of teachers' work? How is control exercised and by whom? None of these questions are value neutral, and they cannot be disconnected from the wider policy environment and the pressures that drive the policies described in the opening chapter. Control of teachers' work does not take place in a vacuum and is not exercised for its own sake. Control is exercised within a specific context and for a purpose, and this study seeks to make explicit the connections between teachers' work, the manner in which it is organised and controlled and the wider policy environment that drives these changes. The implications of workforce reform for teachers' work is discussed by identifying and analysing three inter-dependent themes—the changing nature of teaching, the re-ordering of institutional hierarchies and the development of new managerial roles. In this chapter these themes are developed and linked it to the empirical data presented in previous chapters.

The starting point of the analysis is a recognition that the significant impact of workforce reform on teachers' work is not in terms of its stated aim—'progressive reductions in teachers' overall hours' (DfES 2003: 2), but rather how teachers' work itself has changed *within* those hours. The justification for this focus is that there is now growing evidence that workforce reform has not secured any appreciable reduction in teachers' working hours; on the contrary, more recent evidence points to a reversal of any trend towards reduction. School Teachers' Review Body evidence (STRB 2008), for instance, points to teachers' hours increasing and no significant net reduction in hours since the introduction of the National Agreement. These findings appear to be confirmed by other studies such as that conducted and reported by the *Times Educational Supplement* (Stewart 2008), and by the National Association of Schoolmasters Union of Women Teachers (NASUWT 2008). These are important and substantial studies and they form an important backdrop to the analysis presented here. They also justify a focus on changes in the labour process of teaching *within* the overall hours worked by teachers. This chapter presents an analysis that seeks to draw together the key developments in the labour process of teaching, and in so doing offers a framework that begins to explain why attempts to reduce the overall hours worked have proven to be so ineffective.

THE FOCUS ON TEACHING AND LEARNING—RE-DEFINING TEACHING

Workforce remodelling, and the 'new professionalism' agenda that emerged from it, places considerable emphasis on creating the conditions in which teachers can focus on the 'core task' of improving teaching and learning. By stripping away the extraneous duties that teachers undertake that are peripheral to their core tasks, teacher effectiveness can be enhanced. Teachers should focus on those areas where they add most value, and leave 'non-essential' tasks to support staff. Our data, presented in earlier chapters, indicated that teachers welcomed many aspects of these changes, such as the removal of the 25 tasks. However, it was also clear that there were skirmishes around some elements as teachers resisted a ceding of personal control over aspects of their professional life they considered important. The task most frequently cited to us, and reported elsewhere (Hammersley-Fletcher 2007), was that of display work. Many teachers, predominantly but not exclusively in the primary sector, took the view that the use of physical space in their classroom was an important part of their pedagogical repertoire and they saw the use of displays as a learning resource, or a means to celebrate student achievement, and as part of the teaching process. Displays are obvious manifestations of a creative impulse in the classroom and teachers reported resentment at the apparent closing down of this creative space. However, there was also resistance around other features of the 25 tasks, and in these cases the reasons for resistance are less obvious, but no less significant. For example, it was reported that some teachers regretted the new rules relating to the collection of monies and felt that the removal of these types of contacts with students denied many of the informal exchanges between teacher and student that allow relationships to build. In these instances teachers regretted an apparent growing disconnection between the teacher and student as teacher concerns are increasingly related to, indeed restricted to, 'student performance'.

In another case a headteacher reported that he had not enforced rules on bulk photocopying because he felt teachers valued the respite and the social exchanges with colleagues that sometimes came with a queue for the photocopier. Here the issue raised relates to the intensity of teachers' work—the pressure teachers experience within any given period. One of our interviewees described teaching as a 'pin-down job'—'if you are in the middle of conveyancing or, or having hospital treatment or trying to get your child into a school, you can't leave the room to make a phone call. You know, it's a very tough job' (NUT Local Officer 2, London Borough). In these cases the queue for the photocopier can provide a momentary relief from the 'pin-down', but when this is taken away there becomes nowhere to hide from the pressures of the job. Instead continued pressure is placed on teachers to focus on the 'core task'—the high value-added activities which require the specialist contribution of a qualified teacher. The ability to not undertake bulk photocopying is very welcome if this frees up time to sit in the staff room, relax and have discussions with colleagues—but if the time created simply propels the teacher back into the high octane environment of front-line teaching, then the benefits are less clear-cut. The result is that teachers experience no significant diminution of overall hours worked (a proposition that emerges clearly from the studies referred to earlier), but instead an intensification of their work. In this sense workforce remodelling may be adding to workload pressures, by failing to tackle the issue of total hours spent working, whilst increasing the intensity of effort *within* the hours worked. This is an issue of key importance and suggests that problems of teacher workload have not been addressed fundamentally. Indeed it may have merely postponed the moment at which issues of (un)sustainability reappear as major sources of conflict. Certainly if there is an increase in intensification, without any reversal of the trend towards extensification, it is difficult to see significant problems and conflicts in the future being avoided.

The focus on the 'core task' of teaching and learning not only appeared to increase the intensity of teachers' work, but also narrowed the range of tasks undertaken. This narrowing was highlighted, particularly within the secondary sector, in relation to the pastoral roles of teachers and the traditional provision of promoted posts for those with pastoral responsibilities. Within the primary sector there was little evidence of a significant break in the pastoral relationship between teacher and pupil—the nature of those links remains strong in the professional psyche of the primary school teacher. But within the secondary sector, the emergence of a new division of labour between teaching and support staff created opportunities to re-define the academic-pastoral divide within the teachers' role. This tension was most sharply focussed during the period of pay restructuring when teaching and learning responsibility points (TLRs) replaced management allowances (MAs). TLRs were intended to reward teachers who had a clear role beyond that of the ordinary classroom teacher in promoting student achievement, and at this point several schools used this as an opportunity to pass some, or all, of the responsibility for pastoral leadership to support staff. As evidenced in Chapter 7, there was no uniform approach to this issue within the case study schools, and at the time of the research, the situation across the schools was fluid. There was evidence of schools embracing the idea of support staff replacing teachers in pastoral positions, but then retreating from this—whilst in one of the schools the headteacher was seeking to overcome teacher opposition to making further progress in this direction. Significantly, even where pastoral roles were retained these were often 're-designed'. Sometimes it was suggested that this was purely cosmetic, in order to 'fit' with the language of the TLR restructuring criteria, but in other cases it was clear the shift in role was more than superficial. Posts were re-titled, as 'Director of Learning' for example, and increasing emphasis was placed on 'Year Heads' monitoring student performance and achievement. This re-designing of teachers' role was clearly illustrated by one headteacher:

> So we've tended to say well, the Directors of Learning, who are teachers, their job is to track, monitor, focus on student progress . . . and to commission strategies to support students who are under-achieving. We have in addition got those people who aren't teachers who are doing some of that practical learning mentoring, behaviour support work.
>
> (Headteacher, London Borough Secondary 3)

This headteacher's comments provide a consummate example of the separation of conception from execution that is at the core of Braverman's (1974) analysis. The role of the Director of Learning is to 'commission strategies', whilst others become 'implementers'. However, the change described is even more significant as it exemplifies how the work of teachers begins to be re-designed in an era of remodelling. 'Caring', what the headteacher in the previous quotation described as the 'social work aspect' (Headteacher, London Borough Secondary 3) is increasingly uncoupled from the teaching role, and re-allocated as the responsibility of others—learning mentors, counsellors and behaviour support workers. As far as the role of the 'new professional teacher' is conceived, caring is considered a 'non-essential' task, and work therefore to be the responsibility of others in the school. This is not to suggest that teachers 'don't care': teachers in this study presented themselves as caring about their students passionately, which is precisely why these changes are challenged and struggled over. However, 'caring' in the pedagogical sense—the sense that effective teaching involves the teacher integrating the academic and pastoral needs of students—is being removed from teachers. This is not an abrupt change in teaching—it is slow, uneven and contested. But it is happening, and is hastened by workforce remodelling. Instead of the traditional unity, teaching is re-cast as the technical task of improving students' (narrowly defined) academic performance. Professionalism in turn is re-defined as an ability to focus on the 'core task'—the 'real job' of teaching, unfettered by concerns for students' emotional needs or behavioural 'problems'.

Schools as institutions *are* concerned with students' emotional needs—and are held accountable in this regard. Indeed, a number of recent initiatives, for example the *Every Child Matters* agenda (DfES 2004) and the initiative to support the social and emotional aspects of learning (DCSF 2008b), have strengthened schools' responsibilities for the caring of pupils, but in a remodelled school someone who is not a teacher increasingly fulfils these responsibilities more 'efficiently'. Caring is disconnected from teaching and becomes 'someone else's job'. Whilst there may be some merits in the use of dedicated support of this type, it appears that something is being lost from teaching as a result of this development. It is possible to identify teachers who indicated they were developing new skills, particularly in relation to data interpretation, but it is also possible to identify important skills relating to students' pastoral welfare being stripped out of the teachers' job—suggesting a complex process of simultaneous 'up-skilling' and 'de-skilling', in which skills associated with measuring performance are privileged, whilst skills associated with 'caring' are diminished.

The consequence of these developments is that teachers are becoming increasingly disconnected from the children they teach—students are an output, a score, something to be measured, benchmarked and compared in a league table. This is particularly the case in the secondary sector where teachers see students for limited periods of time. However, it may be an increasing tendency in the primary sector also where there the primary curriculum, with its emphasis on 'subjects', has often assumed an increasingly secondary school appearance. The danger is that this weakening of the relationship between teacher and student is further undermined as the emphasis on performance and league tables corrupts the 'trust' between teachers and students and their parents. Not only is care for students 'some-one else's job', but also the real risk is that students see teachers as caring only for 'the result', rather than the student. In an environment of league tables and performance pay the danger is that students perceive teachers' interest in 'results' as being self-interest, a concern to maximise pay or insti-tutional reputation. Rather than a relationship of trust and service, the relationship becomes one of self-interest and exchange.

The notion of a re-ordered division of labour within schools is also fundamental to both the provision of 10% of time for planning, prepara-tion and assessment, and the limits on requirements to cover for absent colleagues. These developments were broadly welcomed by teachers and, without underestimating their support, it should be noted that both gains depended heavily on the use of support staff without qualified teacher status to provide cover, and using staff in this way *was* controversial. As noted, the National Union of Teachers (NUT) had presented this as the defining issue over which the union had refused to sign the National Work-load Agreement (NUT 2003), and there was considerable evidence in the case study schools of staff being opposed to the use of support staff in these roles. However, opposition to the principle was not universal and in prac-tice was limited. In some schools the use of cover supervisors was seen as unproblematic and indeed an improvement on previous arrangements. The use of staff that knew the children and school procedures was often seen as preferable to a supply teacher who may have no such knowledge. In most cases teachers appeared willing to accept the use of support staff in teach-ing type roles as a price to be paid for planning, preparation and assessment time or restrictions on cover. In some schools these issues did raise ques-tions of quality, and in particular an impact on pupil behaviour, but the economic rationale for employing cheaper alternatives to qualified teachers proved difficult to resist. One assistant headteacher responsible for organiz-ing cover arrangements presented the argument in the following terms:

> It's clearly an economic argument. I employ somebody from the agen-cies and it costs me £180 a day. I employ somebody from the [school] office who will come and work as a supervisor at £70, £80 a day, you know the economics are very, very difficult to argue against. Whatever my beliefs are about the quality of the workforce.
>
> (Assistant Headteacher and Cover
> Organiser, London Borough Secondary 3)

The argument presented by the interviewee in the previous quotation high-lights the importance of the principle of labour substitution for workforce remodelling. Workforce remodelling 'creates time' in schools by using less qualified, and cheaper, staff to undertake some of the tasks previously undertaken by more qualified, and more expensive, staff. However much this process of substitution may be welcomed in some areas of teachers' work, the use of support staff to perform 'non-essential tasks' previously performed by teachers begins to re-define teaching and the role of the teacher, by re-drawing the boundaries between essential (qualified teacher) work and non-essential (support staff) work. 'Teaching' may be considered a core task of the qualified teacher, whilst 'supervision' of pupils is defined as non-essential and therefore a legitimate area for the use of support staff. Previously 'supervision' was a term restricted to something undertaken in playgrounds during breaks and lunchtimes—now it extends to what takes place in classrooms during the formal working day.

Attempts to maintain and extend the distinction between teaching and supervision are significant precisely because the distinction is blurring. In many ways it is more rhetorical than real. Whilst it may be important for teacher unions to claim that support staff are not 'teaching', but 'supervising', this is not an easy argument to sustain when it is subject to sustained scrutiny. The reality is that almost all the fundamental tasks of teaching—planning and delivering learning activities, and assessing their impact—are now undertaken by teaching assistants in some form and with various levels of training and support. The complexity of this issue is highlighted by the cover organiser quoted in Chapter 7:

> . . . they teach. I do think they teach . . . I don't want babysitters, I want teachers, and this is what we said about cover supervisors . . . *I think they do a really good job at teaching*
>
> (Cover organiser, City Secondary 4). (Emphasis added)

The consequences for teachers of the developments we have described is that a new division of labour is emerging within the labour process of teaching in which the teachers' role is being restructured both vertically and horizontally. Horizontal restructuring narrows the task of teaching at all levels, with pastoral roles eliminated or diminished, and concentrates the focus on 'the core task' of teaching and learning. Vertical restructuring increases demarcation between those with teaching roles. Taken together it is clear that not only is teaching being re-defined, but so is what it means to be a teacher. In the first instance teaching becomes defined as a narrow focus on technical improvements to secure higher scores in standardised tests. In the second instance the concept of the teacher is re-cast as a much broader occupational grouping involving 'teachers' and 'teaching assistants', with both clearly involved in 'teaching'. Although there is a diminishing distinction between teacher and teaching assistant, it is nevertheless the case that at the same time there is a corresponding *increase* in the level of differentiation and distinction *within* these occupational groups. There is now increased complexity in the school workforce with new occupational structures emerging and these require further analysis.

WORKFORCE FRAGMENTATION AND
THE NEW DIVISION OF LABOUR

The shifting emphasis from 'teachers' to the 'school workforce' when considering the organisational structure of schools reflects the substantial increase in support staff numbers in English schools, combined with the expanded roles many support staff now have. The emphasis on looking at the whole school workforce aligns with much of the discourse in schools about flatter and more flexible structures, in which rigidity and hierarchy are eschewed in favour of structures that are considered fluid and enabling. This approach is identified strongly with the discourse of 'distributed leadership' (Harris 2004, Harris and Muijs 2004), which has established roots in school effectiveness and school improvement research, and which is increasingly reflected in policy orthodoxy as, for example, promoted by the National College for School Leadership. However, contrary to the claims associated with discourses of distributed leadership, teaching reforms over several years, of which workforce remodelling represents one phase, work to increase hierarchy and demarcation in teaching as they are based on an increasingly fractured and fragmented division of labour. Despite rhetoric to the contrary, the reality is that teachers have experienced reforms as formalising structures and hierarchy.

In the years under New Labour in particular a relatively simple salary structure for teachers has become increasingly complex and hierarchical. This represents a shift from an organisational structure with some basis in a shared professionalism towards one based much more on the management of performance in which managerial roles become more explicit and rewards are linked more closely to performance. This process started in earnest with the publication of Labour's Green Paper *Teachers: Meeting the Challenge of Change* (DfEE 1998), although efforts to introduce performance related pay pre-date that report. The reforms to teachers' pay, resulting from this Green Paper, not only embedded a national system of performance-related pay, but also established new hierarchies within the profession. Principally this was achieved by establishing a performance-related pay threshold, thereby creating a division between those above and those below this dividing line. However these reforms created further division by creating the conditions in which 'leadership' positions might be increased. A new category of assistant headteachers was created, whilst the role of Advanced Skills Teacher was further enhanced. The significance of these roles is that post holders are not covered by the teachers' contractual requirement to work a maximum of 1265 hours on any 195 days in a year.

In effect these posts create a management team, members of which can be required to assume responsibilities that have no working time limits. Key divisions therefore began to develop between those above and those below the performance threshold, and between those covered by the 1265 hours element in the teachers' contract and those not covered (a growing number given the creation of roles described previously). In the latter case, this group emerged effectively as the 'leadership group'—a nomenclature that not only reinforced a distinction between 'classroom teacher' and 'manager', but also signalled the morphing of 'management' into something new and different. 'Management', with its emphasis on maintenance (Cuban 1988) is often diminished, whilst 'leadership', with its connotations of 'transformation', is to be esteemed.

Workforce remodelling reforms have since accelerated the trend towards increasing and reinforcing the complexity of the hierarchy within schools. This expansion has in part been achieved by formalising the roles of teaching assistants, with a much-expanded group of school staff now playing a significantly more important role in the learning experience of students. It is quite clear that these individuals are involved in teaching with no clear argument to be found suggesting they do not 'teach'. Teaching assistants may work under the supervision, directly or indirectly, of a teacher—but they teach. There are therefore, perhaps paradoxically, growing status differentiations within the workforce between teacher and teacher assistant, as roles have become professionalised, codified and graded. Within the organisational hierarchy, the expanded numbers of support staff has increased the significance of the divide between teacher and teacher assistant, but at the same time the demarcation between the work of qualified teachers and those without qualified teacher status has become more blurred. Increasingly the distinction between staff is defined not by their role in teaching (the argument that teachers teach, support staff do not, is not sustainable), but by an individual's degree of accountability for student performance. This distinction is intimately linked not to a new professionalism, but to a new form of managerialism.

THE FOCUS ON PERFORMANCE AND CONTROL—CREEPING MANAGERIALISM

The emphasis on student performance and the drive to raise 'standards' has been the dominant theme of Labour's education policy since 1997 (Ball 2008, Bell 2007, Tomlinson 2001). The previous Conservative administration had put in place a powerful quasi-market mechanism which had already sought to link institutional survival to student performance through the construction and publication of 'league tables', coupled with measures to make it easier for parents to choose an alternative school to the local one to which their child was allocated. The consequence of this framework was the imposition of a powerful disciplinary mechanism on teachers, with a premium placed not only on increasing student test scores, but also on focussing systematically on those students considered to have most 'value' in the market—for example, those students whose performance was at, or around, the key benchmark thresholds used for published results (Level 4 SATs for students aged 11, and grade C GCSE for students aged 16).

Labour's approach to education policy has endorsed this general approach, whilst recognising its limitations. First it has endorsed inter-school competition as the key to raising standards, whilst recognising that markets generate inequalities that are in conflict with Labour's declared commitment to social justice (Whitty 2008). Second, it has recognised that markets and parental choice provisions have only limited impact on school choice. The experience in the UK, as elsewhere (see the impact of No Child Left Behind legislation in the US), is that parents do not automatically seek the school with the highest performance in league tables. Parents make choices about schools based on more complex criteria (although some criteria, such as travel costs, serve to deny choice rather than extend it). What is significant is that even where schools are labelled as 'failing' there is strong evidence to demonstrate that the local community often keeps faith with the school, even when the inspectorate and local authorities do not. For these reasons Labour has developed its focus on driving up student test scores, by not solely relying on the Conservatives' quasi-market structures that it has left largely intact, but by buttressing these with a whole host of additional measures to increase the pressure to perform. These measures include: the publishing of national targets (fractured into local authority and school level targets); the increased use of the Inspectorate (including various 'naming and shaming' initiatives); and the extension of published performance data to include more subjects, at more levels and the impact of 'value-added'. The environment in which schools are under a relentless pressure to improve student scores in standardised tests creates a 'culture of performativity'. Performativity can be described as framing the context within which schools, and thereby teachers, function. It is experienced as a continuous pressure to 'get better', to 'improve' both on past performance and relative to the performance of others, whether it be the neighbouring school or the global competitor on the other side of the world. At its core is the visibility of the individual teacher and the constant need to measure performance in order to be able to quantify and benchmark it relative to the performance of others. Performativity is central to the neo-liberal ortho-doxy in education policy as it is about much more than output—it is about 'efficiency' and the notion of 'value for money'—that output only has value when it is measured relative to inputs.

If a 'culture of performativity' frames the context in which schools func-tion and teachers work, Gewirtz (2002) has argued, then the mechanism that operationalises this at an institutional level is 'managerialism'. Mana-gerialism is not a concept unique to education, although it has become pervasive within it (Thrupp and Wilmott 2003), but rather it reflects a particular ideology of rationality imported from the private sector as part of new public management (Pollitt 1990). While it is a broad concept, with different emphases highlighted by different writers, it has a number of characteristic features. Gewirtz highlights within schools: 'target-setting, performance monitoring and the closer surveillance of teachers' (2002: 6). More recently, Gunter (2008) has suggested that managerialism, as it has developed in schools, has emerged in four different forms. First is the 'identification of new work that is not directly educational' for example, business planning. Second is the use of staff in schools without qualified teacher status to undertake this work. Third is the privileging of business objectives over pedagogical considerations, and the translation of pedagogic objectives into business style output, best illustrated by the development and use of targets to monitor performance. Fourth is a blurring of the private-public divide in the management of schools in which schools increasingly both work with, and mimic, private sector structures and practices.

The value of Gunter's analysis is that it emphasises that managerialism is about much more than the transformation of a headteacher from a 'leading professional' to a 'manager', but that managerialism is ultimately about how control is exercised and experienced across an institution. In much the same way that orthodox thinking argues that 'leadership' is about more than individual leaders, and that 'distributed leadership' is about how power and responsibility are exercised across the institution (Harris and Muijs 2004), then managerialism must similarly be viewed as a feature that is steeped within the structure and organisational culture of an institution, rather than something that is the product of the behaviours of certain key individuals (although this is how it might manifest itself).

New Labour did not invent the culture of performativity, nor the managerialism that is a key feature of it, and both were well established prior to the introduction of workforce remodelling. The crude focus on performance originated with the introduction of standardised testing, league tables of results and the use of quasi-markets to impose a discipline on teachers and the teacher workforce. New Labour did, however, build on this pattern by reinforcing the centrality of standardised testing, supported not only by quasi-markets, but also by more sophisticated 'benchmarking' and use of comparative data. Remodelling extends managerialism and performativity by providing a series of middle management posts that provide the means of further measurement and accountability. The consequence of the urge to measure and make teachers accountable represents a further narrowing of the focus of teaching activity and its direction towards 'learning outputs', that is, standardised test scores. It is the emergence of new accountabilities that are at the heart of a reinforced and 'creeping' managerialism.

Understanding the link between workforce remodelling and the development of a strengthened managerialism requires a brief return to the Workload Agreement itself, and the analysis presented in Chapter 4. The Workload Agreement exemplifies a model of integrative bargaining (Walton and McKersie 1965) that aims to generate gains for both parties in the bargaining relationship. This 'something for something' approach is encapsulated in the title of the Agreement itself—'*Raising Standards and Tackling Workload*'. Whilst this is often referred to in shorthand as the 'National Workload Agreement', acknowledging the Agreement's full title is absolutely central to understanding how the remodelling agenda is likely to impact on schools and teachers. The Agreement itself has little to say, directly, about raising standards—it is not concerned, for example, in explicitly introducing pedagogical issues into the bargaining agenda. However, at the heart of the *quid pro quo* that underpins the Agreement, and the subsequent work of the Social Partnership, is a conviction that reforms that tackle workload will also raise standards—there is therefore an implicit link between conditions of service issues and standards. The nature of this link needs exploring further. Within the remodelling agenda the Workload Agreement sought to achieve improved standards through a sharper focus on teaching and learning, and a more efficient deployment of the school workforce. However, it is the later work of the Social Partnership, and in particular the transition to TLR points, followed by the introduction of new performance management (PM) arrangements, that provide the link between remodelling and school improvement. Improvements in standards will follow not only from a focus on teaching and learning, and a more effective deployment of labour, but crucially from increased accountability, buttressed by a strengthened and extended managerialism in schools.

The pay restructuring associated with the movement to TLRs has played a key role in increasing teacher accountability for student performance, and specifically the roles of those with 'middle leadership' positions. Our research suggested that the pay restructuring was often a contested process, presented as a struggle between 'restructuring and assimilation'. In many of our case study schools headteachers opted to assimilate, based on either their own convictions or a reluctance to challenge staff opposition (specifically, but not exclusively, the NUT, whose comprehensive advice to members was effectively a campaign for assimilation). However, the tendency to assimilate on paper underestimates the cultural shift that still took place, as even assimilated posts were re-engineered to reflect the national criteria for awarding TLRs.

Posing the question as to whether middle manager posts were restructured or assimilated therefore fails to capture the extent to which the move to TLRs re-focussed the management structure in schools and reinforced its alignment with the 'standards agenda', and the drive to improve student scores in standardised tests. This development in itself represents a significant strengthening and extending of managerialism within schools by focussing attention on narrow and relatively crude 'outputs' and by increasing the accountability of 'middle leaders' for the improvement of student test scores. However, this analysis can only be considered partial until broadened to include the new PM arrangements that were agreed by the Social Partnership and introduced in 2007. Unions welcomed the PM arrangements as it was argued these significantly enhanced teachers' access to continuing professional development. Enhanced access is undoubtedly an important development for teachers, although it may simply represent access to continuing professional development that is itself narrow and utilitarian, instrumentally committed to helping teachers 'deliver' national strategies (Stevenson, 2008). However, more significant than this was the emphasis in the new regulations placed on increased numbers of lesson observations as part of performance evaluation, the continued emphasis on targets based on pupil outcomes and the consolidating of the link between pay and performance. Most significantly, 'middle leaders' were to be expected to make recommendations on pay progression for their team members.

All of these developments taken together begin to radically re-position the role of the staff with TLRs. Previously MAs were spread broadly across the school with allowances awarded for being a Head of Department (or assistant), a Subject Co-ordinator or for pastoral or cross-curricular roles. Workforce remodelling and the new professionalism agenda has resulted in fewer posts, but often with enhanced responsibility and accountability. In particular the new 'middle leader' has been re-positioned within the school hierarchy. The new restructuring emphasises their leadership role, it aligns their goals much more closely with the organisation's objectives (as determined by externally imposed targets) and it makes them much more responsible for the performance of their 'team'.

This movement is not 'distributed leadership' in the sense that centralised management is dispersing power and the capacity to innovate across the institution. Rather this is 'creeping managerialism', the upward transferral of power within schools (by reinforcing the management control mechanisms that teachers experience and that compel them to conform to standardised practices) and in which managerial authority is extended beyond the senior management, or leadership team, and is increasingly exercised by those at 'middle' levels. A likely consequence of all these developments is increasing division and differentiation within the teaching force as a significant group of teaching personnel are annexed from their classroom colleagues in terms of their loyalties and affinities—and instead identify increasingly with the leadership team of which they have become an extended part. A headteacher quoted in Chapter 7 suggested that in schools there's always been "them" and "us": workforce remodelling has begun to re-draw the lines of that boundary by pushing the bearers of managerial authority lower down the school, and thereby creating increasing numbers of 'mini-headteachers' (Headteacher, London Borough Secondary 4). In Chapter 1, Michael Apple's (2006a) work was cited arguing that a 'new managerialism' had succeeded in drawing in a broad range of those with leading roles in teaching into a tacit support of the neo-liberal restructuring of school education. Apple argued that whether willingly or otherwise, the new managerialists had become part of the conservative modernisation alliance in support of the neo-liberal agenda. Careers depended on 'signing up' to the key principles of school reform. This group within the workforce is extended, as middle leaders increasingly have to make the same ideological shift if they are to survive, let alone thrive, in the new performativity culture.

RESTRUCTURING TEACHERS' WORK—CONCLUSION

This chapter has drawn together evidence exploring the impact of workforce remodelling on teachers' work, and the labour process of teaching. It suggests that workforce remodelling is not a 'watershed moment', or a major turning point in the changing nature of teachers' work, but part of a longer term restructuring in which increased control has been asserted over teachers and what they do. However, it is important to recognise that, because of the pace and magnitude of the changes that have taken place within the aegis of workforce remodelling, the period of change being discussed must be one that is considered both significant in political terms and substantial in scale. Workforce remodelling impacts on the labour process of teaching in three distinct but interdependent ways:

- The focus on teaching and learning and the re-definition of teaching
- Workforce fragmentation and the new division of labour
- The focus on performance and control and creeping managerialism

The focus on teaching and learning is at the heart of the remodelling reforms and underpins the claims to a new professionalism by suggesting that teachers can now focus on where their expertise is best utilised (Stevenson *et al.* 2007). It is equally arguable that viewed in a wider framework the 'focus on teaching and learning' disguises a narrow commitment to a support for school improvement that is driven by the neo-liberal commitment to improve student performance in standardised tests. The system is driven by a desire to maximise 'efficiency', as measured by evaluating the value of inputs against performance in internationally moderated league tables. The impact on teachers therefore is not a question of a technical re-direction of their labour, but one that fundamentally challenges a pedagogic philosophy that has its roots in teaching approaches that were developed within a commitment to comprehensive education. The focus on teaching and learning is not a neutral re-definition of what it means to be a teacher but a politically driven imperative to weaken the influence of comprehensive values in the education system and to replace these with a functional utilitarianism that is considered much more aligned to the needs of capital in a global economy. Whilst many of these developments are uneven, such as the bifurcation between academic and pastoral responsibilities, there is a narrowing of the conception about what it means to teach and that these developments create a potential for teachers to experience an alienation in their work as they become increasingly disconnected from the education of the whole child and more concerned with the impact of their own contribution to the student's 'value-added'. 'Professionalism' is technicised, whilst values associated with 'caring' and a pastoral concern for the child are stripped away and re-presented as the work of 'others'.

The re-casting of teaching in this way is partly secured by the creation of a new and much more complex hierarchical structure in schools in which support staff play an increasingly significant role. Whilst in many respects this is welcomed there is no doubt that processes of labour substitution are taking place. The emphasis on an 'efficient' deployment of labour, the idea that teachers' expertise is wasted doing necessary but routine tasks, necessitates an increasing division of labour, in which the work of teachers is scrutinised in detail and significant elements of the job are then redistributed—not only within the teaching force, but across the whole, and expanded, school workforce. Whilst some teachers clearly experience this process positively (with benefits in terms of increased status, esteem and remuneration), for many the consequence is an increasing hierarchy in which those at the lower end lack status and security. For some, such as supply teachers, levels of reward and job security are directly threatened by the increase in school support staff and the emergence of an expanded section of the school workforce who, in some cases, are directly replacing the work of teachers.

Pay reforms introduced before and during the period of workforce remodelling reflect and reinforce increasing complex divisions within the school workforce. At the centre of the expanded hierarchy are those sometimes referred to as 'middle managers' upon whom are placed increasing expectations. One of the defining features of this new hierarchy is the way in which responsibility for operationalising managerialist forms of control, in particular the use of PM including performance-related pay, are effectively shunted further down the organisational hierarchy. The separation of 'conception from execution' is thus further reinforced. Previously the preserve of the headteacher, middle leaders find themselves increasingly drawn into managerialist structures as they play a key role in evaluating the performance of their peers and determining how pay is used to reward and sanction performance. This development represents a 'creeping managerialism' as managerialist structures and forms of control are extended and operationalised by new strata within the workforce. Headteachers long ceased to be *primus inter pares*. One of the most significant consequences of the re-ordering of managerial roles is the way in which this alienation from colleagues is being extended so that middle leaders become annexed from their 'team'. Middle leaders now face considerable pressure to deliver their contribution to the standards agenda. In this way the workforce fractures with the potential for middle leaders (now rewarded through the pay restructuring) to become co-opted into a wider managerial group within the workforce—responsible for managing and controlling the performance of others.

Taken together we argue that these developments represent a continued 'Taylorisation' of teaching in which principles that underpin the division of labour are increasingly applied to the efficient management of the school workforce. Teachers' work is increasingly fragmented and re-allocated to other members of the workforce who are not teachers, as lower cost labour is used to perform tasks of 'low value'. In Braverman's terms by 'dividing the craft' it becomes possible to 'cheapen its individual parts' (1974: 80). Within this process new hierarchies are created in which a narrow band of managers assume greater control of the labour process of others. Again, drawing on Braverman, it is possible to argue that workforce reform represents a further 'separation of conception from execution' in teaching, whereby those with managerial roles assume increased importance in the designing and monitoring of teachers' work, whilst the majority of the workforce find their work increasingly codified and intensively policed. This destruction of the 'craft as a process under the control of the worker' (Braverman 1974: 78) and its reconstitution as a process under the control of management threaten to further alienate teachers as they find themselves less and less connected to the education of the whole child, and increasingly seen as one part of a process to maximise output—measured in terms of student performance in standardised tests.

9 Industrial Relations and Trade Union Renewal, *Rapprochement* or Resistance

INTRODUCTION

Teacher trade unions at the end of the period of Conservative Governments were politically marginalised and seemingly powerless to stop a wave of educational reforms that left teachers with deteriorating conditions of service and with less control over key elements of their work. Nevertheless, in organisational terms, teacher unions remained intact with levels of membership and density envied by unions in other sectors. After some initial coldness when first in office, New Labour offered them the prospect of engagement over workload issues, presenting them with an opportunity to reassess their oppositional strategies. As outlined earlier, the responses of the two main unions differed, symbolised by the signing, or otherwise, of the National Workload Agreement, and hence membership of the Social Partnership. Confronted with the recognition of their differing perspectives and trajectories, the possibility of merger and cooperation between the two largest unions, the National Union of Teachers (NUT) and the National Association of Schoolmasters Union of Women Teachers (NASUWT), receded further. The aim of this chapter is to examine the present state of, and future prospects for, school sector industrial relations through the findings at national, local and school levels presented in previous chapters. This multi-level analysis will also allow an examination of the affect of workforce remodelling on the state of the main teacher unions. One area of focus will be an attempt to understand the dynamics of teacher trade unionism and specifically whether they can be captured through the competing strategies of renewal, *rapprochement* and resistance.

SOCIAL PARTNERSHIP

Earlier, in Chapter 2, it was established that although union renewal was not as evident as Fairbrother implies, nevertheless, the concept has tended to dominate discussion of the prospects for unions in the public sector. One consequence is that, although there has been wide academic discussion of social partnership, and it has found its advocates (see, for instance, Ackers and Payne, who see partnership as giving trade unions 'a hand in shaping their own destiny') (1998: 529), on the whole there is little academic consideration of public sector social partnerships. Support for social partnerships was ushered in with New Labour in 1997 but was soon apparent that by 'social partnership' the Government did not have in mind the macro-social arrangements associated with many continental European governments. Indeed, New Labour's stance was dominated by the motive of increased competitiveness and this focus was regarded as antipathetic to macro-social agreements, as indicated by *Fairness at Work* (DTI 1998: para 1.10) which stated: 'Some aspects of the social models developed in Europe before the advent of global markets have arguably become incompatible with competitiveness'. The model of partnership that the Government had in mind was much closer to what might be described as micro-corporatism, in which the interests of labour at the enterprise level are subordinated to capital in order to raise profitability and competitiveness, thereby holding out the possibility of increased worker security (see Wells 2001 for one elaboration of the concept). This was the core of New Labour's 'Third Way', characterized by Stuart and Lucio (2002: 179) as 'coerced pluralism'. McIlroy's (2000: 6) similarly critical judgement of the significance of the rhetoric of social partnership is that it has provided a mechanism for employers to secure unions as 'junior partners in change management'.

There have been attempts at enterprise level within the public sector to construct social partnerships. For example, Stuart and Lucio (2002), as part of a wider study, looked at the advent of partnership in an National Health Service (NHS) Trust. Introduced into a strongly trade union organized environment, the management initiative was greeted with resistance: 'the trade union side was concerned that the introduction of partnership could undermine the existing institutional relations and collective forms of representation within the organisation' (Stuart and Lucio: 194). Furthermore, there is evidence elsewhere that where union representatives are incorporated into management through partnership agreements, this can have the affect of undermining their representative role and change their relationships with their constituencies. Danford *et al.* (2002) looked at a number of local government and hospital sites engaged in partnership agreements and found a number of variations in the patterns and effects of engagement. In an argument that parallels the thinking of unions in the Social Partnership, Danford *et al.* record that shop stewards at one site believed that members' interests were best served by working with management and influencing policy rather than mobilising against it. This belief did not accord with the findings:

> The upshot of this was that senior stewards became intensively engaged with processes of consultation but secured much less scope for hard bargaining on concrete membership concerns. Discussions with departmental stewards highlighted how this approach acted to distance

the senior stewards from the rank and file and undermine any col-
lectivisation of discontents. In the context of work restructuring and
decentralisation, the failure of the senior stewards to establish a robust
decentralised activists' organisation and consequent absence of any infrastructure for membership participation meant that their leadership
style tended to be of a 'detached' nature.

(Danford *et al.* 2002: 76)

In contrast to this example, in other instances, union organisation remained
more independent from the employer and 'where necessary adopted adver-
sarial strategies involving membership mobilisation around critical inci-
dents' (Danford *et al.* 2002: 23). Taylor and Ramsay (1998) and Taylor and
Bain (2004) drew similar conclusions about both the downside of social
partnership and efficacy of organising strategies. In all of these cases, the
relations between union officials, activists and members crucially influence,
and are affected by, union strategies towards employers; these are examined in this chapter, with reference to our findings on the Social Partnership
as it has played out in the specific context of school sector industrial relations and the teacher unions.

TEACHER TRADE UNIONISM AND SOCIAL PARTNERSHIP

As established earlier, the Social Partnership was ushered in with the
workforce remodelling agenda. Referring back to the typology of union
strategies presented in Chapter 1, signing up to the Social Partnership falls
easily into the idea of *rapprochement*. Social Partnership assumes a large
degree of common interest with employers and it has a powerful draw for
some sections of public sector workers, especially professional ones. Just
as the idea of patient care frames the outlook and actions of many nurses
and medical practitioners, so does the notion of 'doing the best for the
pupils' have a strong attraction for teachers and leads to large elements of
cooperation at school level. The good relations at school level tended to be
relatively constant even as the post-war settlement unravelled. Disputes at
school level remained rare and action, when it did take place, tended to be
over national issues, and especially pay. Cooperation extended to the local
authority (LA) level but, before the development of the Social Partnership,
confronted with increasingly hostile governments and marginalisation, the
idea of trade union cooperation beyond this remained remote.

Presented with both an immediate recruitment and retention problem
and the wish to secure fundamental changes in staffing structures, New
Labour was faced with a choice: continue a relatively hostile stance and
risk disruption, especially in a context of rising teacher shortages and elec-
toral sensitivity, or incorporate teachers into an agenda where the long-
term gains were greater than the short-term concessions. Experiencing

marginalisation from debates and consultation, the teacher unions equally faced a strategic choice: either to continue with what appeared to many to be ineffectual opposition or to find ways to accommodate and ameliorate Government policies. The dilemma for most unions was solved by entering the Social Partnership.

The Association of Teachers and Lecturers (ATL) appears to have adopted an almost entirely pragmatic position on membership. The members are not enthusiastic promoters of the Social Partnership and have fundamental criticisms of the Government's educational agenda, but coming from a tradition that made industrial action unlikely, and lacking the workplace organisation and membership activity to be able to pressure for changes in direction, any alternative position is extremely difficult to envisage. They therefore recognise that they can influence only within certain parameters. If one of its senior officials could postulate that education unions as a whole 'have had absolutely no clout whatsoever' then it highlights the even weaker position of ATL. It is little surprise therefore that an official openly acknowledged that the ATL's position inside the Social Partnership was 'calculated acceptance of incorporation' (National Official 2, ATL)

Despite in places being talked up by the union, the advantages of being members of the Social Partnership are themselves not enormous and the demands quite onerous. There is a certain amount of irritation with the Government, for instance, over the use of the unions to delivery policy; a number of the substantive outcomes are also questioned. Echoing the arguments advanced by the NUT, the previously quoted official raised serious concerns about the rationale for and deployment of teaching assistants (TAs):

> I think some of the argumentation in favour of having support staff solely in charge of a class for a while is a bit dodgy . . . If you move into a situation where people with no training, no qualifications, are assumed to be capable of delivering quality lessons, then why waste so much money on the teaching force?
>
> (National Official 2, ATL)

Despite the obvious formal loyalty to the Social Partnership and the claim that the benefits of membership outweigh the disadvantages, critical assessment of its achievements is never far from the surface. Thus commenting on the introduction of new performance management arrangements, it was stated that they threaten to introduce a 'completely different culture of schools . . . One of authoritarianism and bullying, management bullying, systematised' (National Official 2, ATL). The introduction of TLRs was another issue badly handled and as a system was 'a nonsense in primary schools' (National Official 2, ATL). Workload was the key reason for working with the Government and here the judgement is that there is a long way to go:

What we say frequently is we're a long way from making significant progress on that core issue. We've done some stuff, it's had some effect, PPA [planning, preparation and assessment] has had a big effect in primary schools. That's our main win so far. Overall working hours have reduced, not for school leaders but for others, a bit, but don't let's pretend we've cracked it . . . I think the ATL's view is that we're not going to crack the workload until we come back to the notion that teachers need to be given more professional autonomy on curriculum, assessment and pedagogy.

(National Official 2, ATL)

The wish for the expansion of professional autonomy is totally at variance with the direction of successive governments, and in particular with the performance management brought in through the Social Partnership. By its very founding nature, moreover, the Social Partnership excluded discussion of wider educational issues. Following discussion of educational philosophy, policy and direction with the ATL official, areas where the ATL has real strengths, he concluded: 'Actually you know just to repeat and I'm sure you've heard this, what we're talking about now is a long way away from what we ever talk about in the Social Partnership' (National Official 2, ATL). It may be for this reason that the official was quite open in wanting the NUT, with its focus also on professional matters, to be part of the Social Partnership.

The ATL holds out a sober analysis of the achievements of the Social Partnership together with the possibility that it might not be the vehicle to gain significant change. No such doubts are apparent in the position of the NASUWT, the largest and most enthusiastic of the Partnership's union supporters. Its identification with the substance and process of reforms was signalled early in the research when it was made clear to us that we were incorrect in describing workforce remodelling as part of the Government's agenda. On the contrary, it insisted that it was the union's agenda. Having a reputation for, and a background of, militant action and being traditionally the least amenable to pressure from arguments stressing the need to consider the wider effect of action on student performance and welfare, the acceptance of mutual gains perspective would appear surprising at first view. The union sees no radical change from its traditional orientation and joining the Social Partnership is presented as merely a different way of pursuing the same interests. In place of marginalisation and lack of influence, the union stresses that it no longer has to conduct campaigns by media announcements: 'So we're now in a position, rather than me talking to the press and saying this is all terrible and they all do their stuff on it, we can actually take that to the Secretary of State' (National Official 1, NASUWT). Tactics change but there is a claimed continuity of focus as evidenced in the statement of the same official in Chapter 4: 'We have no identity crisis in our union—we are a trade union representing the interests of teachers'.

What the union has been able to do is use the newly found access to the Government to give itself enhanced authority, confidence and advantage:

> Well, as a union of course we're using the whole of workforce remodelling and the pay agreements as an organising tool, because for us it is a really good opportunity to get into schools to talk to members of what we're doing and organise around the issues that they are facing in the schools. So it's an extremely good organising tool for us . . . it's increased probably the base level of case work now, because one of the things that people are having to do is to monitor and make sure that people are getting the benefits of what we've secured. And there's still a long way to go to make sure all the teachers are getting that.
>
> (National Official 1, NASUWT)

Tellingly the result of this perspective is increased casework, traditionally seen in organising unions as antipathetic to organising (Carter 2000). The union recognises the need for effective workplace representation, on the one hand, and Social Partnership, on the other, as synergistic (see Heery *et al.* 2003 for a similar claim). On closer examination, however, although there is a clear wish to increase the competence of school-level representatives, the model is some distance from fully fledged, more radical organising strategies. There is, for instance, no obvious recognition of the need to build wider competence and structures at school level to begin workplace bargaining. Developing school-based representatives is essentially conceived as training individuals to implement union policy rather than developing workplace organisation as evidenced by the reference to case work and the role of representatives being to 'monitor to make sure that people are getting the benefits of what we've secured in schools' (National Official 1, NASUWT). There are perspectives about building teams that are explicitly linked to the idea of organising, but these teams are to be built at the level of the LA rather than the school, reinforcing the local centralism of the organisation.

To portray the commitment of the union to Social Partnership as representing merely a change of circumstances and tactics, however, is not to capture some of its significance. The union's position is not just advanced in a different manner, the very position is altered and its independence is questioned:

> One of the things that we've been doing as Social Partners is when we go out now we talk on behalf of the Partnership. We put all the pieces of the jigsaw together, or as many as we've got . . . Because one thing that schools are frustrated about, they can't see how things join up and we set ourselves the issue of saying 'We're going to show how things join up'. So we started with remodelling, we started with the pay structure to support staff . . . And we kept telling people that this is a

way of working, this is not a new initiative, this is a way of working in which when 14–19 [curriculum reform] comes on, if you get remodelling, you've developed capacity to do it.

(National Official 1, NASUWT)

In framing the union's role in this way, in terms of capacity building, it closely resembles the statements by Pat Collarbone, Director of the National Remodelling Team, who also claims that the welter of changes in education are more coherent than many realise: 'it's simply that few people have bothered to work out and describe that coherence' (Collarbone 2005a). No more it seems.

By virtue of the National Agreement the union has to promote and promulgate the decisions made and hence cannot reveal divisions and differences. As noted, this stance makes the union further vulnerable to accusations that it is no longer independent—accusations not only from the NUT, but also from within—and the union is very conscious of this:

I've had to put my leadership on the line more than once over Social Partnership because it is high stakes and it's a very fine line between people accusing you of being in the pocket of Government and losing your independence and we fiercely guard our independence.

(National Official 1, NASUWT)

But as well as stressing that the union remains independent and still takes industrial action, it also counters with:

At the start of Social Partnership there were some who were saying 'Well it's a gagging clause' or 'we can't do this' and now you don't get that as much. From time to time though they'll say 'We think you should have given them a kicking over that' . . . I vent my sort of spleen on things like GTC or Ofsted and so on. I can just go to town on them (laughs), say what I like on those. So that balances it out a little bit.

(National Official 1, NASUWT)

What is in effect rhetorical opposition to issues outside the Social Partnership does not negate key concerns about the core areas covered by the Partnership and the way in which the methods of working change the relationship of the union to its membership. The union acknowledges, for instance, that it has curtailed its public criticisms of Government initiatives because it 'can go down to the DfES and have a conversation and influence it' (National Official 1, NASUWT), or instead of talking to the press can take the issue to the Secretary of State, but it could be argued that the former actions inform and help mobilise the union and its members and gives clarity to its position, whereas essentially private talks make union pressure invisible and render the possibility of a democratic deficit within the organisation. The union can of course keep its members informed but even here there are serious constraints. The following indicates that whereas the National Executive (NE) is taken into confidence, that confidence does not extend to the membership:

> In the early days we did have some problems, we did have leaks from time to time which could be very, very difficult. We had to find ways of working within our organisation and I have to say I have nothing but praise for the way that NASUWT leadership worked on this. I shared things with the NE in great detail, never once in all these years did anything go outside because my view was they needed to know the detail because in the end they had to make the decision we were going in the right direction. And they made some very courageous leadership decisions when it's much easier to sit on the sidelines sniping. But if you're determined to make a difference to your members, it's no good being on the sidelines sniping and having policies intact that you know are as far from implementation as they ever were.
>
> (National Official 1, NASUWT)

For members of the Social Partnership, 'being on the sidelines sniping' would be an apt characterisation of the NUT, the only teacher union not to sign the National Agreement. No doubt there were mixed rationales within the union for this. Obviously, the expansion of the roles of TAs was a central issue, but there is a view expressed by London NUT branch official that this need not have been a sticking point and the refusal was characterised as a calculated ploy on the part of the then NUT leadership to embarrass the NASUWT, believing that without the NUT the Social Partnership would subsequently fold. Current senior officers do not subscribe to this view, maintaining that there was principled opposition to the idea of signing an open-end commitment when so much of education policy fell outside of the agreement and was counter to sound education practice. This judgement is reflected in the following view:

> The political circumstances behind not signing the agreement however emerged from the previous GS and the executive's concern that it was expanding beyond what would be a deal, that it would actually be much more, that the commitment that was being asked for was open-ended, not an agreement which actually concentrated on specifics. That was the general reason. The specific reason was the real concern about substitution of teachers by support staff.
>
> (National Official 1, NUT)

Moreover, the idea that one or two people could have taken the decision to sign up to the Social Partnership is contested:

> We couldn't have delivered this anyway. I mean even if we'd thought it was a good idea. Or even that there was a *real politik* in signing the agreement, there was no way we could have delivered it. Members would be just rock solid in their opposition to the attack on their professionalism as they saw it.

> (National Official 1, NUT)

Present NUT criticism of Social Partnership continues to reflect these concerns, centring on both its form and the outcomes. Not least of the objections to its form is the fact that the Social Partnership agreement (SPA) 'has led to the exclusion by the social partners and the Westminster Government from normal bi-lateral discussions of unions which have chosen not to be party to the SPA' (Bangs 2006: 206). The union objects to the fact that the Government has continually refused to consult the NUT on matters that affect its membership, triggering the 'wider question about whether pluralism as a feature of a democratic society is undermined by the nature of such a partnership (Bangs 2006: 207). The union also believes that the Government has found support from other unions in taking this stance:

> Those who are involved with RIG [Rewards and Incentives Group] and WAMG [Workload Agreement Monitoring Group], there will be unions there who for years have smarted that the NUT was the leading union and ran things. Suddenly there's an opportunity for them to reverse that position. They're the ones who are going to talk to the DfES and so on and so forth. There's huge political agenda to that.

> (National Official 2, NUT)

There is therefore within this view an implicit criticism of opportunism. The NUT has also consistently accused the other unions in the Social Partnership of being subordinate to the Government's agenda. This sentiment was evident in the union's motion to the Trades Union Congress (TUC) annual meeting in 2007, which was a barely disguised attack on the Social Partnership approach. It read:

> Congress agrees that the independence of our trade union movement and the independence of every affiliate is one of our guiding principles.
>   Congress will oppose any move to incorporate affiliated unions into any form of government or employer-based structure that would limit our ability to act independently, properly represent our members and develop the organising agenda to which the TUC is committed. Congress will oppose any attempted isolation of unions refusing such incorporation. Congress urges all unions seeking to recruit the same body of workers to explore ways to establish new, united and independent organisations, using the good offices of the TUC in this direction.

> (TUC 2007)

The successful motion is unlikely to have had the desired effect. Not only is the TUC still committed to the idea of social partnership, but it was also instrumental in facilitating the setting up of the Social Partnership. As it happened, the Social Partnership unions did not rise to the bait—no union contested the motion; it was passed unanimously without contention and, no doubt, has been quietly buried.

The fate of the motion indicates a wider problem for the NUT. Outside the Partnership it has been unable to frame a strategy to influence the agenda. Its continued criticism of the Social Partnership and the policies emanating from it are largely addressed to its own membership and have little in the way of practical impact. The union's successful mobilisation for higher annual pay settlements is another case in point. Despite impressive support from its members in 2008, the union appears hesitant in its direction of further action. Having acted in enforced isolation from the other teacher unions, which despite initial protests and threats of ballots for action, have accepted below inflation level settlements, the NUT does not have the momentum for effective widespread action. The union has continued to resist the Government agenda, but within traditional frameworks and organisational forms and it is difficult to discern an evaluation of the union's position and recognition of the need for new strategies and tactics. It has yet to feel the necessity, for instance, to respond organisationally to the additional decentralisation that accompanies workforce remodelling. The union in short has continued resistance without attempting a renewal strategy, as is evident at LA and workplace level.

INDUSTRIAL RELATIONS AT LA LEVEL

Industrial relations at LA level have been an enigma since the implementation of local management of schools in 1988. As the earlier review of Ironside and Seifert (1995) indicated, the traditionally close relations between unions and local education authorities were expected to be disrupted. Any impetus in this direction should have been strengthened by the remodelling requirements placed on headteachers and the need to innovate and increase managerialism at school level. Instead, the mechanism of workforce remodelling agenda, the Social Partnership, has been replicated, if unevenly, at LA level, throwing employers and unions closer together through the formation of local WAMGs and the attempt to expand them into standing local social partnerships (LSPs). Rather than being abolished, within these new initiatives, LAs have become more clearly transformed into transmission belts for national priorities. WAMGs are a perfect example of this: supported and sponsored by the DfES, they are an attempt to mirror at local level the policies determined at national level.

Whatever the intention, however, the situation is rather more complicated and LSPs remain one weak point in the Social Partnership perspective.

Firstly, closer to the actual practice and realities of schools, LSPs, of necessity, included the NUT. Although relations are normally good among LA officials, other unions and the NUT, the latter's opposition to many aspects of workforce remodelling can have the effect of stalling progress. Attempts by the NUT, where it is strong, to begin to develop local perspectives on issues raised by the remodelling agenda have been met by resistance from the LAs (as in London Borough) and by the NASUWT (as in City). In the former example, the dominance of the NUT locally encouraged the LA to close the WAMG as soon as the statutory period for implementation of the agreement was reached. Where they have continued, WAMGs' role was widely interpreted as monitoring the implementation of the agreement, a role of WAMG that was reduced to regarding the agreement as narrow and contractual, a matter for national not local determination. This interpretation weakened the impetus of the unions. Unable to negotiate changes, the role was restricted to monitoring implementation. There were those who saw little point in a body that had no power to make decisions of note or take action. Unison in City, for example, withdrew for a period precisely because of this factor.

Teacher and support staff unions in the Social Partnership followed the logic of this non-negotiation by placing expectations on consultants and employers to straighten out errant practice at school level, rather than increasing independent trade union representation and activity within schools. Indeed, consultants having a quiet word with headteachers about offending practices sometimes met these expectations. The NASUWT representative in Shire, for instance, when hearing of non-compliance with terms of the National Agreement would make it clear that the LA had a responsibility to police the National Agreement, complaining that the agreement was a shared one, not a trade union one. But in this instance, he was also prepared to go into the school to orchestrate industrial action if necessary, a position not open to everyone.

The lack of clarity over the role and jurisdiction of WAMGs was exacerbated by the fact that they never supplanted the existing institutions for consultation and negotiation within LAs. Nor could they solve a further problem, which was the lack of direct representation of schools and the poor attendance of the headteacher unions. These factors limited WAMG authority, especially in the eyes of secondary school headteachers who often held their LA in low regard. It is difficult to see how these fundamental problems will be resolved without a reconfiguration of LA-level institutions and widening the remit of the LSP. In doing so it is likely that collective bargaining would begin to be prioritised over Social Partnership–inspired mutual gains perspectives, especially in urban areas and in London Borough where the NUT is dominant.

If the concept of Social Partnership becomes weaker as it moves from central to local government, it becomes even weaker in some respects at school level. However, any contention that workplaces are the crucible of union formation is also not uniformly true, at least in the sense of having formal institutional presence beyond a representative. The union is visible in most schools and in secondary schools the union tends to have regular meetings or consultations with the headteacher. The position is different in primary schools where union consciousness and activity are relatively low. In City Primary 1, a school where the head has some prominence as an advocate of distributed leadership, there appeared to be in construction an environment that would make the coalescence of union consciousness even more difficult. All staff were given areas of responsibility and development and staff meetings were conducted on professional development lines with staff reporting on their areas. The demarcation of different management and classroom teacher interests becomes very difficult to articulate in this context and all the time standing above individual staff is a headteacher with the practice of 'intense monitoring'. Difficult as it is to see the construction of workplace organisation in this context, however, unions are always present in the background in the form of local lay officials as a resource that teachers can call on and headteachers are very aware of this.

The locus of union power is therefore very much outside the schools, and there has been little movement to share the roles of lay officials or to develop the range of competences of the school representative. Several examples were noted in earlier chapters of how headteachers, particularly in London, were able to manipulate their own membership of the NUT in order to gain support of the local union and to strengthen their position against the school-based representative. Conversely, there were also examples whereby the desire of the NUT to maintain uniformity of policies across the LA encouraged the union to limit the role of school-based representatives who could lead them into disputes or cause a fragmentation of conditions of service. As a result, the phrase 'business as usual' (Stevenson and Carter 2004) continues to have some relevance here, albeit under new conditions.

There is no uniform trade union consciousness and schools are very different places from one another with different styles of leadership and culture. NASUWT representatives tend to identify strongly with the Social Partnership but regard it as a national agreement to be implemented and policed at LA and school level and any failure will stoke anger and possibly action. The NUT representatives are more critical of the effects of the agreement on the ground but feel largely powerless to affect its consequences on a school-by-school basis. Where schools have resisted for some time, for instance over the use of cover supervisors, resistance has been worn away, especially where members' own, immediate conditions are threatened by successful resistance. Given ATL's concentration on education policies and principles, ATL members might be equally critical of some new aspects of school policy but their lack of organisation on the ground meant that we did not encounter ATL representatives despite requests.

THE PROSPECTS FOR TEACHER UNIONS

One noted feature of teacher unionism is its multi-unionism and particular unions' uneven density across the wider system. In contrast, nearly every sector of employment in Britain over the past two decades has seen significant merger activity and this consolidation is not a feature restricted to the private sector. The public sector has witnessed the formation through merger of three significant unions: Unison in 1993, covering health, local government and education (Terry 2000); the Public and Commercial Services Union (PCS) in 1998, covering largely Civil Service areas (Undy 2002); and University and College Union (UCU) in 2006, covering lecturers in higher and further education (Carter 2008). Factors that commonly drive mergers are membership decline in at least one of the merging unions and deterioration in unions' financial position (Waddington 2006). These factors are not necessarily linked to a third factor—that of increasing ineffectiveness in relation to employers' policy initiatives adversely affecting members' conditions.

Arguably, the main teaching unions up until 1997 were in a position analogous to that which encouraged the Association of University Teachers (AUT) and National Association of Teachers in Further and Higher Education (Natfhe) to merge: they were not losing members and there was no institutional crisis to propel them into each other's arms, but they were increasingly ineffectual in representing their members' interests. In part this was a result of competition between them and, as Barber (2006: n.p.) has argued, 'if you're in government in the U.K., you have to be particularly obtuse to have all six of our teachers unions opposing you at any given moment'. Mergers held out the possibility of changing this situation. For the teaching unions, however, the accession of New Labour to power lessened the perceived need for merger for a number of reasons. Firstly, more money has flowed into the schools system and teacher numbers and pay have improved. Secondly, the framework of relations with the Government was changed by the working arrangements that grew up around the workforce remodelling agreement and their formalisation into the Social Partnership. The Partnership arrangements had the effect of dividing the NASUWT and the NUT, exacerbating differences based on ideology and constituency bases. The future relations between them, and therefore the possibility of merger, rest in many ways on the future of the Social Partnership. Despite the NUT's attack on the Social Partnership, the arrangement retains strong support from the leadership of the other main teacher unions, and particularly the NASUWT. Moreover, the Government continues to support it as an effective mechanism of consultation, negotiation and dissemination of new initiatives. The fractured nature of teacher unionism therefore seems set to continue in the short term at least.

There are, however, a number of potential threats to the Social Partnership's long-term position. Firstly, despite support for the Partnership there does appear to be a large pragmatic element to it. Unions can maintain membership support as long as it holds out the possibility of improvements in workload. Here results have been marginal and deteriorating. According to a Times Educational Supplement (TES) poll of 3453 teachers, only 3.6% said the workforce agreement had led to a 'substantial reduction' in their workload, 48% said that there had been no effect and 10% that it had actually increased workload (Stewart 2008: n.p.). The School Teachers' Review Body (STRB 2008) found across the board increases in teacher working hours for the first time since 2000. The response of NASUWT to the results was to claim that 'where all aspects of the agreement have been implemented—and that is in a lot of schools—it is working well' (cited in Stewart 2008: n.p.). The Government's response similarly blamed the problems on non-implementation 'with ministers poised to announce a crackdown on non-implementation' (Stewart 2008). However, no correlation was demonstrated between non-implementation and the negative responses of teachers. The schools in our study displayed no reluctance to implement the agreement, and the responses of teachers suggested exactly the spread of results in the TES survey. The conclusion is that, whether or not the agreement has been implemented, the trend has been towards the intensification of labour and it appears from recent STRB findings (2008) towards the re-appearance of the extension of hours as well.

What positive assessment of the reforms there is might be further undermined over the next few years as the additional funding that has lubricated reform lessens or is reversed. As the impact of the economic crisis feeds through into public spending cuts and pay freezes, the landscape is likely to change significantly. The position of particular schools in these changed budgetary constraints might then cause headteachers to make decisions on such issues as class sizes, the availability of TAs, or the replacement of teachers with TAs, that make the implications of the reforms look very different. This could lead to what, in many areas, looks like resigned acceptance of the reforms becoming more active opposition to them and unions would have to reflect these conditions on the ground. The second threat is that wider issues that are not covered by the Partnership might undermine teachers' attitudes to union cooperation with the Government. Planned limits to salary increases that in the context of higher rates of inflation effectively reduce salaries year by year met with limited strike action by the NUT in 2008, and there is little doubt that there is some resonance with this opposition in other unions. It is not impossible to imagine members asking why their leaders are cooperating with the very people reducing their salaries.

Thirdly, it is possible to project current developments into a future where the Social Partnership has little jurisdiction. At present. part of the Government's attraction to academies is that they are outside the control of LAs and do not have to abide by the same nationally stipulated teacher terms and conditions. With the determined expansion of academies and the extension of their remit to primary schools, the Social Partnership will cover arrangements in fewer and fewer schools. Alternatively, and despite pressing on the Conservatives that the Social Partnership is delivering change and stable, amicable Government-union relations, trade union members of the Social Partnership are far from convinced that the arrangement will outlast the New Labour Government. Conservative policies towards further de-centralisation and differentiation of schools will make school-level coop-eration between different unions more necessary and significant.

CONCLUSION

In terms of the triad of strategic orientations open to teacher unions—*rap-prochement*, resistance and renewal—it is clear that the *rapprochement*, and its outcome Social Partnership, are dependent not only on union will-ingness but also willingness of the Government. The progressive erosion of the number of schools covered by national terms and conditions threat-ens in the long term to render the Partnership largely redundant. Deprived of decision-making for schools nationally, its weak institutional base at both LA and school level would almost certainly signal the demise of the Social Partnership. In addition, of course, the election of a Conserva-tive Government might ensure that the long term never arrives. Trade union resistance continues at many levels despite the Social Partnership as evidenced by attempts to use the Partnership agreements as a weapon to resist or further limit workloads within schools. Resistance, born of greater antagonism, may well increase in the context of greater financial stringency and the need for schools to save money through staff cuts. Moreover, to the resistance of teachers is now added the potential of resis-tance of support staff. The insertion of support staff into the school labour process has not solved industrial relations problems. Support staff have taken from teachers a range of jobs that are not core to teaching but are nevertheless core to running schools, including roles covering health and safety. In the event of support staff taking action, and there is widespread frustration with their pay levels, it is inconceivable that the main teaching unions will sanction their members covering these roles and schools will close. If the Social Partnership were to cease, all the tendencies towards greater resistance would be strengthened and would no doubt be further buttressed by greater trade union cooperation between the NUT and the other unions.

Finally, the distinction was made earlier between trade union resis-tance and union renewal. 'Resistance' is a term used here to reflect action taken within an existing, traditional framework of relations. 'Renewal', on the other hand, is a term coined to capture transformed union forms and relations based more on the workplace organisation and membership participation. At present there is no evidence of de-centralisation of trade union organisation and no national or local lay officials' support for radical changes in distribution of resources and the locus of union power and representation. Despite 20 years of local management of schools, and now workforce remodelling, the unions are as far away as ever from feeling the need to develop site-based organisation and bargaining, as opposed to having representatives who largely transmit and transfer problems to LA-based branch organisations.

Appendix
Schedule of Interviewees

Interviews were conducted at three 'levels'—national, local authority and individual school. An explanation of how individuals are identified in the text is presented in Chapter 1. Not all interviewees listed are quoted directly in the text. Further details about the number of interviewees and their role are provided here.

NATIONAL LEVEL

Association of School and College Leaders (ASCL)	1 Interviewee
Association of Teachers and Lecturers (ATL)	2 Interviewees
Local Government Employers (LGE)	2 Interviewees
National Association of Headteachers (NAHT)	2 Interviewees
National Association of Schoolmasters Union of Women Teachers (NASUWT)	2 Interviewees
National Union of Teachers (NUT)	4 Interviewees
Training and Development Agency for Schools (TDA)	2 Interviewees
Unison	1 Interviewee
Voice (previously Professional Association of Teachers) (PAT)	2 Interviewees

LOCAL AUTHORITY LEVEL

City Authority

Remodelling Advisers	2 Interviewees
Local Authority Officer	1 Interviewee
Elected Councillor	1 Interviewee
Local Authority Headteacher	1 Interviewee
ASCL Officer	1 Interviewee
ATL Officers	2 Interviewees

NAHT Officer	1 Interviewee
NASUWT Officer	1 Interviewee
NUT Officers	2 Interviewees
UnisonOfficer	1 Interviewee
Voice Officer	1 Interviewee

London Borough Authority

Remodelling Advisers	3 Interviewees
Local Authority Officers	2 Interviewees
ASCL Officer	1 Interviewee
ATL Officer	1 Interviewee
NASUWT Officer	1 Interviewee
NUT Officers	2 Interviewees
Unison Officer	1 Interviewee

Shire Authority

Remodelling Advisers	2 Interviewees
Local Authority Officers	2 Interviewees
ASCL Officer	1 Interviewee
ATL Officer	1 Interviewee
NAHT Officer	1 Interviewee
NASUWT Officer	1 Interviewee
NUT Officer	1 Interviewee
Unison Officer	1 Interviewee

SCHOOL LEVEL

City Primary 1

Headteacher	1 Interviewee
Classroom Teachers	3 Interviewees

City Primary 2

Headteacher	1 Interviewee
Deputy Headteacher	1 Interviewee
Classroom Teacher	1 Interviewee
Higher Level Teaching Assistant	1 Interviewee

City Secondary 3

Headteacher	1 Interviewee
Business Manager	1 Interviewee

Cover Manager	1 Interviewee
Assistant Headteacher	1 Interviewee
Classroom Teachers	2 Interviewees (including NUT Representative)

City Secondary 4

Headteacher	1 Interviewee
Business Manager	1 Interviewee
Cover Supervisor	1 Interviewee
Headteachers' Personal Assistant	1 Interviewee
Classroom Teachers	2 Interviewees

London Borough Primary 1

Headteacher	1 Interviewee
Deputy Headteacher	1 Interviewee
Classroom Teacher	1 Interviewee (NUT Representative)

London Borough Primary 2

Headteacher	1 Interviewee
Business Manager	1 Interviewee
Classroom Teachers	3 Interviewees (including NUT Representative)
Support Staff Member	1 Interviewee (Unison Representative)

London Borough Secondary 3

Headteacher	1 Interviewee
Assistant Headteacher	1 Interviewee
Business Manager	1 Interviewee
Cover Organiser	1 Interviewee
Classroom Teacher	1 Interviewee (NUT Representative)

London Borough Secondary 4

Headteacher	1 Interviewee
Business Manager	1 Interviewee
Classroom Teachers	2 Interviewees (including NASUWT Representative)

Shire Primary 1

Headteacher	1 Interviewee
Classroom Teachers	2 Interviewees

Shire Primary 2

Headteacher	1 Interviewee
Bursar	1 Interviewee
Classroom Teacher	1 Interviewee

Shire Secondary 3

Headteacher	1 Interviewee
Assistant Headteacher	1 Interviewee
Business Manager	1 Interviewee
Classroom Teacher	1 Interviewee (NASUWT representative)

Shire Secondary 4

Headteacher	1 Interviewee
Bursar	1 Interviewee
Classroom Teachers	2 Interviewees (including NASUWT representative)

References

Ackers, P. and Payne, J. (1998) 'British trade unions and social partnership: rhetoric, reality and strategy', *International Journal of Human Resource Management*, 9(3): 529–550.

Apple, M. (1983) 'Work, class and teaching', in S. Walker and L. Barton (eds.) *Gender, Class and Education*. Lewes: Falmer Press.

Apple, M. (2003) *The State and the Politics of Knowledge*, London: RoutledgeFalmer.

Apple, M. (2006a) *Educating the 'Right' Way: Markets, Standards, God and Inequality*, London: Routledge.

Apple, M. (2006b) 'Interrupting the Right: on doing critical education work in conservative times', in G. Ladson-Billings and W. Tate (eds.) *Education Research in the Public Interest: Social Justice Action and Policy*, New York: Teachers' College Columbia University.

Bach, S., Kessler, I. and Heron, P. (2006) 'Changing job boundaries and workforce reform: the case of teaching assistants', *Industrial Relations Journal*, 37(1): 2–21.

Ball, S. J. (1988) 'Staff relations during the teachers' industrial action: context, conflict and proletarianisation', *British Journal of Sociology of Education*, 9(3): 289–306.

Ball, S. (2003) 'The teacher's soul and the terrors of performativity', *Journal of Education Policy*, 18(2): 215–228.

Ball, S. (2007) *Education PLC: Understanding Private Sector Participation in Public Sector Education*, London and New York: Routledge.

Ball, S. (2008) *The Education Debate: Policy and Politics in the Twenty-first Century*, Bristol: Policy Press.

Bangs, J. (2006) 'Social Partnership: the wider context', *Forum*, 48 (2): 201–207.

Barber, M. (1992) *Education and the Teacher Unions*, London: Cassell.

Barber, M. (2005) 'Informed professionalism: realising the potential', speech given at ATL conference, London, 11 June.

Barber, M. (2006) 'Education reform lessons from England: an interview with Sir Michael Barber'. Online. <http://www.educationsector.org/analysis/analysis_show.htm?doc_id=344385> (accessed 11 January 2009).

Barker, B. (2008) 'School reform policy in England since 1988: relentless pursuit of the unattainable', *Journal of Education Policy*, 23(6): 669–683.

Barker, I. (2008) 'Assistants are now a force to be reckoned with'. Online <http://www.tes.co.uk/article.aspx?storycode=2646972> (accessed 12 September 2009).

Barmby, P. (2006) 'Improving teacher recruitment and retention: the importance of workload and pupil behaviour', *Educational Research*, 48(3): 247–265.

Bates, J. and Carter, B. (2007) 'Workforce remodeling and the limits to "Permanent Revolution": some responses of English headteachers'. Online. *International*

Electronic Journal for Leadership in Learning, 11(18) <http://www.ucalgary. ca/~iejll/> (accessed 11 January 2009).

Becker, G. S. (1964). *Human Capital: A Theoretical and Empirical Analysis, with Special Reference to Education,* New York: Columbia University Press.

Bell, L. (2007) *Perspectives on Educational Management and Leadership,* London: Continuum.

Bell, L. and Stevenson, H. (2006) *Education Policy, Process, Themes and Impact,* London: RoutledgeFalmer.

Bernstein B. (1971) 'Education cannot compensate for society', in B. Cosin, I. Dale, G. Esland and D. Swift (eds.) *School and Society,* London: Routledge and Kegan Paul.

Blandford, S. (1997) *Middle Management in Schools,* London: Prentice Hall.

Boddy, M. and Fudge, C. (1984) *Local Socialism? Labour Councils and New Left Alternatives,* London: Palgrave.

Bottery, M. (2000) *Education, Policy and Ethics,* London: Continuum.

Bottery, M. (2006) 'Education and globalization: redefining the role of the educational professional', *Education Review,* 58(1): 95–113.

Bottery, M. (2008) 'Towards the branded technician? Changing conceptions of the education profession', keynote presentation at *Remodelling Teaching: Rethinking Education* conference, 5 June, University of Lincoln, UK.

Braverman, H. (1974) *Labor and Monopoly Capitalism: The Degradation of Work in the Twentieth Century,* New York: Monthly Review.

Brenner, B. (1998) 'The economics of global turbulence', *New Left Review,* 229: 1–24.

Brighouse, T. (2001) 'New Labour: could do better', *Political Quarterly,* 72(1): 19–29.

Brighouse, T. (2002) 'The view of a participant during the second half—a perspective on LEAs since 1952', *Oxford Review of Education,* 28(2&3): 187–196.

Brighouse, T. and Woods, D. (1999) *How to Improve Your School,* London: Routledge.

British Educational Research Association (2004) *Revised Ethical Guidelines for Educational Research (2004).* Online. < http://www.bera.ac.uk/blog/category/ publications/guidelines/> (accessed 11 January 2009).

Busher, H. and Saran, R. (1992) *Teachers' Conditions of Employment: A Study in the Politics of School Management,* London: Kogan Page.

Butt, G. and Gunter, H. (eds.) (2007) *Modernizing Schools: People, Learning and Organizations,* London: Continuum.

Callaghan, J. (1976) 'The Ruskin College speech', in J. Ahier, B. Cosin and M. Hales (eds.) (1999) *Diversity and Change: Education, Policy and Selection,* London: Routledge.

Cameron, D. (2005) *The Inside Story of the Teacher Revolution in America,* Lanham, MD: Rowman and Littlefield Education.

Carlson, D. (1987) 'Teachers as political actors: from reproductive theory to the crisis of schooling', *Harvard Educational Review,* 57(3): 283–307.

Carlson, D. (1992) *Teachers and Crisis: Urban School Reform and Teachers' Work Culture,* New York: Routledge.

Carter, B. (2000) 'Adoption of the organising model in British trade unions: some evidence from Manufacturing, Science and Finance (MSF)', *Work, Employment and Society,* 14(1): 117–136.

Carter, B. (2004) 'State restructuring and union renewal: the case of the National Union of Teachers', *Work, Employment and Society,* 18(1): 137–156.

Carter, B. (2008) 'When unions merge: the making of UCU', *Capital Class,* 96: 85–112.

Carter, B. and Poynter, G. (1999) 'Unions in a changing climate: MSF and Unison experiences in the new public sector', *Industrial Relations Journal,* 30(5): 499–513.

Cassidy S. and Hodges, L. (2001) 'Blunkett admits failure on teacher recruitment', London: *The Independent,* April 5.

Center for Union Facts (2008) Teachers Union Facts. Online. <http://www.teacher-sunionexposed.com/> (accessed 12 January 2009).

Certification Officer (2006) *Aunnual Report of the Certification Officer 2005–2006* <http://www.certoffice.org/annualReport/pdf/2005-2006.pdf> (accessed 13 October 2008).

Chitty, C. (2002) 'The role and status of LEAs: post-war pride and *fin de siècle* uncertainty', *Oxford Review of Education*, 28(2&3): 261–273.

Chitty, C. (2008) 'The school Academies programme: a new direction or total abandonment?' *Forum*, 50(1): 23–32.

Coates, R. (1972) *Teachers' Unions and Interest Group Politics: A Study in the Behaviour of Organised Teachers in England and Wales*, Cambridge: Cambridge University Press.

Collarbone, P. (2005a) 'Education 2010: A World of Difference (Views from a Modernisation Agent of Change)', Manchester Metropolitan University, September 2.

Collarbone, P. (2005b) 'Remodelling leadership', speech given at North of England Education conference . Online. <http://www.tda.gov.uk/upload/resources/doc/n/neec_conf_collarbone2.doc> (accessed 11 January 2009).

Collarbone, P. (2005c) Target 2010 Conference, November 30. Online. <http://www.tda.gov.uk/upload/resources/pdf/t/target2010_collarbone.pdf> (accessed 11 January 2009).

Collarbone, P. (2005d) 'Touching tomorrow: Remodelling in English schools', *Australian Economic Review*, 38 (1): 75–82.

Colling, T. (1995) 'Renewal or rigor mortis? Union responses to contracting out in local government', *Industrial Relations Journal*, 26: 134–145.

Compton, M. and Weiner, L. (2008) 'The global assault on teaching, teachers and teacher unions', in M. Compton and L. Weiner (eds.) *The Global Assault on Teaching, Teachers and Their Unions: Stories for Resistance*, New York: Palgrave Macmillan.

Crompton, R. and Jones, G. (1984) *White-Collar Proletariat: Deskilling and Gender in Clerical Work*, London: Macmillan.

Connell, R. (1985) *Teachers' Work*, London: Allen & Unwin.

Cuban, L. (1988) *The Managerial Imperative and the Practice of Leadership in Schools*, Albany, NY: State University of New York Press.

Cummings, C., Dyson, A., Papps, I., Pearson, D., Raffo, C., Tiplady, L. and Todd, L. (2006) *Evaluation of the Full Service Extended Schools Initiative, Second Year: Thematic Papers*. Online. <http://www.dcsf.gov.uk/research/data/upload-files/RR795.pdf> (accessed 11 January 2009).

Cutler, T. and Waine, B. (1997) *Managing the Welfare State: Text and Sourcebook*, Oxford: Berg.

Danford, A. Richardson, M. and Upchurch, M. (2002) '"New unionism", organising and partnership: A comparative analysis of union renewal strategies in the public sector', *Capital & Class*, Spring: 1–27.

Demaine, J. (1993) 'The new right and the self-managing school', in J. Smyth (ed.) *A Socially Critical View of the Self-Managing School*, London: Falmer Press.

Denison, E. F. (1967). *The Sources of Economic Growth in the United States and the Alternatives before Us*, New York: Committee for Economic Development.

Department for Children, Schools and Families (2008a) *About the National Challenge*. Online. <http://www.dcsf.gov.uk/nationalchallenge/> (accessed 11 January 2009).

Department for Children, Schools and Families (2008b) *Social and Emotional Aspects of Learning . . . Improving Behaviour . . . Improving Learning*. Online. <http://nationalstrategies.standards.dcsf.gov.uk/primary/publications/banda/seal/> (accessed 11 January 2009).

Department for Education and Employment (1997) *Excellence in Schools* Cmd 3681, London: HMSO.

Department for Education and Employment (1998) *Teachers: Meeting the Challenge of Change* Cmd 4164, London: HMSO.

Department for Education and Skills (2002) *Time for Standards: Reforming the School Workforce*, London: DfES.

Department for Education and Skills (2003) *Raising Standards and Tackling Workload: A National Agreement*. Online. <http://www.teachernet.gov.uk/docbank/index.cfm?id=3479>(accessed 11 January 2009).

Department for Education and Skills (2004) *Every Child Matters: Change for Children*. Online. <http://www.everychildmatters.gov.uk/_files/F9E3F941D-C8D4580539EE4C743E9371D.pdf> (accessed 11 January 2009).

DTI (1998) *Fairness at Work*. Online. <http://www.berr.gov.uk/files/file24436.pdf> (accessed 11 January 2009).

Devine, P., Pearmain, A., Prior, M. and Purdy, D. (n.d.) *Feel Bad Britain: A View from the Democratic Left* . Online. <http://www.compassonline.org.uk/publications/thinkpieces/item.asp?d=257> (accessed 11 January 2009).

Dhillon, K. (2006) *Schools of Thought: How Local Authorities Drive Improved Outcomes in Education*, London: New Local Government Network.

Easton, C, Wilson, R. and Sharp, C. (2005) *National Remodelling Team: Evaluation Study (Year 2). Final Report*, Slough: National Foundation for Educational Research.

Edwards, G. (2008) 'Workforce remodelling and union activism in the NUT', paper presented at the *Remodelling Teaching: Rethinking Education* conference, 5 June, University of Lincoln, UK.

Ellis, T., McWhirter, J., McColgan, D. and Haddow, B. (1976) *William Tyndale: the Teachers' Story*, Essex: Anchor Press.

Fairbrother, P. (1994) *Politics and the State as Employer*, London: Mansell.

Fairbrother, P. (1996) 'Workplace trade unionism in the state sector', in P. Ackers, C. Smith and P. Smith (eds.) *The New Workplace Trade Unionism*, London: Routledge.

Fairbrother, P. (2000a) 'British unions facing the future', *Capital and Class*, 71: 47–78.

Fairbrother. P. (2000b). *Trade Unions at the Crossroads*, London: Mansell.

Ferlie, E., Ashburner, L., Fitzgerald, L. and Pettigrew, A. (1996) *The New Public Management in Action*, Oxford: Oxford University Press.

Fitz, J., Gorard, S. and Taylor, C. (2002) 'School admissions after the School Standards and Framework Act: bringing the LEA back in?' *Oxford Review of Education*, 28(2&3): 373–392.

Fitz, J. and Halpin, J. (1994) 'Ministers and mandarins: educational research in an elite setting', in G. Walford (ed.) *Researching the Powerful in Education*, London: University College London Press.

Fitzgerald, T. (2007) 'Remodelling schools and schooling, teachers and teaching: a New Zealand perspective', in G. Butt and H. Gunter (eds.) *Modernizing Schools: People, Learning and Organizations* London: Continuum.

Fletcher, B. and Gapasin, F. (2008) *Solidarity Divided: The Crisis of Organized Labor and a New Path Toward Social Justice*, Berkeley: University of California Press.

Fletcher-Campbell, F. and Lee, B. (2003) *A Study of the Changing Role of LEAs in Raising Standards of Achievement in Schools*, Nottingham: DfES.

Fosh, P. (1993) 'Membership participation in workplace unionism: the possibility of union renewal', *British Journal of Industrial Relations*, 31(4): 577–592.

Foster, D. and Scott, P. (1998) 'Competitive tendering of public services and industrial relations policy: the Conservative agenda under Thatcher and Major', *Historical Studies in Industrial Relations*, 6 (Autumn): 101–132.

Gall, G. (1998) 'Evaluating Fairbrother's union renewal thesis', *Capital and Class*, 66: 149–157.

Gamble, A. (1988) *The Free Economy and the Strong State: The Politics of Thatcherism*, London: Macmillan.

Gewirtz, S. (2002) *The Managerial School: Post-welfarism and Social Justice in Education*, London: Routledge.

Gewirtz, S. and Cribb, A. (2007) 'What to do about values in social research: the case for ethical reflexivity in the sociology of education', *British Journal of Sociology of Education*, 27(2): 141–155.

Gilbert, N. and Gilbert B. (1989) *The Enabling State: Modern Welfare Capitalism in America*, New York: Oxford University Press.

Grace, G. (1978) *Teachers, Ideology and Control: A Study in Urban Education*, London: Routledge and Kegan Paul.

Gramsci, A. (1971) *Selections from Prison Notebooks*, London: Lawrence and Wishart.

Green, A. (1997) *Education, Globalization and the Nation State*, Basingstoke: Macmillan.

Gunter, H. (2008) 'Policy and workforce reform in England', *Educational Management, Administration and Leadership*, 36(2): 253–270.

Gunter, H. and Butt, G. (2007) 'Introduction: the challenges of modernization', in G. Butt and H. Gunter (eds.) *Modernizing Schools: People, Learning and Organizations*, London: Continuum: 1–16.

Hall, S. (1987) 'Gramsci and us', *Marxism Today*, June: 16–21.

Hammersley, M. (2007) 'The issue of quality in qualitative research', *International Journal of Research and Method in Education*, 30(3): 287–305.

Hammerlsey-Fletcher, L. (2007) 'Engaging staff in change—experiences in schools in England'. Online. *International Electronic Journal of Leadership for Learning*, 11 <http://www.ucalgary.ca/~iejll/> (accessed 22 January 2009).

Hannon, V. (1999) 'On the receiving end: New Labour and the LEAs', *Cambridge Journal of Education*, 29(2): 207–217.

Harden, I. (1992) *The Contracting State*, Milton Keynes: Open University Press.

Harris, A. (2004) 'Distributed leadership and school improvement: leading or misleading?' *Educational Management, Administration and Leadership*, 32(1): 11–24.

Harris, A. and Muijs, D. (2004) *Improving Schools through Teacher Leadership*, London: Open University Press.

Hartley, J., Rashman, L., Radnor, Z. and Withers, E. (2008) *Learning, Improvement and Innovation in Local Government: Final Report of the Beacon Scheme Evaluation—Executive Summary*, London: Department for Communities and Local Government.

Harvie, D. (2006) 'Value production and struggle in the classroom: teachers within, against and beyond capital', *Capital and Class*, 88(Spring):1–32.

Heery, E. (1998) 'Campaigning for part-time workers', *Work, Employment and Society*, 12: 352–366.

Heery E., Simms, M., Delbridge, R., Salmon, J. and Simpson, D. (2003) 'Trade union recruitment policy in Britain: form and effects', in G. Gall (ed.) *Union Organizing: Campaigning for Union Recognition*, London: Routledge: 56–78.

HM Government (2004) *Every child matters: change for children*. Online. <http://publications.everychildmatters.gov.uk/eOrderingDownload/DfES10812004.pdf> (accessed 17 July 2008).

HM Government (2007) 'Extended schools: building on experience'. Online. <http://publications.teachernet.gov.uk/eOrderingDownload/extended%20services%20prospectus%2012.07.07.pdf> (accessed 19 July 2008).

Holland, S. (2008) 'The world after Keynes', *Red Pepper*, 163(Dec/Jan): 22–24.

Ingersoll, R. (2003) *Who Controls Teachers' Work? Power and Accountability in America's Schools*, Cambridge MA: Harvard University Press.

Ironside, M. and Seifert, R. (1995) *Industrial Relations in Schools*, London and New York: Routledge.

Ironside, M., Seifert, R. and Sinclair, J. (1997) 'Teacher union responses to education reforms: job regulation and the enforced growth of informality', *Industrial Relations Journal*, 28(2): 120–135.

Jeffrey, B. (2002) 'Performativity and primary teacher relations', *Journal of Education Policy*, 17(5): 531–546.

Jesson, J. and Simpkin, G. (2007) 'New Zealand's education reforms: 20 years engendering changes in the teacher unions'. Online. *International Electronic Journal of Leadership for Learning*, 11 <http://www.ucalgary.ca/~iejll/> (accessed 22 January 2009).

Jessop, B. (1994) 'The transition to post-Fordism and the Schumpterian workfare state', in R. Burrows, and B. Loader (eds.) *Towards a Post-Fordist Welfare State?* London: Routledge: 13–37.

Jessop, B. (2002) *The Future of the Capitalist State*, Oxford: Blackwell.

Johnson, T. (1972) *Professions and Power*, London: Palgrave Macmillan.

Kasten, R. and Fossedal, G. (1996) Teacher union 'concentration' in 21 countries. Online. <http://www.adti.net/new_zuberi_uploaded/teacherchoice/21countries.html> (accessed 22 January 2009).

Kean, H. (1990) *Challenging the State: The Socialist and Feminist Educational Experience 1900–1930*, London: Falmer Press.

Keane, W. (1996). *Win-win or Else: Collective Bargaining in an Age of Public Discontent*, Thousand Oaks, CA: Corwin Press.

Kerchner, C. and Koppich, J. (eds.) (2003) *A Union of Professionals: Labor Relations and Educational Reform*, New York: Teachers College Press.

Kerchner, C., Koppich, J. and Weeres, J. (1998). *Taking Charge of Quality: How Teachers and Unions Can Revitalize Schools*, San Francisco: Jossey-Bass.

Kerchner, C. and Mitchell, D. (1988). *The Changing Idea of a Teachers' Union*. London: Falmer Press.

Kerr, L. (2006) *Between Caring and Counting: Teachers Take on Education Reform*, Toronto: University of Toronto Press.

Kershaw, S. (2004) 'School workforce remodelling: role of LEAs'. Online. <http://www.teachernet.gov.uk/_doc/4807/LEA.0285Letter.2003.pdf> (accessed 11 January 2009).

Knights, D. and Willmott, H. (1989) 'Power and subjectivity at work: from degradation to subjugation in the labour process', *Sociology*, 23(4): 535–558.

Kyriacou, C. (2001). 'Teacher stress: directions for future research', *Educational Review*, 53(1): 28–35.

Lansley, S., Goss, S. and Woolmar, C. (1989) *Councils in Conflict: The Rise and Fall of the Municipal Left*, London: Palgrave.

Lawn, M. (1996) *Modern Times? Work, Professionalism and Citizenship in Teaching*, London: Falmer Press.

Lawton, D. (1992) *Education and Politics in the 1990s: Conflict or Consensus?* London: Falmer Press.

Lawton, S., Bedard, G., MacLellan, D. and Li, X. (1999) *Teachers' Unions in Canada*, Calgary: Detselig Enterprises.

Leopold, J. and Beaumont, P. (1986) 'Pay bargaining and management strategy in the NHS', *Industrial Relations Journal*, 17(1): 32–45.

Lipsett, A. (2008) 'Government defends National Challenge target', *Education Guardian*, 25 June. Online. <http://www.guardian.co.uk/education/2008/jun/25/schools.gcses/print> (accessed 9 December 2008)

London Edinburgh Weekend Return Group (1979) *In and Against the State*, London: Pluto.

Lowe, R. (2002) 'A century of local education authorities: what has been lost?', *Oxford Review of Education*, 28(2&3): 149–158.

Maclure, S. (1992) *Education Re-Formed*, London: Hodder and Stoughton.

Marx, K. (1990) *Capital: Critique of Political Economy*, vol.1, Harmondsworth: Penguin.

McIlroy, J. (1997) 'Still under siege; British trade unionism at the turn of the century', *Historical Studies in Industrial Relations*, 3: 93–122.

McIlroy, J. (2000) 'New Labour, new unions, new left', *Capital & Class*, 71: 11–45.

Meier, D. and Wood, G. (eds.) (2004) *Many Children Left Behind*, Boston: Beacon Press.

Miles, M. and Huberman, M. (1994) *Qualitative Data Analysis: An Expanded Sourcebook*, Thousand Oaks, CA: Sage.

Milne, S. (2008) 'Not the death of capitalism, but the birth of a new order', *Guardian*, 23 October. Online. <http://www.guardian.co.uk/commentisfree/2008/oct/23/creditcrunch-economics> (accessed 11 January 2009).

Morris, E. (2001) *Professionalism and Trust: A Speech by the Rt Hon Estelle Morris MP Secretary of State for Education and Skills to the Social Market Foundation*, London: DfES.

Morton, R. (2005) *Transforming the School Workforce—A New Professional Respect? The Beacon Scheme 2004–2005*, Slough: EMIE at NFER.

Murphy, M. (1990) *Blackboard Unions: The AFT and the NEA 1900–1980*, Ithaca, NY: Cornell University Press.

National Association of Schoolmasters Union of Women Teachers (2008) *Workload Audit: the Workload of Teachers and Headteachers in England and Wales*, Birmingham: NASUWT.

National Education Association (2003) *Interest-Based Bargaining in Education: A Review of the Literature and Current Practice*, Washington DC: NEA.

National Remodelling Team (2004) NRT Newsletter Issue 7. Online. <http://www.hants.gov.uk/education/eps/workforce-remodelling/nrt-newsletter-7.pdf> (accessed 29 April 2008).

National Union of Teachers (2003) *A Price Too High?* London: NUT.

O'Connor, J. (1973) *The Fiscal Crisis of the State*, New York: St. Martin's Press.

O'Doherty, D. and Willmott, H. (2001) 'Debating labour process theory: the issue of subjectivity and the relevance of poststructuralism', *Sociology*, 35: 457–476.

Ofsted (2008) *Every child matters: framework for the inspection of schools in England from 2005*. Online. <http://www.ofsted.gov.uk/assets/Internet_Content/Shared_Content/IIFD/SchoolsFramework/Framework_For_Inspection_Of_Schools.doc> (accessed 8 August 2008).

Ozga, J.(ed.) (1988) *Schoolwork: Approaches to the Labour Process of Teaching*, Milton Keynes: Open University Press.

Ozga, J. and Lawn, M. (1981) *Teachers, Professionalism and Class: A Study of Organized Teachers*, London: Falmer Press.

Passy, R. (2003) *Children and family values; a critical appraisal of 'family' in schools*, unpublished PhD thesis, University of Plymouth.

Pollard, A. and Bourne, J. (eds.) (1994) *Teaching and Learning in the Primary School*, London and New York: Routledge/Falmer in association with the Open University.

Pollitt, C. (1990) *Managerialism and the Public Services: The Anglo-American Experience*, Oxford: Blackwell.

Poole, W. (2007) 'Neo-liberalism in British Columbia education and teachers' union resistance'. Online. *International Electronic Journal of Leadership for Learning*, 11, <http://www.ucalgary.ca/~iejll/> (accessed 11 January 2009).

PricewaterhouseCoopers (2001) *Teacher Workload Study: Final Report*, London: DfES.

PricewaterhouseCoopers/Department for Education and Skills (2007) *Independent Study into School Leadership: Main Report*, Nottingham: DfES.

Pring, R. (2000a) 'The "false dualism" of educational research', *Journal of Philosophy of Education*, 34(2): 247–260.

Pring, R. (2000b) *Philosophy of Educational Research*, London: Continuum.

Public Services International (2008, 27 March). 'Colombia: Impunity continues. Assassination of four trade unionists; threats against a trade union activist', 27 March. Online. < http://www.world-psi.org/TemplateEn.cfm?Section=Urgent_actions2&Template=/UrgentActionsEmailer/EN_UAColombia6March_form.htm> (accessed 11 January 2009).

Reid, A. (2003) 'Understanding teachers' work: is there still a place for labour process theory?' *British Journal of Sociology of Education*, 24(5): 559–573.

Rewards and Incentives Group (2005) 'STRB: *Evidence from the Rewards and Incentives Group: 25th May 2005*'. Online. < http://www.teachernet.gov.uk/_doc/8454/20050526 STRB JOINT EVIDENCE Final.doc> (accessed 11 January 2009).

Rewards and Incentives Group (2007) '*Performance Management for Teachers and Headteachers: Guidance*'. Online. <http://www.teachernet.gov.uk/_doc/10405/PM%20Guidance%20print%20final%20Nov%2006.pdf> (accessed 11 January 2009).

Robertson, S. (2008) ' "Remaking the world": Neoliberalism and the transformation of education and teachers' labour', in M. Compton and L. Weiner (eds.) *The global assault on teaching, teachers and their unions: Stories for resistance*, New York: Palgrave Macmillan.

Ryner, M. (2007) 'US power and the crisis of social democracy in Europe's second project of integration', *Capital & Class*, 93(Autumn): 7–26.

Schultz, T. W. (1981) *Investing in People—The Economics of Population Quality*, Berkeley: University of California Press.

Scott, D. (2000) *Realism and Educational Research: New Perspectives and Possibilities*, London and New York: RoutledgeFalmer.

Scott, D. & Usher, R. (1999) *Researching Education: Data, Methods and Theory in Educational Enquiry*, London and New York: Continuum.

Seifert, R. (1984) 'Some aspects of factional opposition: Rank and File and the NUT 1967–1982', *British Journal of Industrial Relations* 22(3): 372–390.

Seifert, R. (1987) *Teacher Militancy: A History of Teacher Strikes 1896–1987*, London: Falmer Press.

Sharp, P. (2002) 'Surviving, not thriving: LEAs since the Education Reform Act of 1988', *Oxford Review of Education*, 28(2&3): 197–215.

Simon, B. (1988) *Bending the Rules: The Baker Reform of Education*, London: Lawrence and Wishart.

Somekh, B. (2007) 'Last words: speculative knowledge', in B. Somekh and T. Schwandt (eds.) *Knowledge production: Research work in interesting times*, London and New York: Routledge.

Smithers, A. and Robinson, P. (2001) *Teachers Leaving*, Liverpool: Liverpool University, Centre for Education and Employment Research.

Smyth, J. (2001) *Critical Politics of Teachers' Work: An Australian Perspective*, New York: Peter Lang.

Smyth, J., Dow, A., Hattam, R., Reid, A. and Shacklock, G. (2000) *Teachers' Work in a Globalizing Economy*, London: Falmer.

Spooner, A. (2006). *Principles of Public/Private Partnerships in Educational Reform*, London: NRT.

Stevenson, H. (2003). 'On the shopfloor: exploring the impact of teacher trade unions on school-based industrial relations', *School Leadership and Management*, 23(3): 341–356.

Stevenson, H. (2007a) 'Changes in teachers' work and the challenges facing teacher unions'. Online. *International Electronic Journal of Leadership for Learning* , volume 11 <http://www.ucalgary.ca/~iejll/> (accessed 11 January 2009).

Stevenson, H. (2007b) 'Restructuring teachers' work and trade union responses in England: bargaining for change', *American Educational Research Journal*, 44(2): 224–251.

Stevenson, H. (2008) 'Challenging the orthodoxy: Union Learning Representatives as organic intellectuals', *Journal of In-Service Education*, 35(4) 455–466.

Stevenson, H. and Carter, B. (2004) ' "Business as usual"? Assessing trade union responses to school sector restructuring', paper presented at Belmas annual conference, 8–10 October, Yarnfield Park, Staffs, UK.

Stevenson, H. and Carter, B. (2007) 'New unionism? Exploring the development of "social partnership" in English school sector labor relations', paper presented at American Educational Research Association annual meeting, 9–13 April, Chicago, IL.

Stevenson, H., Carter, B. and Passy, R. (2007) ' "New professionalism", workforce remodelling and the restructuring of teachers'. Online. *International Electronic Journal of Leadership for Learning* , 11 <http://www.ucalgary.ca/~iejll/> (accessed 22 January 2009).

Stewart, W. (2003) 'Storm out of blue skies', *Times Educational Supplement*, 5 December, http://www.tes.co.uk/search/story/?story_id=387856 (accessed 2 June 2008).

Stewart, W. (2008) 'Someone still has to do the work'. Online <http://www.tes.co.uk/article.aspx?storycode=6002048> (accessed 12 September 2009).

STRB (2008) *Teachers' Workloads Diary Survey*. Online. <http://www.ome.uk.com/downloads/2008%20Teachers%20Report%20FINAL.pdf> (accessed 12 September 2009).

Streshley, W. and DeMitchell, T. (1994) *Teacher Unions and TQE: Building Quality Labour Relations*, Thousand Oaks, CA: Corwin Press.

Stuart, M. and Lucio, M. M. (2002) 'Remaking involvement and trust at the British workplace, social partnership and the mutual gains organization', *Economic and Industrial Democracy*, 23: 177–200.

Tatto, M. (ed.) (2007) *Reforming Teaching Globally*, Oxford: Symposium Books.

Taylor, F. (1911) *Scientific Management*, New York: Harper and Bros.

Taylor, P. and Bain, P. (2004) 'Failing to organise—or organising to fail? Challenge, opportunity and the limitations of union policy in four call centres', in G. Healy, E. Heery, P. Taylor, P. and Brown, W. *The Future of Worker Representation*, Basingstoke: Macmillan: 62–81.

Taylor, P. and Ramsay, H. (1998) 'Unions, partnership and HRM: sleeping with the enemy?' *International Journal of Employment Studies*, 6(2): 115–143.

Taylor, S., Rizvi, F., Lingard, B. and Henry, M. (1997) *Education Policy and the Politics of Change*, London: Routledge.

Terry, M. (ed.) (2000) *Redefining Public Sector Unionism: Unison and the Future of Trade Unions*, London: Routledge.

Thomas, G. and Gorard, S. (2007) Editorial: quality in education research, *International Journal of Research and Method in Education*, 30(3): 239–242.

Thomas, H., Butt, G., Fielding, A., Foster, J., Gunter, H., Lance, A., Pilkington, R., Potts, L., Powers, S., Rayner, S., Rutherford, D., Selwood, I. and Szwed, C. (2004). *The Evaluation of the Transforming the School Workforce Pathfinder Project*, DfES, Research Report RR541, Norwich: HMSO.

Thompson, P. (1983) *The Nature of Work: An Introduction to Debates on the Labour Process*, London: Macmillan.

Thrupp, M. and Willmott, R. (2003) *Education Management in Managerialist Times: Beyond the Textual Apologists*, Maidenhead: Open University Press.

Tipple, C. (1998) 'Tracking the Phoenix: the fall and rise of the local education authority', *Oxford Review of Education*, 24(1): 35–43.

Tomlinson, S. (2001) *Education in a Post-Welfare Society*, Buckingham: Open University Press.

Trades Union Congress (2007) *Congress decisions*. Online. < http://www.tuc.org.uk/congress/tuc-13720-f0.pdf> (accessed 22 January 2009).

Training and Development Agency (2007) *Professional Standards for Teachers. Why sit still in your career?* Online. <http://www.teachernet.gov.uk/_doc/11525/Professional%20Standards%20for%20Teachers.pdf> (accessed 22 January 2009).

Troman, G. (2000) 'Teacher stress in the low-trust society', *British Journal of Sociology of Education*, 21(3): 331–353.

Tropp, A. (1957) *The School Teachers: The Growth of the Teaching Profession in England and Wales from 1800 to the Present Day*, London: Heinemann.

Undy, R. (2002) 'Negotiating amalgamations: territorial and political consolidation and administrative reform in public sector service unions in the UK', *British Journal of Industrial Relations*, 37(3): 445–463.

US Department of Education (2001) *The Elementary and Secondary Education Act (The No Child Left Behind Act of 2001)*. Online. <http://www.ed.gov/policy/elsec/leg/esea02/index.html> (accessed 11 January 2009).

Vincent, B. (1993) 'No Minister . . . ', *Education Today and Tomorrow*, 45(1):12–13.

Waddington, J. (2006) 'The trade union merger process in Europe: defensive adjustment or strategic reform?', *Industrial Relations Journal* 37(6): 630–651.

Walford, G. (ed.) (1994) *Researching the Powerful in Education*, London: University College London Press.

Walton, R. & McKersie, R. (1965). *A Behavioral Theory of Labor Negotiations: an Analysis of a Social Interaction System*, New York: McGraw-Hill.

Woods, P. and Troman, G. (2001) *Primary Teachers' Stress*. New York: Routledge/Falmer.

Wells, D. (2001) 'Labour markets, flexible specialization and the new microcorporatism: the case of Canada's major appliance industry', *Relations Industrielles*, 56(2): 279–306.

Whitty, G. (2002) *Making Sense of Education Policy*, London: PCP.

Whitty, G. (2008) 'Twenty years of progress? English education policy 1988 to the present', *Education Management Administration and Leadership*, 36(2): 165–184.

Whitty, G. and Edwards, T. (1994) 'Researching Thatcherite education policy', in G. Walford, (ed.) *Researching the Powerful in Education*, London: University College London Press.

Wood S. (ed.) (1982) *The Degradation of Work?* London: Hutchinson.

Workforce Agreement Monitoring Group (2004). Note 8: Local Implementation—Success Factors. Online. <http://www.tda.gov.uk/upload/resources/pdf/w/wamg_guidance8.pdf>(accessed 11 January 2009).

Workforce Agreement Monitoring Group (2007) Note 18: Supporting Local Social Partnership and sustainable reform. Online <http://www.tda.gov.uk/upload/resources/pdf/w/wamg_joint_working_10102007.pdf> (accessed 11 January 2009).

Workforce Agreement Monitoring Group (2008) Note 19: Updating Local Social Partnerships on the programme and priorities. Online. < http://www.tda.gov.uk/upload/resources/pdf/w/wamg_note_19_english.pdf> (accessed 11 January 2009).

Yarker, P. (2005) 'On not being a teacher: the professional and personal costs of workforce remodelling', *Forum*, 47(2&3): 169–174.

Index

A

absenteeism, student 107
academy schools 36, 51, 67, 84, 155
accountability 6, 8, 21, 29, 30, 64,
    114–17, 118, 134
Advanced Skills Teachers 133
agenda setting, Social Partnership
    47–51
American Federation of Teachers (AFT)
    13
anti-union legislation 26
Apple, M. 5, 14, 138
appraisal 35
assimilation 113, 137
Assistant Masters and Mistresses Asso-
    ciation (AMMA) 24
Association of School and College
    Leaders (ASCL) 23, 106, 119
Association of Teachers and Lecturers
    (ATL) 24, 25, 30, 84, 119, 153;
    and Social Partnership 50, 145–6
Association of University Techers
    (AUT) 154
autonomy, professional 8, 20, 21, 126

B

Beacon Scheme 66
benchmarking 6, 22, 136
Bernstein, B. 22
Blair, T. 29
'Blue Sky' staff events 32
Blunkett, D. 33
Braverman, H. 9, 107, 141
bureaucracy 15, 29
Burnham Committee 24–5, 26, 54, 66
bursaries 122
business managers 108
Butt, G. 33, 103

C

Callaghan, J. 20
Canada 13
capability procedures 16, 21, 22, 115
capital 4, 139; accumulation 9; human
    7, 21–2
capital-labour relationship 4
caring 129–30, 140; *see also* pastoral
    work
Carter, B. 67
centralisation: of government 21; of
    trade unions 15, 28
change management 75, 106
change teams 32–3, 106
choice 6; parental 21, 66, 134
class interests 23
Collarbone, P. 31–2, 69, 148
collective bargaining 14–15, 25, 26–7,
    36, 51–2, 53
Colling, T. 28
competition 6; inter-school 21, 135
comprehensive values 139
conditions of service 25, 50, 64, 137
conservative modernisers 5–7, 11, 14,
    20, 138
Conservative Party 20, 66, 134, 142,
    156
constructivism 39
consultation 52–3
Consulting Strategies Ltd 31
continuing professional development
    (CPD) 53, 64, 79, 92, 138
control: of curriculum 6; of teachers'
    work 126–7, 134–9, 139
cover supervision 34, 35, 109–11, 118,
    131, 132, 153
curriculum: control of 6; National 21;
    standardised content 8

D

Danford, A. 143–4
data collection: and monitoring teachers' performance 93–4; research project 40, 41–4
decentralisation 21; of trade unions 15
delegation 107–8
Department of Children, Schools and Families (DCSF) 46
Department of Education and Science (DES) 26
Department for Education and Skills (DfES) 30, 42, 46
deregulation 5
Dhillon, K. 66
display work 34, 107, 128
distributed leadership 133, 136, 138
distributive bargaining 52

E

economic crisis, global 4
Education International 11
Education Reform Act 1988 (ERA) 19, 20, 21, 27, 66
educational output 6
Edwards, T. 37
efficiency 6, 135, 139
equity, and Social Partnership 54–6
ethics 40
Every Child Matters 48, 67, 130
examination invigilation 105, 107
Extended Schools agenda 48, 84

F

Fairbrother, P. 15, 20, 27–8
Fairness at Work 143
Fletcher-Campbell, F. 66
Fossedal, G. 11
funding, workforce remodelling 87–8, 155

G

Gewirtz, S. 135, 136
globalisation 2–7, 39–40
Gramsci, A. 4
grant-maintained schools 27, 36, 66, 84
Great Debate 20
Greater London Council 66
Gunter, H. 33, 103, 136

H

headteachers 118–19; assistant 133
hours of work 30, 34, 127, 128, 133, 134, 146, 155
human capital 7, 21–2

I

ideology 10
industrial action 59–60, 62
Ingersoll, R. 10
integrative bargaining 51–2, 136–7
intensification of work 118, 128–9
interest-based bargaining 14, 51
Interim Advisory Committee (IAC) 26, 27
International Monetary Fund 5
interview process, research project 40
Ironside, M. 20, 28–9

J

Jessop, B. 5

K

Kasten, R. 11
Kerchner, C. 14
Kershaw, S. 68
Keynesianism 4, 19
Klingel, S. 51
knowledge economy 10

L

labour, division of 9, 111–12, 121, 132, 133–4, 139, 140, 141
labour-capital relationship 4
Labour Party, *see* New Labour
labour process of teaching 1, 3, 8–10, 16, 20, 90–5, 107–19, 126–41
labour substitution 131–2, 140
Lawn, M. 26
leadership 136; distributed 133, 136, 138; middle 137, 138, 140
league tables 21, 121, 130, 134, 136, 139
Lee, B. 66
local authorities (LAs) 21, 25, 26, 27, 65–84, 106, 151–3
local education authorities (LEAs) 22, 65, 66–7
Local Government Employers 46
local management of schools (LMS) 21, 27, 29, 36, 66, 67, 151
Local Social Partnerships (LSPs), *see* local Workload Agreement
local Workload Agreement Monitoring Groups (WAMGs) 38, 43, 67, 70, 71, 72–84, 151–2
Lucio, M. M. 143

M

McAvoy, D. 34
McIlroy, J. 143

McKersie, R. 51
management 133–4
management allowances (MAs) 103, 112, 114, 121, 129, 138
managerialism 5, 135–9, 140
market mechanisms 5, 6, 7, 21, 36, 134, 135, 136
Marx, K. 9
middle leaders 137, 138, 140
Mitchell, D. 14
money, collection of 34, 107, 128
Morris, E. 31, 33
multi-unionism 13, 19, 23, 154

N

naming and shaming 22, 34, 135
National Association of Head Teachers (NAHT) 23, 41, 46, 58, 87, 106, 119
National Association of Schoolmasters Union of Women Teachers (NASUWT) 24, 25, 30, 42, 127, 142, 152; and local authorities 73–4, 75, 76, 78, 79–80, 84; secondary schools 119, 121, 123; and Social Partnership 49–50, 55, 60, 62, 63, 146–9, 153, 154; and Workload Agreement 121
National association of Teachers in Further and Higher Education (Natfhe) 154
National Challenge schools 6
National Challenge targets 22
National College for School Leadership 133
National Curriculum 21
National Education Association (NEA), US 13, 51
National Health Service (HNS) Trust 143
National Remodelling Team (NRT) 67, 68–9, 70, 71, 75, 106, 108
National Union of Teachers (NUT) 23–4, 30, 42, 113; and Burnham negotiating structure 24–5; cooperation with other unions 142, 156; and cover supervision 109–10, 131; and local authorities 67, 74, 76, 78, 79, 80, 81, 82–3, 84, 152, 153; primary schools 96, 99–101; secondary schools 119, 120, 124; and Social Partnership 41, 46, 55, 58, 61–3, 64, 149–51, 153,

154; and Workload Agreement 34–5, 41
National Workload Agreement, *see* Workload Agreement
negotiation 52–3
neo-liberalism 2–7, 10, 12, 13–15, 16, 19–23, 39–40
New Labour 7, 21–2, 29, 35, 45, 134, 135, 136, 142, 143, 154, 156
New Left 66
new professionalism 1, 127, 139
new public management (NPM) 21, 135
New Right 4–5
New Zealand 13, 19
No Child Left Behind (NCLB) 6, 135
nursery nurses 88

O

Ofsted (Office for Standards in Education) 64, 95
output, educational 6

P

parental choice 21, 66, 134
pastoral work 30, 103, 104, 107, 111–12, 129–30, 132, 138, 140
pay 23, 25, 26–7, 46, 103–4, 151, 155; dispute (1984–6) 20, 26; performance-related 3, 131, 133, 139, 140; progression 115, 116, 138; restructuring 22, 49, 57–8, 59, 62, 129, 133, 137; *see also* management allowances (MAs); teaching and learning responsibilities (TLRs)
performance 130–1, 134–5, 139, 141; benchmarking 6, 22, 136; pay 3, 131, 133, 138, 140; student 134–5, 137, 139; teacher 21, 30, 93–4
performance management (PM) 22, 35, 46, 49, 59, 64, 94, 114–17, 133, 137–8, 140, 145
performativity 135, 136
photocopying 34, 128
'pin-down' 128
planning, preparation and assessment (PPA) 30–1, 34, 61, 85, 87–8, 89–90, 94, 95, 101, 103, 131
post-structuralism 9
power 3
PricewaterhouseCoopers (PwC) 30–1, 33

primary schools 85–102, 129, 130;
trade unions 85, 96–102, 153
Pring, R. 39
privatisation 5, 6, 21, 66
Professional Association of Teachers
(PAT) 24
professional development, *see* continuing professional development
(CPD)
professionalism 8, 21, 140; new 1, 127,
139
Public and Commercial Services Union
(PCS) 154
public service 8
public spending, reduction of 5

Q

qualified teacher status (QTS) 34, 61, 131
qualitative research 38–9
quantitative research 38
quasi-markets 6, 21, 27, 134, 135, 136

R

Raising Standards and Tackling Workload, see Workload Agreement
rapprochement 13, 14, 16, 63–4, 83–4,
144, 156
Reagan, R. 4
realism 39
recruitment of teachers 30, 90
Reference Group 40–1
remodelling advisers 69–71, 84
research methods 37–44
resistance 13, 14–15, 16, 64, 83–4, 156
retention of teachers 30, 90
Rewards and Incentive Group 35, 46
routine tasks 34, 103, 107, 117–18,
128, 131–2, 140

S

salaries, *see* pay
School Teachers' Review Body (STRB)
27, 35, 46, 127, 155
Secondary Heads Association 23
secondary schools 103–25, 129, 130;
trade unions 119–25, 153
Seifert, R. 20, 28–9
self-regulation 8
Sharp, P. 66
Simon, B. 21
Smith, A. 107
social democracy 4, 26
Social Partnership 2, 31, 35, 36, 41,
45–64, 65, 74–5, 87, 137,

142–56; agenda setting 47–51;
discussing and deciding 51–6;
equity between partners 54–6; as
trust 56–8
standardisation, curriculum content 8
standardised testing 6, 8, 21, 29, 50,
135, 136, 137, 139, 141
standards 6, 8, 29–0, 32, 47, 48, 107,
123, 134, 135, 137
State: rolling back of 5, 19; teacher
unions and 25–9
Stevenson, H. 67
stress 11
Stuart, M. 143
students: absenteeism 107; pastoral
work with 103, 107, 111–12,
129–30, 140; performance
134–5, 137, 139
supply teachers 111, 140
support staff 30, 33–4, 88–90, 101,
133; cover supervision 131,
132; increase in numbers 133,
134, 140; management of 118;
pastoral work 30, 111–12,
129; professionalisation of 118;
resistance 156; and routine
tasks 34, 103, 107, 117–18,
131–2, 140; unions 42, 55;
whole class teaching 34, 61–2,
145; *see also* teaching assistants (TAs)
Support Staff Review 35, 46
supra-national institutions 3–4, 5

T

targets 21, 22, 29, 136, 138, 235
taxation, progressive 5
*Teachers: Meeting the Challenge of
Change* (Green Paper) 33, 133
Teachers' Consultative Groups 67
Teachers' Negotiating Committees 67
teaching assistants (TAs) 31, 32, 87–8,
89–90, 92, 108–9, 132, 134,
145, 149, 155
teaching and learning 127–32, 139
teaching and learning responsibilities
(TLRs) 35, 44, 129, 137, 145;
primary schools 88, 90, 99–100;
secondary schools 103–4, 111,
112–14, 116, 117, 121, 122
teaching unions, *see* trade unions
testing, *see* standardised testing
Thatcher, M. 4, 66
Third Way 143

Times Educational Supplement 127, 155

trade unions 1, 11–13, 19–20, 22–9, 36, 37; bureaucracy 15; centralised 15, 28; decentralisation of 15; and local authorities 66–7, 72–84; mergers 142, 154; multi-unionism 13, 19, 23, 154; primary schools 85, 96–102, 153; *rapprochement* 13, 14, 16, 63–4, 83–4 144, 156; renewal 13, 15, 16, 20, 27–8, 142, 156–7; resistance 13, 14–15, 16, 64, 83–4, 156; secondary schools 119–25, 153; and Social Partnership 45–64, 142–51; and the State 25–9; *see also individual unions*

Trades Union Congress (TUC) 23, 55

Training and Development Agency for Schools 42, 46, 52

training events, workforce remodelling 68, 69

Transforming the School Workforce (TSW) project 31, 32, 33

trust 56–8, 130–1

trust schools 36, 50

'25 tasks' 34, 107–8, 127–8

U

Union of Women Teachers 24; *see also* National Association of Schoolmasters Union of Women Teachers (NASUWT)

Unison 42, 43, 55, 73, 80, 81, 83, 152

United States (US) 5; No Child Left Behind legislation 6, 135; teacher unions 11–12, 13, 51

University and College Union (UCU) 154

V

value-added 135, 140

value for money 6

Voice 24, 25, 43, 50–1, 55, 119

W

Walton, R. 51

welfare state 5

Welsh Assembly 46

Whitty, G. 37

William Tyndale School 20

workforce remodelling 1, 2, 3, 16–17, 20, 29–35, 37–8; advisers 69–71, 84; funding 87–8, 155; implementation of regulations 68, 69; local authorities and 67, 68–84; primary schools 85–102, 129; secondary schools 103–25, 129; and teachers' work 90–5, 107–19, 126–41; training events 68, 69

working hours 30, 34, 127, 128, 133, 134, 146, 155

workload 30–5, 47, 49, 64, 107, 117–19, 123, 128, 145–6, 155

Workload Agreement 34, 35, 46, 47, 48, 57, 121, 131, 136–7, 142, 152

Workload Agreement Monitoring Group (WAMG) 35, 38, 41, 42, 46, 48, 65, 67, 71; local *see*, local Workload Agreement Monitoring Groups (WAMGs)

World Trade Organization 5